Modern Monetary Theory and European Macroeconomics

T0300162

This book provides a new methodological approach to money and macro-economics. Realising that the abstract equilibrium models lacked descriptions of fundamental issues of a modern monetary economy, the focus of this book lies on the (stylised) balance sheets of the main actors. Money, after all, is born on the balance sheets of the central bank or commercial bank. While households and firms hold accounts at banks with deposits, banks hold an account at the central bank, where deposits are called reserves. The book aims to explain how the two monetary circuits – central bank deposits and bank deposits – are inter-twined. It is also shown how government spending injects money into the economy.

Modern Monetary Theory and European Macroeconomics covers both the general case and then the Eurozone specifically. A very simple macroeconomic model follows, which explains the major accounting identities of macro-economics. Using this new methodology, the Eurozone crisis is examined from a fresh perspective. It turns out that not government debt but the stagnation of private sector debt was the major economic problem and that cuts in government spending worsened the economic situation. The concluding chapters discuss what a solution to the current problems of the Eurozone must look like, with scenarios that examine a future with and without a euro.

This book provides a detailed balance-sheet view of monetary and fiscal oper-ations, with a focus on the Eurozone economy. Students, policy-makers and fin-ancial market actors will learn to assess the institutional processes that underpin a modern monetary economy, in times of boom and in times of bust.

Dirk H. Ehnts works as a lecturer in Economics at Bard College, Berlin.

Routledge International Studies in Money and Banking

For a full list of titles in this series, please visit www.routledge.com/series/SE0403

Modern Monetary Theory and European Macroeconomics

Dirk H. Ehnts

Routledge
Taylor & Francis Group

LONDON AND NEW YORK

First published 2017
by Routledge

2 Park Square, Milton Park, Abingdon, Oxon OX14 4RN
711 Third Avenue, New York, NY 10017, USA

Routledge is an imprint of the Taylor & Francis Group, an informa business

First issued in paperback 2017

Copyright © 2017 Dirk H. Ehnts

The right of Dirk H. Ehnts to be identified as author of this work has been
asserted by him in accordance with sections 77 and 78 of the Copyright,
Designs and Patents Act 1988.

All rights reserved. No part of this book may be reprinted or reproduced or
utilised in any form or by any electronic, mechanical, or other means, now
known or hereafter invented, including photocopying and recording, or in
any information storage or retrieval system, without permission in writing
from the publishers.

Notice:
Product or corporate names may be trademarks or registered trademarks,
and are used only for identification and explanation without intent to
infringe.

British Library Cataloguing in Publication Data
A catalogue record for this book is available from the British Library

Library of Congress Cataloging in Publication Data
A catalog record for this book has been requested

ISBN: 978-1-138-65477-8 (hbk)
ISBN: 978-1-138-29992-4 (pbk)

Typeset in Times New Roman
by Wearset Ltd, Boldon, Tyne and Wear

For Josephine and her generation

Contents

Figures

Boxes

Tables

Preface

What this book is about

What is money? How does it arise, where does it come from, by what mysterious process does it disappear again? What do banks and governments have to do with it? Why is there so much debt everywhere? And if Europe is drowning in debt, what is to be done?

Today people use money like ducks take to water, but despite this, knowledge about the origins and nature of money is grossly lacking. Even in academic economics, one can find relatively few professors who are able to accurately explain how money is created. Ask an economics professor who isn't a money and banking specialist about what money is and how it arises, and you'll likely hear tales of barter economies, fables of Robinson Crusoe, or thought-experiments about how central banks could drop money from helicopters to stimulate the economy. These are greatly oversimplified conventional stories recycled from introductory economics textbooks, divorced from a clear empirical understanding of how money and banks work in the real world.

The layperson is left baffled. There is some value to simplification, but do these conventional abstractions lead to useful insights? Do they help us understand how exactly money is created, and who has this extraordinary ability and privilege? Or are they dangerously misleading?

This book addresses these questions. We will need to roam fairly widely, and look back in economic history, though we won't go so far as to examine the entire history of money from ancient Mesopotamia to the creation of the euro. Mostly, we'll explore the issue like forensic accountants examining a bookkeeping system.

The explanations that follow are based on a *balance sheet approach* to understanding how stocks of money and debt arise and flow around the financial economy. This understanding should enable readers to think about monetary policy independently, make them better able to question common talking points recited by politicians and reduce their dependency on opinion leaders.

My hope is that this book might contribute to an improvement in democratic decision-making processes by increasing the number of citizens who have a realistic basic understanding of how the economy actually works.

Structure of this text

Since this book is aimed at readers without prior specialist knowledge, I've left out the copious quotes and footnotes typical of books aimed at academic audiences. At the end of the book, however, the reader can find a list of authors whose work has informed this text.

The book is structured into three main parts.

In Part I we examine the basic social imperatives. What is the economy for, what determines its structure? What are the basic social arrangements?

In Part II the institutional arrangements from which money and credit arise will be made explicit. Both fiscal and monetary policy are examined in detail. A simple macroeconomic model concludes this part.

Part III contains analysis. How does the economy work in terms of macroeconomic aggregates? What are the drivers of GDP growth, and what are the parts that slow the economy down? The Eurozone's economic history since 1999 is discussed in order to highlight the causes for the boom and bust that we have seen.

Part IV contains policy recommendations. Should Europe abandon the euro? If not, which reforms would stabilise the euro and end the economic and social crises in countries like Spain, Portugal and Greece?

Acknowledgements

While creating this book, I have benefited from discussions and comments from many people. I would like to thank them in alphabetical order: Miguel Carrión Álvarez, Stefan Angrick, Nicolas Barbaroux, Long Chen, Winnie Chen, Daniel Detzer, Alfonso Díez Minguela, Nina Dodig, Eckhard Hein, Alex Hofmann, Erik Jochem, Neophythos Kathiziotis, Alejandro Márquez Velázquez, Carmen Marull, Ronny Mazzocchi, Warren Mosler, Jan-Kaspar Münnich, Manfred Nitsch, Jan Priewe, Isabel Rodriguez, Reinhard Schumacher, Achim Truger, Nils Zimmermann, and my students from Bard College Berlin, the Berlin School of Economics and Law, Free University Berlin, and the University of Oldenburg. I would like to thank Nils Zimmermann also for the excellent job he did in improving my writing in English, giving insightful comments on how to improve some arguments and point out crucial issues that needed some more elaboration. Any remaining errors are my own.

Dirk Ehnts
Berlin, March 2016

Introduction

In recent years, the world economy has been lurching from crisis to crisis, amid a general deterioration in economic conditions for millions of ordinary people in the developed world. This book is intended to help the reader understand why these things are happening.

It explains what money is, and how credit and debt arise in a modern economy. It shows how existing mechanisms of credit and debt creation and distribution have led to ever-increasing concentrations of wealth in the hands of a small minority, as well as ever-higher debt burdens on governments and ordinary people, and how excessive private debt accumulation eventually leads to financial crises, economic stagnation or depression.

After explaining the essence of how the monetary system works, this book provides some guidance on what could be done to stimulate economic activity while concurrently overcoming the problem of excessive accumulated debt, with special attention to the European context.

Before we launch into the main body of the text, let's begin by sketching, in this introduction, some of the macroeconomic problems the world faces. We'll also briefly address the question of why so many economists didn't see the global financial crisis coming – and why existing policy prescriptions for overcoming Europe's economic stagnation are flawed.

An increasingly unequal and debt-clogged economy

As this text was being written, the US employment rate – the proportion of adults in work – remained nearly 4 per cent lower than it was in 2007. Median income continued to follow a long-term trajectory of decline, despite average income continuing to rise. This reflected the fact that for many years, nearly all gains in national wealth and income have been going to the wealthiest Americans, even as the income of most workers has stagnated or declined.

In Europe, the Eurozone has been in danger of falling into a third recession in six years, and is hovering on the brink of deflation. In Japan, new policies were being tested – so far with little success – in an effort to stop the stagnation that has plagued the country for 25 years. Globally, oil prices are at record lows, causing massive macroeconomic disruptions in countries strongly dependent on oil production.

China, after a three-decade-long growth spurt, is facing big problems. A huge debt bubble has arisen in Asia's most populous country in recent years, involving both state enterprises and private households. A financial crisis may occur if its twin debt bubbles burst. A big rise in Chinese workers' wages may be the only way to enable Chinese consumers to keep up with debt repayment obligations and, at the same time, give them enough money to afford the products and services they produce without getting even further into debt. Brazil is in recession, its commodity exports having taken a hit in both quantity and value as a result of reduced global demand, especially due to reduced Chinese demand.

Economic growth rates have declined in other emerging and developing economies, too. That's one of the factors that led to the Arab Spring, among other disruptions. The world is re-learning what bitter experience had taught in the aftermath of the Great Depression of the early 1930s: financial and economic crises can lead to political crises, and even to wars.

Avoidable economic storms

One of the questions we address in this book is whether or not financial and economic crises are avoidable. Can something be done to prevent or resolve them, or are they like hurricanes, natural phenomena that can neither be predicted nor prevented?

The answer, as we will see, is that crises can indeed be prevented, but prevention would require structural changes in the financial system. Unsurprisingly, powerful financial sector actors who have shaped current financial regulations and systems, and continue to benefit from them, have strenuously and effectively resisted such changes.

When a debt or deflation crisis hits, and people are motivated to take a close look at the causal factors, it becomes obvious that the origins and structure of accumulated debt – whether of households, firms or states – has played a crucial role. Moreover, the origins of those debts as well as the mechanisms for resolving excessive debts always depend on past and present policy choices. Post-2008, for example, in order to protect banks from going under, enormous amounts of bad debt were shifted from the balance sheets of insolvent banks to the balance sheets of governments – which is to say that rather than requiring bank shareholders and creditors to 'write-down' bad debt and take losses, the losses were imposed on taxpayers instead. This example reminds us that the economy is deeply political, and a politics that claims to be economically neutral is both insipid and dishonest.

In the past few decades, politicians decided on a number of major changes in the financial sector that we now recognise as having been essential factors in generating today's crises.

Deregulation and its consequences

Among the biggest changes was the end, under the Nixon Administration in 1971, of the post-Second World War 'Bretton Woods' global system of exchange-rate-managed currencies, centred on a gold-backed dollar. This was followed up by mechanisms for recycling money from Middle Eastern petro-states into the US financial sector.

Another was the financial deregulation that finally led to the repeal in 1999 of the US Banking Act of 1933, commonly known as the Glass–Steagall Act in honour of the politicians who sponsored it. Glass–Steagall had mandated the institutional separation of major components of the US banking sector, in particular investment banking and commercial banking. Its goals were to reduce the scope for financial fraud by banking insiders, and reduce the risk of debt bubbles and financial contagions occurring via unsound lending by commercial banks to stock- or bond-market speculators.

Glass–Steagall was largely successful in achieving those goals, and was a major contributor to America's financial and economic stability – and by extension, that of the wider world – for several decades after the end of the Second World War. Glass–Steagall was written by policy-makers who had recognised that financial system instability caused by balance sheet entanglements between commercial banks and a variety of unregulated financial institutions, especially 'margin loans' to financial speculators, was what caused the Great Crash of the US economy in the autumn of 1929, which led to the Great Depression.

That deflationary disaster illustrates why sound regulation of financial systems and institutions is important to everyone, not only to bankers. The crash of 1929 was a direct consequence of weak financial sector regulation in the US, and it had world-historical consequences. It caused the economies not only of the US and Canada to melt down, but also those of many other nations financially linked to the US – including the German economy, whose deflationary collapse in 1929 led to the election of Adolf Hitler by a desperate electorate in 1933, the same year Glass–Steagall was passed. Had Glass–Steagall been legislated ten years earlier, the Second World War would most likely never have happened.

After many years of determined lobbying by increasingly influential Wall Street financiers, Glass–Steagall was repealed in 1999 under President Clinton by means of the Gramm–Leach–Bliley Act. At the same time, Secretary of the Treasury Larry Summers and other key members of President Clinton's economic policy team flatly refused to regulate financial derivatives.

The consequences were disastrous. The policies leading to Glass–Steagall's repeal quickly brought about the emergence of banking behemoths of such size and complexity that top management no longer really understood the institutions they supposedly ran. Bank balance sheets became choked with fraud-ridden mortgage derivatives, and the Great Financial Crisis (GFC) of 2007–8 ensued less than a decade later.

From the 1980s deregulation of savings and loan associations under President Reagan and the 'Big Bang' deregulation of the City of London under UK Prime Minister Margaret Thatcher onward, two decades of 'financial innovation' in the deregulated US and UK financial sectors allowed the scale of fraud, toxic debt creation and insider dealing to grow to truly monumental proportions.

The trend towards malfeasance, leveraged speculation and Ponzi schemes was abetted by the loosening of other legal constraints on the US financial sector beyond Glass–Steagall, as well as a long-standing policy of *laissez-faire* at US regulatory agencies like the Securities and Exchange Commission, which were not particularly energetic or serious about enforcing financial regulations that did exist. That was in line with the dominant philosophy of leading figures like long-time Federal Reserve chairman Alan Greenspan, an Ayn Rand disciple who believed with quasi-religious fervour that financial markets 'regulate themselves' out of self-interest. Vigorous enforcement of existing regulations in the lead-up to 2008, or indeed since, could have headed off a lot of trouble.

The entrenchment of financial power

Despite the enormous damage wrought by the GFC and its aftermath, and some half-baked attempts at re-regulation, culminating in the Dodd–Frank Act, passed into law in July 2010, the US has not managed to restructure its financial sector in ways that would effectively prevent fraud and ensure financial power is primarily aligned with the public interest. Nor have other jurisdictions.

That's because the banishment of effective regulation of finance over the past several decades, linked to persistent lobbying by financial interests that grew in scale and effectiveness in a self-reinforcing feedback loop as financiers' wealth increased, has led to an enormous entrenchment of the power and influence of the financial sector. The professional financial management class and its phalanx of lobbyists, think-tanks and beholden politicians has become increasingly able to shield the income and wealth of the well-to-do from state interventions, taxation or other constraints.

At the time of writing, some US politicians, including Vermont Senator Bernie Sanders, a candidate for the Democratic nomination for the US presidential election of 2016, are advocating the re-instatement of Glass–Steagall, i.e. the re-separation of investment banking and commercial banking. But the prospects for financial re-regulation seem dim in political economies as heavily influenced by the power of financial lobbies as those of the US or the UK.

The financial sector has achieved its legislative and regulatory aims in part by directly sponsoring accommodative politicians. It has also relentlessly promoted, through a vast industry of think-tanks, corporate media outlets and PR campaigns, misleading political narratives that have persuaded millions of ordinary voters that any and all government regulations – even regulations mandating minimum wages or consumer finance reforms – are bad for the economy and bad for ordinary workers.

From the 1980s onwards, unions in the US and the UK have been under frontal attack, and the negotiating position of workers has been progressively and durably weakened. Political lobbying campaigns aimed at weakening workers' relative economic bargaining power vis-à-vis major corporations became increasingly brazen after the end of the Cold War, perhaps because the population no longer needed to be persuaded of the relative advantages of the capitalist system over state socialism.

Moreover, 'stagflation' – a combination of stagnation and inflation that charac-terised the 1970s in North America and Europe – had caused many people to lose faith in old-school pro-labour policies by 1980. A backdrop of stagflation enabled 'free-market' politicians in the 1980s to convince ordinary voters that labour unions and regulations constraining corporations were causes of, rather than solu-tions to, their economic malaise. The consequent rise of Ronald Reagan in the US and Margaret Thatcher in the UK ushered in an era of financial sector deregulation and empowerment that culminated in the run-up to the GFC of 2007–8.

For more than a generation, pressure for redistribution of wealth or income from the rich to the poor was glibly dismissed with the aphorism that 'a rising tide lifts all boats', which claimed that if the rich got richer, the poor would do better as well – a claim that empirical data from the past three decades have unmasked as simply wrong.

Powered by faith in this simple aphorism, government policies since 1980 in much of the developed world have actively enabled redistribution in the opposite direction: from the lower- and middle-income classes towards an increasingly wealthy ownership class. Value-added taxes were increased, even as taxes on high incomes and capital were decreased. Sophisticated tax-avoidance schemes enabled many powerful corporations to escape taxation almost entirely. Profits rose even though investment fell as a proportion of gross domestic product (GDP).

Weakened aggregate demand

As a result of the world's collective obeisance to the preferences of the financial sector, advanced economies have not only seen an increased frequency of finan-cial crises and a marked increase in inequality of income and wealth. They've also seen a sustained decline and stagnation in rates of economic growth.

The reason is that the poor and middle classes are the engines of consumer spending. Net take-home income, for most people, is the money left over after taxes, payroll deductions, monthly rental or mortgage payments and other debt payments. As their debt burdens have increased, salaried workers' net take-home incomes have decreased, and they've been left with insufficient disposable income to sustain growth in aggregate economic demand.

It turns out increasing wealth in the hands of a small, wealthy minority reduces the overall level of economic activity. This isn't really surprising: the poor and middle classes quickly spend all the money they take in, whereas the wealthy save rather than spend most of their income. Money sitting idle in a savings account doesn't contribute to GDP. Nor does trading financial papers back and forth on secondary financial markets, bidding up the price of houses, stocks, bonds or Old Masters paintings.

Macroeconomic imbalances

As crucial as the trend towards rising wealth and income inequality has been to generating macroeconomic weakness, other factors have also contributed. They too are inherent to the structure of today's global financial system and the flawed policies that have given rise to it. Moreover, these other factors feed back into the problem of increasing inequality and macrofinancial instability.

One of these factors is the tendency of some countries to run massive trade surpluses. Some countries, like Germany, Japan and China, have in recent decades transformed themselves into strong net exporters that import significantly less than they export.

The first reaction of citizens in those countries might be to say: well done! Unfortunately, however, it turns out that running persistent trade surpluses is not a good thing – and nor is running persistent trade deficits. A balanced trade account is best for all concerned.

Germany's exports are primarily a consequence of the country's ability to produce high-quality goods and services that are in demand globally: cars, machine tools, chemicals, pharmaceuticals, software and many other things. Large exports are not, in themselves, a problem.

The problem arises when the stream of imports coming into a successful exporting country like Germany is persistently smaller in total value than the country's exports. This generates a build-up of debt among Germany's trading partners, and sooner or later, those debts will become so burdensome that they will cause economic problems in the debtor countries. At a minimum, the need to service their debt burdens drains purchasing power from debtor economies and weakens aggregate demand. In extreme cases, countries may become unable to service their debts, as in the case of Greece, and part of their accumulated debt may have to be written off – with potentially destabilising effects on the financial sector in the creditor country as well as the debtor country.

Why has Germany persistently imported less than it has exported?

The country's large export surpluses have been caused in part by falling or stagnating aggregate domestic consumer demand in Germany, due to stagnation of real wages (wages adjusted for inflation) among the lower-middle and working classes.

By keeping wages of German workers stagnant even as productivity per worker increased year-on-year, German corporations were able to offer products more cheaply to export markets, out-competing global competitors on price as well as quality. The consequent redistribution of income from wages to investible net corporate income was a fundamental cause of the German *Exportwunder* of recent years.

Unfortunately, the same mechanism that benefited those German companies contributed to economic stagnation in Italy, France, Spain and other countries, which were not able to suppress wages similarly and so were unable to keep up with German producers' aggressive price competition. Trapped as they were in a currency union with Europe's industrial powerhouse, they faced years of trade deficits vis-à-vis Germany, Austria and the Netherlands, as these countries' relative advantage in unit labour costs steadily increased.

Similar patterns were at work in two other leading global net exporters: China and Japan. These three countries piled up foreign assets (US sovereign bonds and other financial assets) in the amount of their respective surplus of exports over imports, year after year. The accumulated portfolio of foreign financial assets owned by households, corporations, banks or governments based in the world's major net exporting countries grew to gigantic proportions.

Trade surpluses and financial deregulation: a toxic cocktail

This led to growing imbalances in the global financial system – and that was an important factor in the post-1980 boom in the global financial industry, which found itself under sustained pressure to figure out ways to generate financial returns on huge piles of Chinese, German and Japanese savings, as well as those of Middle Eastern oil-producing countries.

That helped contribute to the mania for financial deregulation that began in the 1980s, and to the abandonment of prudential regulations that had been put in place decades earlier, in the wake of the Great Depression of the 1930s.

In the years between 2002 and 2006, a flood of savings looking for financial investment opportunities, combined with the pernicious effects of loose prudential lending regulations, meant that several countries experienced huge increases in mortgage credit lending. Banks lent money to people for the purpose of buying flats and houses on the apparent expectation that real estate prices would rise indefinitely. Enormous real estate bubbles were caused in the US, UK, Spain, Portugal, Ireland, Australia and Canada, and also in Asia, where Chinese real estate prices have reached unbelievable heights.

In 2007–8, real estate prices in several countries stopped rising and then collapsed – including in Spain, Ireland and the US. That caused numerous mortgage loan defaults, which quickly wiped out banks' capital buffers – since in many countries, banks' loan books are composed mostly of mortgage loans. Some banks went under, while governments bailed out others.

Bubbles deflated in some regions but not in others. London housing prices, for example, remain stratospheric. The real estate bubbles in Australia and Canada appear to have stopped expanding, but prices have not yet collapsed.

That doesn't mean no macroeconomic harm has yet occurred in countries where bubbles haven't deflated. In fact, harm is ongoing, as mortgage debtors and renters labour under extremely high monthly payment obligations that rob them of a large chunk of their monthly after-tax income. Rather than getting spent on consumer purchases, big slices of workers' incomes are transferred each month to building owners or to banks – and hence to bank shareholders and senior staff – reinforcing trends towards concentration of wealth in the hands of a small ownership class. That's an important contributor to the weakness in aggregate economic demand in many developed countries.

Bubbles and broken balance sheets

Where real estate bubbles have burst, households and firms that took on big mortgage loans have found themselves between a rock and a hard place. Real estate prices have sunk, but the debt obligations burdening borrowers haven't, leading to 'underwater mortgages'.

The bursting of national or regional mortgage bubbles resulted in a sudden stop to house-building booms and a wave of construction sector unemployment, with knock-on effects in other sectors. A reduction in the balance sheet value of houses also stopped booms in debt-based consumer spending based on people taking out second mortgages. A wave of mortgage and consumer loan defaults caused banks to adopt more cautious lending policies and reduce lending volumes.

As the economy shrank, households collectively had to spend a higher proportion of their income on mortgage payments, and correspondingly less on consumption of goods and services.

Taken together, the result was a spreading wave of unemployment crises, household debt overhangs and a lasting, self-reinforcing drop in aggregate consumer demand across whole economies – i.e. a vicious downward spiral of still lower demand, lower production and lower employment, leading to still lower demand, and so on. Government spending was ramped up to compensate, as automatic stabilisers like unemployment insurance or welfare payments kicked in, responding to the wave of unemployment caused by the sudden end of real estate construction booms and consumer spending sprees.

Dogmas and blindness to real-world causalities

Unfortunately, not everyone recognised that a large drop in aggregate demand caused by legacy debts burdening post-bubble economies was the main reason for flat or shrinking GDP in the wake of the 2007–8 financial crisis.

Instead, many European economists, politicians and journalists have propagated a different explanation. Governments in the European countries in crisis, they proclaimed, had loaded up with debt excessively and lived beyond their means, and so they must now tighten their belts in order to return to a sustainable economy – just like any private household must do when times are tough and credit card debt has to be paid down. Moreover, the reason some economies were in trouble was that they were inefficient, and structural reforms were needed, especially in order to increase the 'flexibility of labour markets'.

This line of argument became the conventional wisdom. In accordance with this doctrine, austerity policies and structural reform agendas were imposed on several countries – Portugal, Ireland, Spain, Greece – in exchange for emergency loans granted to their governments by European institutions when those countries were in dire need of emergency credit after the GFC shrank their economic activity and their governments' revenues. The European Central Bank (ECB), European Commission (EC) and International Monetary Fund (IMF) – the infamous 'Troika' – imposed cuts in wages and tight limits on government deficit spending on all four countries.

The belt-tightening did not, however, lead to a return to economic growth; instead, it led to stagnant or declining real GDP and sustained sky-high unemployment.

The package of austerity policies imposed on debtor nations in Europe was not a legal inevitability. It was a discretionary political choice by the EC. In fact, imposing austerity implicitly entailed ignoring several core policy goals set out in the preamble of the Treaty on European Union – for instance, the requirement for solidarity between European peoples, for maintaining and funding basic social services, for strengthening democracy and developing economic and social progress in Europe. All these goals were harmed by the consequences of austerity policies.

Had austerity policies been necessary – in the sense of necessarily imposing short-term pain for long-term gain – they might have been appropriate. Austerity policies imposed at times when aggregate demand is already weak, during recessions or after lending bubbles have burst, are simply counterproductive. They're neither necessary nor appropriate.

This is a controversial claim, but by the time you've read this book, you will probably agree with it. For now, here are a few additional claims for you to ponder.

Austerity policies throw millions of people out of work. Policies that throw millions of people out of work necessarily reduce the total amount of real goods and services produced by an economy. This is the case provided the people who lose their jobs were actually working while they were on the payroll, not merely drawing a salary and sitting around inactive, pretending to work, or in some cases not even showing up – a phenomenon that has not been uncommon in parts of the civil service of some southern European countries. The proponents of austerity have prescribed various reforms to try to reduce such problems. They're right about the need for such reforms, but they're wrong about the merits of budget austerity, as will be shown in this text.

The lower level of output caused by austerity means there are fewer goods and services available to distribute. Society becomes objectively poorer in material production terms. How can that be helpful – whether to the citizens, or the economy, or the financial system, or even to the creditors?

Mass unemployment is self-reinforcing, because it deprives unemployed people of the income needed to buy goods and services from each other, leading to still higher unemployment, and so on, in a downward spiral.

Some readers may object: what if there just isn't enough money to pay people? If there's just no money, it's no good going ever further into debt. Society has to bite the bullet and accept some unemployment if there's just not enough money to pay people. Right?

Wrong. Money is not actually a limited resource. Money is a scorekeeping tool, nothing more. Governments and central banks can no more run out of money than the scorekeeper of a basketball game can run out of scoring-points. Financial numbers in bank computers are routinely created or destroyed by banks, central banks and governments, limited only by accounting rules and conventions the government itself writes and imposes.

If excessive debts have built up somewhere in an economy, that implies equal amounts of credit have built up elsewhere in the economy. Governments have powers of taxation as well as credit creation that they can use to re-balance the distribution of debts and credits if they choose. Providing appropriate amounts of money, in the right places, for the right purposes, to keep an economy running smoothly is the core purpose of ministries of finance and banking institutions – it's the basic reason societies set them up.

What this adds up to is that unless debts are denominated in a foreign currency, a government and the banking system it ultimately controls cannot 'run out of money'. If politicians say otherwise, they either fundamentally don't understand banking, finance and taxation systems, or they're dissembling to promote a redistributive agenda such as the current emphasis in Europe on 'austerity'.

The real issue is the *distribution* of money and of debt – not its inherent availability or quantity.

Unfortunately, European governments gave up control over the central bank that creates and manages the Eurozone's currency and its stocks and flows of credits and debts. Eurozone countries have thereby given up a very important measure of national sovereignty and of democratic power. They've essentially adopted a foreign currency, the euro, which no single national government has effective control over.

Part of the reason this mistake was made may have had to do with the fact that academic economists advising governments have been misguided, for at least three decades, by an erroneous but dominant theory of macroeconomics that fails to incorporate a realistic understanding of how banking systems, money and debt relate to the functioning of real economies.

Theoretical failures

The surprising reality is that the conceptual analysis of the recent global financial crisis that has dominated the economic policy discourse in Europe in recent years has its roots in mistaken ideas about economics and finance that had already been recognised as incorrect by leading thinkers in the 1930s – mistaken ideas that made a comeback and became accepted as conventional wisdom in recent decades.

If those mistaken ideas could be replaced with a clear and realistic understanding of how the financial system works and how it relates to the real economy of goods and services, Europeans would realise that the continent's public sector could quite straightforwardly obtain and spend the money necessary to get Europe back on the path towards full employment and prosperity.

People would understand that 'lack of money' is not actually a real constraint at all, and that as long as there are underutilised resources in the form of unemployed Europeans who are willing to work, the money necessary to give them useful work can always be made available – whether by transfer of some existing money from idle savings pools to active circulation, or by temporary creation of new money.

The theoretical misunderstanding underlying the 'austerity' doctrine has been in play for several decades now, since the 1970s. However, for a long time, it didn't matter very much, because burgeoning credit creation continued to fuel expansion. In the period prior to the GFC of 2007–8, GDP growth rates were satisfactory and inflation was low. Except for the issue of extreme and rising inequality, and the fact that society was largely ignoring some very big 'externalities' such as atmospheric carbon pollution, the economy seemed to be doing fine. Most Europeans or Americans who wanted a job could find one.

What academic economists (and perhaps even some central bankers) mistakenly believed about how the economy works only became crucially relevant once a major systemic crisis broke out and the credit-generating machinery got stuck.

Prior to 2008, the potential for a massive systemic financial and economic crisis had been building up, yet only a few economists saw the GFC coming. Those who did were unusual in that they had special knowledge and expertise of the empirical workings of financial systems.

Surprising as it may seem to people who are unfamiliar with the dominant paradigms of academic economics, most economists prior to 2008 – and perhaps even today – believed that the details of monetary and banking systems didn't really matter, in the sense that they were thought to have little or no impact on supply and demand, economic growth or employment. They believed, as an article of faith learned in introductory economics courses early in their training, that monetary transactions are merely 'veils over barter' whose internal functioning has little or no macroeconomic relevance, and that 'money is neutral'. So most economists simply ignored the functioning of real banks and financial markets entirely.

Veil over empiricism

Guided by the false 'veil over barter' aphorism, which has been propagated in undergraduate economics textbooks for many decades, most academic economists spent their time making mathematical models of the economy in which money and debt either played no role at all, or in which money was treated as just another commodity – as if money still consisted of weights of gold or silver bullion that could be bartered for other things: a quarter ounce of gold for three horses and a cow.

The main point of this book is to serve as an antidote to the intellectual poison of the erroneous 'veil over barter' aphorism, helping readers understand the basic mechanisms of money, debt and financial systems. This will clarify why the details of financial systems, money and debt do indeed matter to macroeconomic performance, why any macroeconomic model that doesn't incorporate them is unrealistic, and why our financial system is in need of systemic reform.

This book accordingly rejects as erroneous the standard academic macroeconomic model, whose assumptions have been built into complex multivariate abstract mathematical structures called 'dynamic stochastic general equilibrium' (DSGE) models.

Among other conceptual absurdities, such as the assumption that economic actors consist of identical omniscient 'rational agents' all of whom have perfect information about prices and quantities everywhere in the global economy, DSGE models generally incorporate the erroneous 'veil over barter' notion and ignore the functioning of real monetary systems, working instead on the assumption that money is a commodity, something like a heap of gold coins.

DSGE models represent the distilled essence of the past three decades of dominant macroeconomic theory. Yet they are, to put it bluntly, nonsense. There is only one representative agent – no meaningful discussion of debt can take place in such a theoretical frame. These models are worse than useless – they are misleading. It's not just that they consistently generate incorrect macroeconomic projections; if they're used as a basis for guiding economic policy, they can lead to mistaken and harmful policy prescriptions.

Interlinked balance sheets

Instead of the otherworldly mathematical fantasy world of DSGE modelling, this book offers a theoretical framework based on a realistic, empirical understanding of the functioning of money and credit – an understanding which leads to very different policy prescriptions than those currently in vogue in Europe.

As we will see in the course of this book, the global financial economy is composed of a single interlinked network of electronic spreadsheets, distributed over thousands of bank computers. The story of the global economy can be understood by tracking the dynamic creation, destruction and direction of stocks and flows of credit and debt in and between those computers. The fates of individuals, households, corporations and entire nations are recorded in columns of offsetting financial numbers – i.e. the credit and debt numbers stored in electronic spreadsheets within the banking system, manipulated in accordance with accounting conventions governing double-entry bookkeeping.

Those conventions mandate that credit and debt must always be equal in quantity, created and maintained in a precisely one-to-one relationship. However, while credit and debt points are equal in aggregate quantity, they are anything but equal in distribution. Credit vs. debt, blue vs. red, concentrated purchasing power vs. debtors' burdens, freedom in prosperity vs. anxiety in debt-slavery – the story of our lives, and of the political economy of our global civilisation, is told in spreadsheet entries in banks' networked computers.

The balance sheet focused monetary theory underlying this book's perspective is not new, but it has fallen out of fashion in the past three or four decades. It is important to bring it back into the awareness of economists, policymakers and citizens. There is a dearth of texts that explain the background and mechanisms of the Eurozone crisis in plain language. My hope is that the present book will help fill the gap.

Part I

Theoretical foundations

In Part I we examine how essential components of our societies function. We address the question: what is the economy for?

With that question in mind, in Chapter 1, 'Substance and purposes of economic activity', we first identify broad classes of individual and social goals. Given that economic activity is a mechanism for achieving those goals, we'll ask what the implications for the design of a financial system might be.

We'll see that there's no single correct answer to this question. In practice, how a financial system is set up has been historically contingent on the goals of leading groups or networks of influence that exercised political power as the system grew and evolved. Unintended consequences have followed from many institutional changes, ranging from beneficial via trivial to destructive.

For readers mainly interested in understanding money and credit, Chapter 1 can be skipped.

1 Substance and purposes of economic activity

Gossipy stardust, with tools

Some years ago, the space probe *Voyager 1* sent a picture of Earth back to Mission Control. Taken from the edge of our solar system, it showed our planet as a pale blue dot in a nebular mist. On that tiny blue dot lost in the inky blackness of space, at the moment in time when Voyager's camera shutter recorded the image, several billion human beings went about their business, as did uncounted billions of ants, flies, nematodes, mice, plankton and jellyfish.

In the context of billions of years of universal time, mankind seems like a meaningless anomaly. Nevertheless, we're part of the universe – arguably the most interesting part, at least in our particular corner of the Milky Way galaxy. Our connectedness to the rest of the universe can be recognised in the fact that our bodies consist of components similar to those that constitute celestial bodies. We are, in the end, stardust.

Our connectedness to each other can be recognised in a multitude of ways – not only in the similarity of our body chemistry and our genes, but also in our need for company, for communication and for making deals with each other.

As a social species, experience and evolutionary pressures long ago taught us that we cannot long survive as isolated individuals, whereas we can do almost anything if we band together in highly structured groups that divide up specialist tasks and collaborate on projects – whether the project is to hunt down a few zebras in the East African savannah and turn them into meat, leather and clothing, or to build a space probe capable of sending pictures back from the edge of the solar system.

Experience has shown us the extraordinary powers we can gain by making tools and mastering their coordinated use. Other species on our planet also form into teams, gangs, bands or groups, and they too communicate – horses, dolphins, baboons, starlings and meerkats are examples. Some other species, like chimpanzees and ravens, are capable of using primitive tools, such as sticks to poke at things. What's unusual about human beings is our unparalleled sophistication in all three of these domains: social communication, tool-making and group organisation. Taken together, these abilities have turned us, over the past 100,000 years, into a new kind of animal never before seen on this planet. We've become, in effect, a magician species, capable of the most extraordinary tricks. 'Economics' is the study of some of the systems we've developed to help coordinate our efforts and make deals with each other as we set about performing our extended magic show.

Natural laws, artificial rules

The world as we find it, with all the things it contains, organic and inorganic, is subject to natural laws. In that sense, the world is determinate. Some things are possible, even inevitable, whereas other things are impossible. We know that's how the world works, even if we haven't yet figured out what all the natural laws are.

The rules that govern the interactions of human beings, by contrast, are much less determinate and more flexible than the basic laws of physics and chemistry, even if our culturally determined rules are, at the end of the day, also subject to the constraints of basic natural laws.

Clever chimps

Human beings are a species of great ape, closely related to chimpanzees, orang-utans and gorillas, all species whose genes are mostly identical to ours. Great apes are social animals – orang-utans less, gorillas and chimpanzees more, humans intensely so. All the great apes live in social groups, all experience dispute and cooperation, joy and sorrow, alliances and enmities. All use tools to some extent. However, even our closest relatives are animals whose behaviour is mostly instinctual and moment-to-moment, and whose tool use is, compared to ours, negligible.

Humans are the talking, tool-making, long-range-planning, super-sophisticated genius model in our planet's great ape product line: stardust reconfigured for gossip and magic. Our social groups consist of individuals with complex personal histories and narratives. Each of us nourishes hopes and plans, and we're intent on realising at least some of them. We're individuals, yet we don't exist independently of one another. We exist in complex webs of relationships, and we influence each other constantly. We are each other's echo chambers and transformers.

Human beings have an extraordinarily well-developed ability to think, plan and take decisions in accordance with plans, in the context of complex knowledge and social roles, far outstripping that of any other species on our planet.

In a semi-determinate world causally dominated by the past and constrained by basic natural laws, human beings are strongly shaped by their physical and cultural environments. At the same time, we reciprocally shape the trajectory of our own and each others' lives.

It's the exceptional destiny of human beings to investigate our surroundings, and then redesign them, as we attempt to realise some of the inherent possibilities of the world in which we're embedded. And the more we learn about the basic laws of nature, and develop sophisticated cultural and technical recipes for manipulating it, the wider and deeper the range of possibilities.

As we set about this process of exploration and manipulation, we form teams to do things we cannot achieve alone. We collaborate, compete and exchange with others, individually and in groups. We make deals with each other.

Those deals have deal terms, ranging from high-level agreements like the legal and monetary frameworks our deals are embedded in, all the way down to prices and delivery schedules for individual sales. The deal terms – that's what monetary economics is really about.

Filters on our eyes, ears and brains

Having a consistent framework of laws, customs and procedures helps us navigate a complex world which none of us individually can fully comprehend. Each of us possesses only a limited amount of information, and our mental models of the world are necessarily incomplete approximations. Often we rely on rules of thumb and other heuristics to guide our behaviours. Our brains cannot process all the available information coming in through our senses, so they use various tricks to simplify and screen for what's important from moment to moment. Abstractions help us to organise the vast amount of information flooding in.

Our vocabulary is abstract, too, and hence of limited validity. There will never be complete agreement on what different individuals mean by words like 'nice' or 'grotty' or even 'red' or 'green'. Each individual's vision of reality is necessarily influenced by his or her subjective context, each of us has a partial and limited perspective on events and realities in which we're embedded. However, through a long, slow process of acculturation, and systems for resolving ambiguity of definition and interpretation ranging from dictionaries to law courts and a great deal of arguing and discussing, we use language to help us make sophisticated deals with each other.

Even when we slow down and use careful reasoning, we're faced with constraints of bandwidth, abstraction and perception, as well as cultural and personal biases. The processes of perceiving and understanding the world and the factors and relations that constitute it lead to a constant evolution of knowledge (or pseudo-knowledge) – a process which cannot stop, since our world is constantly changing, not least because our collective and individual actions are constantly causing changes.

This constant change affects both the nature of the deals we're able to make with each other, and the frameworks those deals are made within. For example, 50 years ago, nobody was in a position to make deals over internet website access charges, since the internet didn't exist. New laws and a whole new vocabulary have had to be invented to help us make deals around this powerful new technology since it emerged into commercial relevance in the early 1990s.

Goals of individuals and society

The fact that none of us can ever develop a full understanding of reality doesn't limit our collective powers. No single person has the knowledge and skills to build an aeroplane, or even to fully understand all its components and how they were produced – yet by working in teams, we can build excellent aeroplanes that are fast, safe and powerful. Our abilities to master tool use, to communicate and to cooperate, including by making sophisticated and durable deals with each other, has given teams of us powers far in excess of those of any single individual.

Together, we understand enough to have transformed ourselves into the Sorcerer's Apprentice. From modest beginnings as small teams of hunter-gatherer apes in East Africa's savannahs, we've become a race of ultra-collaborative ape magicians. Now rampant possibility defines human existence. The future is open, and we have the freedom to shape it.

Evolution doesn't plan, but it shapes a species' genes in iterative interaction with a complex environment. Evolution didn't 'intend' to turn us into magicians, but that's what emerged as a consequence of evolution's shaping our savannah-ape hunter-gatherer ancestors' genes to enable them to plan ahead, rather than stumble about randomly, and to hunt in teams.

Hunters and gatherers plan their forays. Albert Einstein put it this way: planning means that randomness is substituted with error. As our communications abilities evolved in sophistication, and especially since we invented durable systems for remembering and sharing knowledge – at first by means of tribal sages memorising and repeating traditional wisdom sayings or didactic stories, then by writing, now through films and interactive computer programs, and soon by means of interactive virtual-reality immersion systems – records of past errors have helped us avoid or reduce future ones.

Wondrous conceptual tools in the hands of groups of testy apes

Natural sciences have been enormously useful in our economic and cultural evolution, since an understanding of chemical and physical causalities enables the construction of sophisticated and precise tools and instruments. The cumulated technological progress that has followed on the industrial revolution has radically changed the way we live, and further technological revolutions are most assuredly on their way. It's here, at the interface of knowledge, skills and social interactions, that economics comes into focus.

At the same time, our grasp of physical science is what may eventually kill us all, along with a substantial portion of the rest of the biosphere. We may be genius, talking, tool-making, super-social ape magicians, but we're still apes. Our species, like other mammalian band-forming species ranging from horses to baboons, carries a powerful instinct for dividing the human world into Us and Them, Friend and Foe, and banding together to fight the foe.

As individuals, our cooperative and collaborative social instincts are offset by an instinct for seeking personal gain and dominance. As a result, we have a tendency to sometimes behave as irresponsible, selfish, manipulative game-players with a mean streak, like the demigod Loki in Norse mythology, or the trickster Raven in the mythology of coastal Pacific Northwest native tribes.

By realising that there are physical laws, and recognising that we can discover them and use them to manipulate and redesign our world, we've given ourselves the keys to Pandora's box. We're at one and the same time so extremely clever as to be able to understand nuclear physics and genetics, and so extremely empathy-devoid, stupid and vicious as to use that knowledge to build nuclear weapons and biowarfare agents to aim at our perceived 'enemies' – failing to recognise the really rather obvious fact that the people we class as 'enemies', the Foe, the Other, are really exactly like us, just ordinary people living their ordinary lives. Somehow, by being attached to a different societal group, enormous categories of people become labelled as Them rather than Us.

If a group of Them is further labelled as a Foe, they become unworthy of any empathy whatsoever, and may legitimately be killed and maimed in their millions. Indeed, our leaders sometimes convince us that mass killings of the Foe must be done, and done urgently, as a matter of the highest priority, worthy of the greatest efforts.

Yet we are capable of routinely acting with consistent decency and empathetic reciprocity towards those whom we consider fellow members in various categories of Us.

The reality is that enormous amounts of creative effort, generating some of humanity's most impressive technological achievements, have resulted from frantic efforts of rival groups of Us to develop more effective ways of killing Them efficiently and in large quantities. Notwithstanding this undeniable fact, we might want to give more thought, as we set out to understand 'economics', to the question of whether and how a political economy might be designed in which the prevailing rewards, incentives and institutional processes result in the emergence of a world in which there exists, in this sense, only Us and Us, and no longer Us and Them.

Goods and services

A crucial dimension of the human enterprise is the provision of goods and services. We've understood that we can make or do almost anything that's physically possible, and that the range of physical possibilities is almost infinite. How to individually and collectively form and express specific preferences for goods and services within that vast realm of possibility, and how to effectively satisfy the demand for those goods and services – these are the core concerns of economics.

It's standard to say 'goods and services', yet the range of possibilities and preferences encompasses bads and disservices, too. Fluffy plush toys, tasty meals and hot baths; cigarettes, machine guns, suicide belts and torture services – there's a market for nearly anything.

Not all of these 'goods and services' are things or experiences that can be purchased by single individuals in a free marketplace. There are social-historical 'markets' too, at which only groups or movements can express preferences or demand new types of goods and services.

Caught in the moment, living fragments of our particular time and place, we sometimes forget that there have been enormous social transformations over the course of just the past few generations: the limitation of daily and weekly working hours, the introduction of state-sponsored education for all children, of unemployment and health insurance as well as pensions, the enforcement of higher wages that led to the rise of the so-called middle class.

These achievements didn't just spontaneously happen – they originated from the pressure of organised groups of people who demanded these things, pushing against other organised groups who didn't want to see them emerge, in the socio-political marketplaces of cultural evolution.

Models and dogmas

The foundations of the progressive collective demands that emerged in recent centuries are built on Enlightenment-era humanism. Oddly, this humanism has in recent decades faded from the spotlight in the narratives we tell about how our economy and society work. It has been replaced to a large extent by a simplified narrative of a mythical 'rational economic agent', a cartoonish, primitive story that claims the profit motive, or a mysterious 'utility maximisation function', as the prime mover of all human behaviour.

It's a false narrative. Extremely oversimplified, mathematised caricatures of human behaviour, invented by nineteenth-century economic theorists intent on developing tractable mathematical models of marketplace exchanges, somehow evolved into ideological dogmas, assumptions that 'utility-maximising rational economic agents' are what human beings actually *are*, or if not, it's what they *should be*.

In the English-language world, this ideological perspective has attained popularity in significant part through the writings of Ayn Rand. Her 'positivist' philosophy, expressed in didactic novels, preached that altruism is evil and total selfishness is the highest form of morality. She rejected all pro-social or empathetic behaviour as inconsistent with the Invisible Hand of capitalist endeavour that guides selfish behaviour to result, allegedly, in the highest advancement of humanity. Her novels, which promoted adulation of particularly ruthless capitalists as successful Nietzschian superheroes, have become something akin to the sacred texts of the American 'libertarian' movement.

Bolstered by the propagation of ideological writings like Rand's novels, the mathematical simplifications of nineteenth-century economic theorists who caricatured economic actors as utterly selfish 'utility-seeking rational economic agents' – mostly in order to simplify their mathematical games with systems of equations, rather than out of any conviction that humans lack pro-social instincts – took on a teleological dimension.

In so far as humans do not actually behave according to their free-market rational-economic-agent model schema, neoclassical economists apparently grew angry with reality for failing to correspond to the assumptions built into their mathematical models. They began to insist that legal frameworks and financial systems should be changed to incentivise human beings to behave as much as possible like the caricatures in those models. Rather than change their elegant mathematical oversimplifications, they wanted to change the world itself, so that it would behave as much as possible like a system of individual representative 'rational economic agents' interacting as utility-maximising free agents in perfectly free markets.

Only recently, with the emergence of more empirically realistic methods and approaches such as 'behavioural economics' that take into account the insights of decades of research into social psychology and anthropology, has this dogma begun to lose some of its allure.

History and ideology

Had history lessons, including lessons on the history of academic economics itself, been included in standard economics-major college curricula during recent decades, the rather odd collective sojourn of mainstream academic neoclassical economics down a conceptual and methodological blind alley might have been avoided.

Economics students would have known that the Enlightenment project of compulsory school attendance for all children, for example, was not originally based on a plan to maximise GDP by training more disciplined workers with useful skills like reading and writing. It was based on the premise that more education is ennobling, that it would enable people to live better, culturally and intellectually richer lives. Productivity and GDP have increased as a by-product of improved education, but that wasn't the original purpose of the drive to provide all children with basic education.

Yet we have become so accustomed to thinking about everything related to public policy in terms of maximising economic metrics like GDP that, today, it might seem slightly controversial to suggest that universal education would have been worthwhile even if it had *not* increased GDP as a side effect.

The reality is that our civilisation's processes for arriving at decisions about what goods and services (or bads and disservices) to produce are complex and politically charged. They are not merely the result of individual 'rational economic agents' in utilitarian free spot-markets, and attempting to model human behaviours and systems as if this were the case is unrealistic, disingenuous and burdened with crushing loads of ideological baggage.

It's not difficult, by means of a simple thought experiment, to see that trying to induce the world to set up spot-markets in everything, the better to conform to academic mathematical models assuming perfectly rational utility-maximising agents, would be unrealistic. Should there be a spot-market in hugs? Should mothers refuse to change their babies' nappies unless the broke little buggers can offer an acceptable price for the service?

Aggregating this sort of thought experiment to a macroeconomic scale, wouldn't it be more rational to euthanise ageing workers after they're too old to efficiently provide productive services in competitive spot-markets? That would probably maximise society's aggregate utility curve, especially since aged people's utility curves go negative with illness and disability anyway, right?

As we say goodbye to legends of notional 'rational utility maximisers' based on excessively abstract nineteenth-century economic models, and set out to develop a more empirically grounded understanding of economics, it's worth developing our awareness of just how complicated, multi-layered, historically contingent, path-dependent, socially determined, politically contested and feedback-ridden our processes for generating 'demand' for 'goods and services' really are.

Looking back towards one of history's most successful and durable political economies drives this point home, and reminds us that, just as the past looks very different from the present, political economies of the future may look very different from those of today.

Economic activity as a central mechanism of societal design

Organised groups of people can achieve astonishing things. That has been true for a long time. The pyramids of Giza – giant tombs for absolute monarchs – are an example of the enormous creative energy of antiquity, but also, perhaps, of how the focus of a civilisation can be misdirected to an astonishing extent. An entire civilisation spent several thousand years devoted to building ever larger, more grandiose tombs for the leading members of its 'royal' family. Hmm. Apparently this worked well as a device to maintain political, economic and cultural stability and continuity – but considered in the round, at least from our own era's cultural perspective, was it a good choice?

Today, the state generally finances projects of more obvious use to the general public, and workers generally enter voluntary rather than forced labour contracts. And today, the material-technological limits of the possible are expanding further and further into fantastical realms, reminding us of science-fiction writer Arthur C. Clarke's beautiful and profound observation that 'any sufficiently advanced technology is indistinguishable from magic'.

The sheer scope for ambitious projects made possible by the abundance of human, technical and material resources that could be mobilised in the context of a modern civilisation is mind-boggling. This should motivate us to take a closer look at how we make decisions about what projects to embark on, and how we allocate resources to them.

With an eye towards the example provided by Egypt's Pharaonic civilisation, and what most of us today would probably consider its exuberantly misallocated focus of collective effort, we can observe with some relief that cultural evolution continues. We have not arrived at the end of history, nor at the final, definitive political-economic ideology.

History suggests that achieving a very durable political-economic system, a systemic stable state capable of perduring for millennia in the manner of Pharaonic Egypt, is quite unlikely in an era of rapid technological change and multicultural interaction. The example of old Egypt, a largely isolated civilisation in which technology, culture and political economy changed very little over millennia, shows that this is just as well: great political-economic systemic stability may not be particularly desirable.

Given our survey of a sampling of economic problems in our own era in the introduction, and the examples of past civilisations whose institutions were fiercely defended at the time but in retrospect seem to us curious or misdirected, we might want to ask whether our current systems and mechanisms for deciding on projects and allocating resources are as good as they could be at meeting our most important needs first – and whether they are sufficiently attuned, also, to the necessity of avoiding the provision of the most fatefully dangerous and damaging bads and disservices which we are all too capable of delivering as well.

What are some of the basic features of our contemporary civilisation's allocative systems and mechanisms? A few pertinent observations:

- The mechanisms by which the state enables its own access to domestic resources, including the rules by which it finances infrastructure investment and other public expenditures, are formally determined by constitutional law.
- The potential output of the present has been determined by investments made in the past.
- Today's investments and expenditures by the state, the private sector and the rest of the world determine the potential output of the near future.
- A key to optimising today's investments, and hence to optimising the intended design of the future, is the constitution and direction of the monetary system.
- *Where the money flows, there too the future goes.*

This last point is the reason why this text, starting from Part II, is centrally concerned with how stocks and flows of money and debt are generated and directed.

Before we go there, let's wander a little further over the civilisational terrain whose monetary system we'll be picking apart, and consider some other factors that influence the evolution of political economies.

Geography and endowments

Geography obviously plays a role in how a society's economy develops. Some raw materials are only available in certain regions, and some regions might lack certain key raw materials altogether.

Interestingly, however, poverty of raw materials does not necessarily lead to economic underdevelopment. In fact, the opposite may be the case. Countries endowed with rich raw material resources are often relatively poor. They focus on exporting those raw materials in trade for manufactured or consumer goods, and produce relatively little in the way of high-value-added products domestically. This leaves them vulnerable to downturns in the price of their main commodities. Moreover, the earnings from commodity exports tend to be concentrated in the hands of relatively few people.

In contrast, proximity to big markets can transform small countries with few natural resources into important industrial or trading powerhouses, as the examples of Switzerland, the Netherlands, Singapore and Hong Kong show. As long as commodity prices are high enough, commodity-dependent economies like Russia or the Gulf Arab states can provide a large source of demand for manufactured products from countries that are poor in natural resources yet rich in organisational, human-development and technical terms.

Technology trumps commodities

This reminds us that there are always three essential ingredients in an economy: natural resources, skilled people and organisation. If nature is very generous to a human population in terms of its endowment of local natural resources, those populations needn't work quite so hard as the other two. On balance, that's probably not an advantage.

These three ingredients have always been essential to civilisation's progress, and they remain so today. Before the Pyramid at Giza was built, a mighty tomb emblematic of an ancient civilisation's power, the physical substance of that pyramid was already in existence. It was composed of 5.5 million tonnes of limestone embedded in the crust of the earth near the Nile River. What made that limestone into a fabulously ostentatious monument to a ruler's ego was a grand plan, organised teams of workers, supply chains for provisioning them, social systems for retaining, leading, motivating, rewarding and disciplining them, and a great deal of digging, chiselling and heaving.

In essence, the Pyramid was made of dug-up dirt plus skilled human labour organised into effective teams in the service of a detailed plan, a plan that in this case was ultimately motivated by some very base human instincts.

Dirt plus a plan plus people organised in teams to make the plan happen.

That's how the smartphone in your pocket is built, too.

Socially embedded individuals

Let's return for a moment to the topic of the openness or indeterminacy of the future, and how its unfolding is influenced by tangled webs of reciprocal interaction between individuals and social groups.

The fact that society is composed of individuals has triggered an extensive ideological contestation over the past couple of centuries, and inspired different experiments in collectivism and radical individualism. Some thinkers have emphasised that individuals are shaped by society, others that individuals shape society. In reality, of course, both views are correct, and a realistic understanding of an economy, or of history, cannot be achieved by overemphasis on one perspective or the other.

A paramount fact about our contemporary world, in stark contrast to the world in which the Pharaoh's pyramid-building work crews lived, is the pressure of rapid change in the key variables driving the evolution of the future. Technological and demographic changes continually drive civilisational evolution, with added influence from intensive and extensive interactions with foreign cultures. As a result, the rules of contemporary societies must frequently adjust to new circumstances and technologies.

People's ideas about their environment are also constantly being updated in our era of massive information flows and technological acceleration. Ideas exert an influence on society, but the rules and norms of society also exert an influence on individuals. Individuals are changed by their changing technological and informational context, but they also can become change agents. Moreover, in many modern societies, a broad range of subcultures is available, with which people can affiliate if they choose. Taken together, all this provides the individual with much more freedom of manoeuvre regarding the future than was the case in static societies such as ancient Egypt.

The resulting reflexive processes between individuals, groups and societies are very complex, and an assessment of the merits or demerits of individual changes is not easily possible. Even societies that cling to 'bad' ideas can sometimes do well. Monarchies of any kind, for example, are a 'bad' idea from a meritocratic standpoint. However, the transition from absolute to parliamentary monarchies in Europe over the past few centuries has led to material improvements for large parts of the population. This change led to one of many possible futures – better than what existed before, perhaps, but not necessarily the best we could do.

In this sense, changes of institutions are only improvements in relative terms, without any claim to perfection. In contemporary Europe, we're trained to think that a liberal representative democracy with free competitive markets complemented by well-financed social insurance safeguards is the best possible civilisational system. Leaving aside the question of whether this is indeed the best possible system, we can observe that it probably would have been impossible to set up democratic nation-states corresponding to this model in the Europe of 2,000 years ago, given the technological and social conditions of that earlier era. But this doesn't imply that no improvements of society would have been possible in classical Rome. There's also no good reason to think we couldn't improve quite substantially on the system we have now.

While we're on the topic of 'we', let's take a moment to acknowledge how profoundly important the many forms of 'we' are in our lives, and how remote from reality the neoclassical economists' model of humanity as a collection of isolated individual utility-maximisers really is.

The many forms of 'we'

Individuals attempt to understand the world they're embedded in, and also to manipulate it. However, the influence of any single individual in isolation is limited. This is why we organise ourselves into various groups – for instance, political parties, firms, families, clubs and religious communities. Team efforts make it possible to achieve purposes and projects that no single individual could hope to achieve alone. Moreover, in many cases, our 'individual' aims are defined by our wanting to make a contribution to an organisation. A sense of belonging, and of having a valued role in a group to which one belongs, or wants to belong, is what gives meaning and purpose to most lives.

Some individual or group goals are largely independent of inputs of material goods or services (e.g. an a-cappella choir's goal to put on a concert on the evening of the Winter Solstice), while others are overwhelmingly concerned with material processes and outputs (e.g. a car company's plan to produce half a million minivans for sale in Europe next year). Invariably, however, achieving any of our aims requires material inputs at least indirectly.

Teams and their goals are found at many different levels, from bottom-up efforts agreed by a few individuals – like the a-cappella choir – all the way to highly organised multi-level hierarchical social structures like the sort of corporate entity needed to build half a million minivans.

Some group aims are so high-order that they encompass enormous amounts of resources, with myriad sub-goals and specialist teams organised to work in collaboration. The desire of a nation to avoid being subject to intimidation by a neighbouring nation, for example, may require conscription of a million-man defensive army supplied by abundant goods and services. This example reminds us of the vast power and scope of top-down structured collaboration.

By the same token, if societies are structured to carry out projects decided on by top-level leaders in hierarchies that have the authority to mobilise a substantial fraction of society's total resources, as is the case in well-functioning nation-states, the end result can be quite absurd, and in some cases horribly dystopian, even if the members and leaders of all the subordinate teams are intelligent, honourable people simply performing their duties competently and conscientiously, achieving assigned sub-aims. The top leadership may have decreed, for example, that the bundled resources of society are to be allocated to building a giant tomb for the Leader to be buried in after his death, as did the Pharaohs, or that a vast military organisation be assembled not for the purpose of defence, but rather for the conquest and enslavement of neighbouring peoples, as did Genghis Khan or Hitler.

Surveying the field of human endeavour and organisation, we see that social and individual goals are invariably linked inextricably to each other. Speaking about them as if they were in separate categories is really a form of verbal simplification more than a reflection of reality. And no matter how 'non-materialistic' our goals may seem, they always have economic consequences.

Ethical economics, and the economics of ethics

Non-materialistic aims and desires have come to include concepts like 'freedom' and 'equality'. These notions are based in ethical principles that recognise fundamental human rights. These are based, in the end, on the Golden Rule: the recognition that each person is at the centre of their own world, and that we should avoid doing to others what we wouldn't want done to us. If we set out to rework our civilisation in a quest to honour these ethical principles, we face the challenge of creating circumstances enabling the coexistence of people under humane conditions, regardless of their individual characteristics and differences.

This is why, for instance, in most countries slavery has been at least formally abolished, because it isn't justifiable in ethical terms. This choice was made despite the fact that for thousands of years, slave states were economically successful civilisations – at least from the perspective of the slave-owning class. Slavery was one way of seeing to the organisation of teams of skilled workers able to make useful things out of dirt and detailed plans.

But it has turned out that the abolition of slavery and serfdom didn't cause economic disaster, as slaveholders in the pre-civil-war US South had warned. The end of slavery was an important contributing factor to economic growth in the gradually industrialising world, since greater freedoms and incomes for larger numbers of people stoked aggregate demand. This example shows that acting on lofty ideas about ethics or justice can have powerful consequences in the economic sphere – whether intentionally or as a side effect.

Institutionalisation of ethical principles

A crucial issue in contemporary economics is equality of opportunity. It's a natural extrapolation of the same impulse that lends to the banishment of slavery. Should all people have the same quality and abundance of opportunities to do something meaningful with their lives? How does one establish equality of opportunity? The motto of the French Revolution, 'Liberty, Equality, Fraternity', has to be backed up by institutions if the words are not to remain empty shells.

Since the European Enlightenment era, there has been growing agreement that institutions should provide for the realisation of fundamental ideas of justice, individual freedom, peaceful coexistence and cooperation. The constitutions of European states accordingly guarantee irrevocable fundamental rights to individuals, and states have set up a variety of institutional mechanisms to foster movement in the direction of equality of opportunity.

The public education system provides children with free schooling to provide a basis for at least some degree of equality of opportunity. Police and the judiciary try to ensure that laws are respected, and although the reality doesn't always meet the ideal, the same laws are supposed to apply impartially to everyone, rich or poor, peasant or proprietor. Those laws are the outcome of carefully structured democratic processes, stabilised by the constitution.

The economic machine

Meanwhile, the monetary system hums along in the background, enabling all the myriad transactions between the players in the daily theatre of life in modern states. Commercial banks, coordinated through the central bank, ensure the smooth operation of payment and credit systems. The institutional machinery churns through its complex and often inscrutable processes, enabling us to make deals with each other, as individuals and in teams, and finding ways to encourage us to honour the terms of the deals we've made. That's a big part of what the economic machinery is really for. Most of our needs and wants can only be met through collaborative efforts, and countless deals have to be made in order to achieve complex systems capable of supplying myriad goods and services.

It's clear that there is a huge diversity of individual and social desires that require goods and services to be provided. In addition to meeting basic needs like housing, clothing and food, people seek individual fulfilment in various ways. Some learn to play an instrument, some to master a sport or a game. Others buy an expensive new car to show off their financial success. Society's collective goals require supply chains for everything from road, school and hospital construction to police and other armed forces. Given the multitude of demands and desires, some sort of mechanism is required to supply appropriate amounts of goods and services to fulfil those desires. How, in broad terms, does that work?

Let's think about the division of labour, the role of markets and how money fits into the picture.

The division of labour and functions of money

The production of goods and services depends on many different factors, but the most important are technology, environment and social organisation – i.e. we're back to our magic formula again: detailed plans, dirt and organised teams of skilled workers. These are the basic ingredients with which we make everything, including aeroplanes, pyramids, football games, armies in the service of totalitarian dictators bent on conquest, organic farms and factories pumping out plushy toys.

The first order of business, always, is to set up farms. They're the base of every other supply chain. The foundation of human civilisation is an abundant supply of agricultural products.

Imagine a tribe so poorly equipped in terms of agricultural technology that it takes all of a family's full-time labour to produce a food supply sufficient to keep starvation at bay. In that civilisation, people would have to work for subsistence every day. It would be impossible to build villages or cities. One year's work output would be one year's food output, and nothing more.

If we increase agricultural labour productivity by a factor of ten, however, then one farming family can produce an annual food supply sufficient to nourish ten families. That leaves nine families in a position to follow other occupations. How is it determined what these occupations will be?

In this scenario, we're already past the stage of Stone Age farming villages, and we're well removed from the hunter-gatherer way of life in which humanity spent most of the past 100,000 years. In early villages, nearly every family was a farming family, and most continued doing a bit of hunting and gathering on the side. A scenario in which there are nine non-farming families for each farming family puts us in a fairly advanced civilisation, with towns and skilled trades.

Since all of its members need food, they want to be in a position to barter with the farmer, directly or indirectly. This is why they're likely to produce something the farmer wants or needs, or something which people want or need who have, in turn, already received some food from the farmer. How does that work?

The barter story

This idea of a barter economy is routinely raised in introductory economics texts. It's proposed that money evolved as early townies settled on some standard, divisible, easy-to-measure and easy-to-carry commodity with which to barter for various goods. Grain would meet the description, except that it spoils easily. Gold or silver dust, eventually cast into standardised coins, became standard, so the story goes, because these metals are divisible, easy to carry, extremely durable and sufficiently rare and difficult to get hold of so as to have intrinsic scarcity value.

However, barter was not in fact the historical origin of money. The rise of modern money goes hand in hand with taxation by the state. In the earliest Mesopotamian civilisations, taxes were paid in kind – farmers and bakers surrendered a tithe in grain to the lords of their estate or the chiefs of their village. This kind of system continued on for millennia, well into feudal Europe, where some number of bushels of grain or sheep or pigs were due to the local lord from each farming family every year. At some point, however, the local population was obliged to supply 'money' rather than actual goods like grain or sheep to the tax collectors.

The monetary circuit

In the modern world, if the state wants to buy some of the labour power of its subjects, it must first introduce a monetary system, and then a tax that is to be paid in the state's particular form of money.

The state determines which forms of money it will accept in payment of taxes – e.g. tally sticks in medieval England, the state's currency more recently – and establishes a unit of account: for example, pounds, dollars or euro. It also passes laws asserting that all financial contracts within the realm are to be denominated in that unit of account. A monetary system established in this way is a fundamental component of the operating system of every sovereign state. No state that lacks such a system is truly sovereign.

A sovereign government uses its powers of law-making and coercion to create demand for a specific form of money – a particular money or a system that it controls. It asserts that its subjects have to pay taxes in the state's particular form of money, on pain of punishments or sanctions if they fail to do so, and it also creates a system to collect those taxes.

Once it has done these things, the only thing left to do for government is to spend money into circulation so that the people can do business with each other, and also obtain the means to pay their taxes. One way the state could do this would be to pay a monetary wage for labour services, using the money it has decreed as the official currency within its sovereign realm, and in this way start up a monetary circuit.

What taxes are really for

If the government establishes a monetary system and defines some arbitrary unit of account, like the pound or euro, which can easily be produced in unlimited quantities by the government itself, why does it levy taxes?

It's true that a sovereign government with its own money can always produce more of it, in whatever quantities it likes, subject only to laws and rules it has itself set up. However, there are two excellent reasons to demand payment of taxes.

First, obliging citizens to pay taxes in the government's money, with a credible threat of serious punishments for failure to do so, forces citizens to do whatever they can to acquire such money. It 'establishes demand' for that particular kind of money. Second, tax payments reduce the amount of money in circulation, and thereby prevent inflation.

Let's consider the coercive aspect first. Compulsory taxes lead people to accept the government's money as the thing they need in order to deal with future tax liabilities. For example, a farmer in medieval Europe will have had an awareness that several of the duke's armed henchmen would stop by around the time of the first full-moon after the Winter Solstice, and demand ten pieces of silver coin with the duke's head stamped on them in profile. Moreover, the farmer was acutely aware that the duke's tax collectors would be violently angry with him if he didn't have ten ducal silver coins to give them.

This is a caricature, a 'stylised fact' as economists like to put it, and the details of how the state today coerces acceptance of its money are more complex and subtle than they were when ducal henchmen rode from village to village, but at bottom the principle remains the same. The state's particular form of 'money' is necessary for the reduction of tax liabilities vis-à-vis the state, and in functional terms, this generates a promise of its wide acceptance. It makes sense for private households to decide to enumerate prices and fix debt contracts in the currency units of the state. This makes state money doubly useful: it can be used to clear private debts vis-à-vis households or firms, as well as pay one's taxes to the state.

The second purpose of taxes is to reduce the number of currency units in circulation, and thereby ensure that money is appropriately scarce. Properly tuning the scarcity value of money is crucial to its effectiveness in lubricating transactions. That's what all the fuss over 'inflation' or 'deflation' is about.

The point of a taxation bureaucracy's and a central bank's work, when considered in combination rather than separately, is to dynamically adjust monetary quantities through taxation, interest rates and other fiscal and monetary policy tools to ensure that there is enough money around, but not too much, at any given time.

These agencies generally measure their performance in this regard by means of consumer price inflation (CPI) indices. Working in tandem, they remove money from circulation by means of taxes and by selling bonds to investors. Conversely, they pump money into circulation by means of a combination of government spending and central bank purchases of bonds from bondholders, complemented by central bank manipulations of interest rates. The latter are aimed at encouraging or discouraging people from taking on new bank loans, since – as we will see in Part II – when private actors borrow money from banks, this has the effect of putting fresh money into the system.

The foregoing few paragraphs were just a sneak preview. We'll get into these mechanisms in much more detail in Part II.

Private savings imply government deficits

In an uncertain world, there is an incentive to hoard money – that is, to 'save'. One can never be sure what the future will bring. The state must thus bear in mind that out of all the money spent into the economy, both by paying for labour services and buying goods and services, a significant part will flow into savings, set aside for a rainy day rather than spent back into circulation.

For that reason, it isn't sufficient for the state to expend money at the level of its anticipated annual tax revenues, and no more. In any normal year, the state has to spend *more* than it plans to recoup in tax payments, because every time the state takes in some money in taxes and re-spends it into circulation, some of the money it spends will be diverted from circulation and 'saved' in inactive pools of savings, leaving less available for the next cycle of taxing and spending.

One way for the state to increase its purchasing power is to levy taxes on inactive savings, or 'wealth taxes'. In practice, however, it's politically very difficult for the state to confiscate people's savings. For that reason, the state usually only taxes income or transactions, not wealth (with the exception of inheritance taxes, which are often rather low or even zero). Given that pools of inactive savings tend to grow (the more money a saver has, the easier it is to accumulate even more), the state's access to available money will gradually decline unless it either (1) creates new money to spend into existence, or (2) 'borrows' money from the owners of those pools of savings and spends it back into circulation.

This is the reason why the state normally runs a deficit: it spends more than it can collect in taxes so that the private sector can build up savings. The difference between the state's spending and its tax revenues, i.e. the state's deficit, ends up as the aggregate net savings of households and businesses, i.e. the private sector's surplus.

Conversely, if the state runs a surplus, by taking in more in taxes than it spends, the result is necessarily a private sector deficit – i.e. the pool of aggregate private sector savings must decline, assuming a fixed money supply. It's a zero-sum game, a matter of simple accounting.

Again, the foregoing paragraphs are a sneak preview. All this will be explained in more detail in Part II.

Economies of scale

When planning production of goods, so-called 'economies of scale' are important. Mass production is often less costly than the manufacture of small batches. The same goes for the provision of services. Deployment of a passenger aircraft with ten seats will lead to higher ticket prices than deployment of an air-craft with 250 seats. The reason is that fixed costs, such as the basic costs of building aeroplanes (hiring engineers, building an aircraft factory, etc.) or charges for the use of a runway, will be a higher proportion of total costs per passenger per flight if the aeroplane has fewer seats.

Given this, an evolutionary process gets going in which the companies pro-ducing the biggest quantities tend to win out over their competitors. Economists speak of 'increasing returns to scale'. This can lead to situations in which only a few firms, or even just one, exist in a given industry. Early entrants that achieve big scale and low unit costs tend to develop an insurmountable price advantage and lock out most of the competition.

Corporate planners and entrepreneurs understand this very well, so they have an incentive to outspend their rivals and seize market share even before their business is profitable. That means they cannot rely on net earnings from sales to power their early-stage growth. Instead, they must raise external money, either from equity investors or by borrowing. This helps explain why financial markets, venture capitalists and investment banks exist: specialisation of labour leads to specialist work-teams, or 'companies', whose aim is to conquer market share in particular goods or services – but early on, they generally cannot self-fund their own establishment and expansion.

We're used to thinking about market economies in general terms as eco-nomies in which many small firms compete for many customers, so the whole game is intensively competitive, which tends to drive down prices and drive up quality. Successful firms create profits by producing and selling goods more effi-ciently and cheaply than their rivals, and thereby out-compete them. If an indus-try is characterised by increasing returns to scale, however, it will tend to end up as an oligopoly or monopoly. In a mature industry, the competitive mechanism will often have been weakened or sidelined.

It turns out that in the real world, a great many markets are characterised by increasing returns to scale, and end up dominated by oligopolies. As long as products of a given category – breakfast cereals, say – are not wholly identical, however, at least in the perception of customers, it's possible for smaller firms to exist alongside sectorally dominant firms: they can attempt to achieve 'product differentiation' as a reason for customers to spend a bit more than they would for a similar product from the dominant established brand in the sector.

Competition between comparable products or services generally forces firms to offer low prices, though firms can also compete on other factors, like quality or a perception that a given product will confer enhanced status to its buyer compared to functionally similar products.

In confronting price competition from rivals making similar products, a firm can employ one or both of two basic strategies. The first option is for a firm to maximise output given some quantity of inputs. This is done through an increase in unit productivity – i.e. the total financial cost involved in producing a unit of product, making it known to potential buyers and getting it to the point of sale. Total costs can be reduced at any point along the supply, sales or marketing chain. More efficient machines or processes can be employed, for example.

Economies of scale mean that for a given amount of fixed inputs such as production machinery, a rise in production volume will lead to cheaper output on a unit-cost basis. It's better for a factory manager to run the factory's production machines for 16 hours per day rather than 8 hours per day – the amount of money initially spent to buy the machines is the same either way, although they'll likely have to be replaced sooner if they're working double shifts.

A second strategic option is to lower the variable costs of production. Either wages or the costs of other variable inputs can be decreased. This strategy relies on political power, since wages, in Europe at any rate, are usually set in negotiations between employer associations and unions. The result determines how the fruits of production are distributed among entrepreneurs, employees, financiers and owners of capital.

There is a problem with this second option. If all firms engage in lowering wages, total demand will fall accordingly as workers have less money to spend. Since entrepreneurs spend less of their income, the fall in demand from the workers is not compensated by a rise in demand from those getting the profits. Hence, production will fall if too many firms cut their wages. Deflationary problems might create a negative cycle of circular causation as firms react to falling prices by lowering their wage costs further.

Public or private efficiencies? Both

For decades, a sterile debate has raged between advocates of private sector economies versus state-dominated economies, each pointing to the problems with an economy that's entirely private or entirely state-run as an argument against the other side.

In reality, efficient and effective structuring of the internal processes of businesses is best done decentrally and locally, incentivised by market competition driving efficiencies and quality improvements. At the same time, there are many cost efficiencies and business-enhancing systemic conditions that private businesses cannot achieve on their own, and for which public infrastructure provision is necessary.

For example, better education and training of workers enables them to work more productively. The provision of better transport infrastructure can lead to lower transport costs, which helps lower the retail price of goods at the point of sale as well as the total costs associated with obtaining the inputs used for production. An improvement in communication infrastructure can lower costs as well.

Most of these improvements are partly financed by the public, either in the form of institutions like universities or the internet, or investments in research and development, or in transportation and communications infrastructure. Without these, doing business at a sophisticated level would be nearly impossible. Places with weak public institutions and investment, like Somalia or Honduras, can be contrasted with places with strong institutions, like Switzerland or Singapore, in order to show in very practical terms why public investment and infrastructure are necessary for modern businesses to thrive. In this sense, all business enterprises are public–private joint enterprises – just like the monetary system itself, which requires a government to set up, maintain and enforce it, and a wider public to use it.

The question of whether the private or public sector should be responsible for providing or improving inputs to particular production processes requires a differentiated answer on a case-by-case, contextualised basis. It depends on which strategies have the best probability of success given the problem at hand. There are many different possible solutions for any given problem, and sometimes it makes sense for more than one solution to exist side by side.

Complementarity of public and private transit solutions

Public transport and racks of key-card-accessible public bicycles, for example, are on offer in cities like Barcelona or Valencia in Spain, where many people don't own their own car or bike. In contrast, in the north of Germany, for instance in Bremen or Oldenburg, people own more than one bicycle, on average, so there's a less compelling case for key-card-accessible public bicycles. Both public and private solutions can work efficiently, and they can also coexist. Another example is car-sharing services, which complement public buses or trains.

Regardless of the details, what's important is that ready availability of bicycles as well as safe, reliable shared motorised transport options in urban areas tends to enable people to commute to work in a way that's more environmentally friendly and often faster and cheaper than driving through congested streets in private, single-occupancy automobiles, hunting for an elusive parking spot. Among other benefits, affordable public transit indirectly enhances the productivity of private firms by reducing the amount of time and energy people waste in traffic jams.

Why firms exist

Why do firms, and hence entrepreneurs, employees and capital owners, exist? As was explained above, the unit costs of production depend crucially on the volume of production. Entrepreneurs need more employees in order to establish larger production runs. They also constantly seek ways to increase the productivity of each employee. Division of labour has proven to be useful in this regard. An employee who specialises in a single production stage is more productive than a generalist. That's why most employees are highly specialised.

Another reason why production is organised into companies is the need for long time horizons and skilled teams whose members are accustomed to working with one another. The firm determines what its employees will do in the course of organising its production processes, which are often complex. Firms deal with this complexity by planning, and planning works best if a group of employees stays with the firm for a long time. In an uncertain world, this is much more useful then hiring employees in the morning and seeing them off in the afternoon, as one might imagine in a hypothetical 'perfectly flexible' labour market driven entirely by spot-prices for daily labour.

The trade-off is that once an employee has signed a labour contract and joined a firm, he or she is, for the duration of that contract, no longer a free agent. Nor is the firm free to re-orient its cash flow away from wages on a moment's notice. Both parties trade a significant amount of freedom for an increase in security and effectiveness.

Labour contracts, then, are institutional mechanisms whose purpose is to circumvent the market mechanism of daily price formation. Long and complex labour processes require specialised employees, and engaging in a long-term commitment is rational for both sides of a labour contract. Employers don't have to fear their employees will leave from one day to another, and employees value the security of a regular income stream of known or predictable size.

The state as a market maker and player

The discussion in the past few pages has made it clear that markets don't consist merely of firms and consumers. The state and its various agencies, as well as other firms, are key constituents of markets for goods and services, and of the systemic services that provide the environment for markets to function reasonably effectively.

The state also comprises specialist markets within its ambit – that's what a public service job market is, for example. Departments in the public sector, like skills-intensive businesses in the private sector, have strong reasons to hire people on long-term contracts. Long-dated employment contracts ensure planning security, which is necessary for a variety of reasons. It would be silly for the state to hire judges on Monday and let them go on Friday, for example. A lawsuit normally lasts weeks, and constantly changing judges would require each new judge to learn their way into a case afresh. Likewise, a company wouldn't hire a law firm on a one-day contract if it needs help with a lengthy lawsuit about the validity of some patents.

Limits to competition

We've already pointed out that competition is important and salutary, but also that many markets naturally tend towards the emergence of dominant firms, due to economies of scale and network effects.

There are additional reasons why no market is ever perfectly competitive. In most markets, households can choose from a variety of products and services.

Many different brands, colours and features of washing machines, for example, are available. But for any given family looking for a new washing machine, transport, search and transaction costs limit the scope of competition to what happens to be in stock at suppliers that are easily accessible.

On the other hand, in line with our previous discussion about the dynamic nature of real economies and the importance of technology, it's also true that online markets coupled with cheap transportation and easily accessible online information are making proximity less of a factor. Some people are comfortable choosing even quite large and expensive consumer products based on peer evaluations or consumer reports, and ordering them online, sight unseen (except for online pictures).

But there are still some markets that are inherently local. People looking to pick up some tasty fresh bread rolls for breakfast won't necessarily buy from the very nearest baker, but nor will they go on a five-hour hike in an effort to get to the best baker in the city, and fresh bread rolls are not something one is likely to order online.

Such constraints on the effective number of competitors in a market are especially strong for services rendered on location. No one travels to a foreign country to get a haircut (unless they happen to live right next to an international border).

In contrast, in some markets, firms face truly borderless competition – for example, the business-to-business market for call-centre services is global, since telecommunications technology makes distance irrelevant.

The formation of demand

Whether or not international competition applies in a given market, it is ultimately demand that determines what will be produced in which amounts. So, what determines demand?

There's no answer to that question that's both simple and accurate. The details of consumer demand depends on everything from the availability of purchasing power to potential customers' awareness of the existence and availability of particular products, to peer pressure or fads generated by advertising, to cultural traditions, among many other factors. But despite all this, there's a simple story told in introductory economics textbooks that's worth recalling – not because it's the whole truth, but because there's some important truth in it.

Many goods markets work through the adjustment of prices. Let's take the market for fish and chips as an example, and tell the classic tale of a market 'clearing' through the price mechanism's ability to generate bottom-up adjustments in supply and demand. We'll assume that debt plays no role – there are no credit cards in our scenario – and consumers only spend money they've previously earned.

Let's assume a portion of fish and chips costs three euro in a Spanish city. Then a large influx of British migrants to the city increases local demand for fish and chips, which leads to higher prices in the short run. When sellers realise that their fish and chips are consistently sold out, and they find themselves turning away customers on a daily basis, some react by increasing their prices.

This increases the industry's profits, which brings imitators into the arena. Pizza parlours and bocadillo shops might think about adding fish and chips to their assortment. The supply of fish and chips meals rises, which, given a fairly constant level of demand, eventually leads to a fall in the price of those meals.

The price of the inputs used in the production of fish and chips might also rise (alternatively, some input prices might actually fall, if economies of scale come into play), which could create an increase in costs. Lower revenues per unit sale and higher input costs would lead to lower profits. Taken together, a rise in supply should cause prices and profits to eventually fall back to their initial level, more or less.

This is the classic tale of the workings of the price mechanism in competitive markets. While it's a simplification, there's enough truth in it to recognise that in generic terms, a tendency for competitive markets to automatically tend towards 'equilibration of supply and demand' is one of the basic mechanisms in market economies.

However, it's only one of several basic mechanisms. To achieve a rounded understanding, other basic mechanisms need to be included in our model of the economy as well – including economies of scale, imperfect, bounded information, geographically limited markets, the importance of location, network effects, the power of advertising and limitations on aggregate demand caused by ebbs and flows in the availability of money, among other factors.

It's also worth keeping in mind that while competitive markets comprised of private firms fighting for market share are generally a good thing, that's not always the case. It depends on the nature of the market. Competitive markets for heroin or for illegal weapons, for example, are not a good thing. Nor are poorly regulated pharmaceutical markets.

Moreover, as we've seen, the phenomenon of increasing returns to scale means that most markets eventually are dominated by a small number of powerful firms. The concentrated power of such firms can interfere with the democratic process – for instance, when lobbyists write laws, finance the electoral campaign of a political party or exert influence on the shaping of domestic and foreign policies in secretive trade negotiations. We conventionally speak about the 'public sector' and 'private sector' as if these were two completely distinct categories, but in reality the line that separates them is blurred.

Firms can also cause harm through monopoly or collusion, fixing their prices to gain unearned profits, or shifting parts of their costs onto the public or the environment, for example by releasing toxic pollution into the air or water in order to dodge having to make investments in pollution abatement equipment.

The time factor

Another problem a modern economy has to solve is the distribution of the fruits of production over workers' lifespans. After all, people want to consume not only when they're working, but also after they've retired. They can't solve this problem simply by setting aside some of what they produce for later – most goods are not durable without limit, and most services are rendered instantly and can't be saved or set aside at all.

That's why people need ways to shift some of their purchasing power into the future. Rather than taking the form of physical goods or services, 'savings' take the form of 'money', which constitutes a claim on goods or services that will be produced in the future.

This brings us back to the main preoccupation of this book, which is to ask: what is money, exactly? How does it arise, how does it disappear, how does it flow? How does it work?

Part II

Money and credit

In Part II we consider the nature and mechanisms of money and debt, and how these make economic activity possible. We use a balance sheet approach to examine the creation of credit and debt through central banks and commercial banks, as well as to understand how the fiscal spending of government functions.

We'll see that the division of labour goes hand in hand with debts. The function of money, in essence, is to serve a kind of transferable IOU accepted by everyone. Debt is not bad per se, but excessive accumulated debt, especially if it has been generated in connection with unproductive purposes, can generate enormous macroeconomic problems. Too much debt in the wrong places is like a severe illness of the body politic: it causes symptoms like mass unemployment, weak growth, stagnation or even depression.

2 Debts and balance sheets

Money and credit have existed for millennia. Coins made from gold, silver or other materials circulated during the Roman Empire, and Roman coins were still in use in Europe centuries after the Empire collapsed. Bank notes were invented centuries ago. Even older than coins or notes is the loan – an entry in a book of accounts recording an enforceable debt. Numerous clay tablets recording liabilities and debts have been found in archaeological sites of ancient Sumer, dating back 4,000–5,000 years.

The fundamental nature of 'debt' is that someone's assets are matched by another's liabilities. The debtor, it is assumed, will extinguish his or her liabilities by transferring either money or goods to the creditor, or by providing services – 'working off' the debt.

Based on this expectation, the creditor possesses an asset that has the same value as the liability of the debtor. Hence if the debtor becomes unable to extinguish his or her liability, or refuses to do so and cannot be compelled, the asset is cancelled along with the defaulted liability. Asset and liability are two sides of the same coin.

This means that monetary assets and liabilities always arise simultaneously, since they're really just two perspectives on the same transaction. In modern banking systems, they arise through the act of 'lending', when banks 'extend credit' to borrowers. The bank's act of granting a bank loan to a borrower creates a debt repayable to the bank, and at the same time, it also creates an offsetting, equally sized deposit of bank credit in the borrower's account.

Bank credit is what we think of as 'money in the bank'. It's the borrower's asset. But from the point of view of the bank, that bank credit in the borrower's account is the bank's liability vis-à-vis the borrower. The two are numerically equal mirror images of each other.

The deposit of bank credit recorded in a borrower's account when a bank grants a 'loan' represents an increase in purchasing power within the financial system. In other words, it's new money. In a modern economy, 'bank credit' and what people think of as 'money' are the same thing. And in the banking system as a whole, the total volume of bank credit is matched precisely one-for-one with the total volume of debt owed by borrowers to banks. Credits and debts, assets and liabilities, are recorded in columns of offsetting figures in spreadsheets according to the conventions of double-entry bookkeeping.

Even physical cash is nothing more than a transportable record of spreadsheet operations that have occurred in the banking system's double-entry bookkeeping system. When cash is issued to people at cash-points, certain accounts are debited; when cash is 'paid in' to one's account at a bank, those accounts are credited.

Cash is used for payments of goods and services as well as for settlement of debts and tax liabilities. Electronic 'deposits' in bank accounts can be used for the same purpose, by means of transferring 'funds' from one account to another. In today's world, payment and credit systems are tightly interconnected.

The power of transferable IOUs

Why did financial systems of this kind become generally accepted? Why can't we design a pure payment system that works without any debt?

In this chapter, we examine in some detail the creation of credit and money – and also the financing of the state, which turns out to be very closely linked to the mechanisms of credit creation.

We need a payment system to enable us to pay each other for goods and services, without which a society based on complex divisions of labour would be unable to thrive. However, there is another function of the payment system, namely taxation. The purpose of taxation is to dynamically re-assign some of the bank credit (purchasing power) recorded in the banking system's private sector accounts towards state spending. Note, however, that as soon as the state spends money, it re-enters the accounts of the private sector. That includes money the state spends on its own employees: their salaries represent an income stream for private households.

Let's look at how the mechanisms of money creation and taxation relate to the question of whether it's possible to design a payments system that works without incurring any debt. The answer is no. Here's why.

As a thought experiment, imagine a simple bookkeeping-based payment system whose function is to enable individuals to spend and receive 'money', i.e. transferable credit. Every individual obtains an account with a debit (–) and a credit (+) side, so that inflows and outflows of credit can be recorded. Let's assume that credits in this system are called 'ducats' (rather than euro or dollars).

individual	
credits (+)	debits (–)

Imagine, first, that a week ago society has completely collapsed. A biowarfare pandemic has wiped out the bulk of the population, and before that a cyberwar and the detonation of electromagnetic pulse weapons has destroyed the entire banking system's records. All gone. A revolution follows in which people decide not to respect claims on ownership of corporate shares or land titles. The world consists simply of people, no longer of employees and owners. Governments have lost credibility. All property contracts, by general consensus, have been declared null and void. Those who remain alive agree it's time for a completely fresh start.

Now suppose a civil-society group, the Public Money Working Group (PMWG), steps up and announces that even though all bank records and money have disappeared, enough solar and wind power equipment remains functional to power computer networks, and enough fibre-optic cabling remains in place to allow the internet and smartphones to reboot. To enable a complex economy to be rebooted as well, PMWG proposes to create a common global electronic money system. Everybody who registers for an account with PMWG's new cooperative bank, the Global Ducats Bank (GDB), will be equipped to do business with other registered members.

People sign up in droves, and everyone gets a simple smartphone app with this bookkeeping system, courtesy of GDB. This permits people to transfer credits securely through the cloud or via Bluetooth.

After everyone has downloaded and installed GDB's ducat-accounting and transfer app, it's time to initialise the system, so that people can do business with each other. In other words, people need to obtain some 'ducats', or GDB credits, in order to be able to do business with each other.

Here's where we encounter a bit of a problem. Where does the system's initial supply of ducats come from? On Day 1 of the launch of the new GDB online electronic wallet system, there is, obviously, no money in the system. No ducats. Nothing with which people can pay each other, since no one has built up any credits in the system.

Under normal conditions, as distinct from the aftermath of a global collapse that wiped out all existing monetary systems, it would seem obvious that all circulating purchasing power, or 'money', took the form of bank credits created through sales of goods, services, valuables or labour in the past.

But at some point in the past, someone must have provided goods or services to someone else without immediately getting compensation with other goods or services of equal value. If they had immediately received such compensation, we would refer to the exchange as 'barter', and there would have been no need for a system for keeping track of 'credits'.

It turns out that the solution to this conundrum is for some people to get into debt and others to correspondingly build up a stake of credits, and for these credits to be transferable to third parties. Transferable credits are what 'money' actually is.

Several centuries earlier...

To help us visualise how 'money' arises as a tool for keeping track of debts that have been incurred, let's imagine a late-medieval farming village in England grappling with the problem of how a farmer can get help with the harvest even if his neighbour, a labourer, doesn't need anything from the farmer just at the moment.

Let's say a labourer named Jock spent 20 hours helping Farmer Brown with the harvest, and the farmer then wrote up a note saying, 'I owe you, Jock, purchasing power equal in value to 20 hours of your labour on my farm.' This meant that Jock could come back any time in the future, present the IOU note, and Farmer Brown would be obliged to give him something of roughly equal value to those 20 hours – for example, two big sacks of potatoes, or one sack of potatoes and half a sack of onions.

Brown would have an incentive to be fair in the value he gave Jock. He'll have been wise to ensure that Jock would be happy enough with what he gets for his 20 labour-hour IOU note, because otherwise Brown might have trouble getting Jock or any of Jock's friends to come help him with planting or harvesting again in future. Reputation is extremely important in a village context, where everyone knows everyone else and gossip is ubiquitous and never-ending.

But there's a serious limitation to the IOU note system as we've described it so far: a note from Farmer Brown to a village labourer promising to repay 'the value of 20 hours of Jock's labour on my farm' would be difficult for Jock to cash in anywhere except with Farmer Brown, or maybe with one or two of Farmer Brown's neighbours who knew the farmer well.

For example, Jock might be able to pass along the written IOU he received from Farmer Brown to Agnes the tailor lady in exchange for her sewing a new pair of trousers for him. That can work if Agnes is willing to accept the IOU Brown had written to Jock. She might be willing if she knew that Farmer Brown would honour the IOU as a 'bearer note' and give her, instead of Jock, a couple of sacks of potatoes in exchange for it.

Assuming that's the case, the IOU note Brown wrote to Jock is in this narrow, local sense 'transferable'. By writing an IOU to Jock, Farmer Brown, in this scenario, has actually issued a type of local currency. Note that it's a *debt-based* currency. Brown's IOU note originated as a record of a debt Brown owed to Jock.

In general, however, nobody outside the neighbourhood would be likely to accept the IOU note Farmer Brown wrote to Jock in exchange for Jock's labour. A transferable IOU only becomes 'money' in the modern sense when it is widely transferable, including between strangers.

Coins and bank deposits are transferable IOUs

Now suppose everyone in this imaginary medieval-era farming economy has a pretty good idea of what an adult's labour-hour is worth, in terms of a generally accepted 'unit of account'. Suppose that a long ten-hour day's farm labour is worth, in the general estimation, one unit of a standard currency – say, a small gold coin of a type commonly traded in the region, called a ducat. Then Jock's 20 hours of labour would be worth two small gold coins, or two ducats. So, the farmer, instead of writing up a note, might agree to give the labourer two ducats for two days (20 hours) of hard work.

Under these circumstances, Jock could take the two gold coins and get a pair of trousers made for him by Agnes. Alternatively, he could also take them to a saddler two towns away, someone he has never met and who has never heard of Farmer Brown, to get his donkey's saddle repaired and a new harness made.

This is more or less how things worked during medieval times – and money in the form of some types of coin was even accepted internationally. A Scottish buyer in AD 1521 – a raw-wool merchant, say, who owned a flock of sheep – might have paid for a crate of wine by handing over a small gold coin to a Portuguese wine-seller. The Portuguese wine-seller would now have more credit and less wine, and the Scottish sheep farmer less credit and more wine. The Portuguese wine-seller could now use his additional credit (represented by the gold coin) to purchase cloth from a British woollens merchant, who owns a loom and can make cloth, provided he has a supply of raw wool to work with.

Now the woollens merchant has less cloth but more credit. Next, assume the woollens merchant takes the gold coin and gives it to the Scottish sheep farmer in order to buy enough raw wool to make a quantity of woollen cloth whose value, it happens, amounts to one gold coin. The Scotsman now has his original gold coin back, and a bit less wool, but he still owns the sheep, who seem endlessly able to convert grass and water into more sheep and more wool. He also has that crate of wine.

After these several transactions, everyone's total credit would have reverted to its original position. Everybody had the same amount of 'money' they began with, yet the welfare of everyone concerned was improved.

The key here is that the transactions were facilitated by exchanges of 'money', or standard transferable credit units, which in our scenario we've called ducats.

But where did the ducats originally come from? Notice that we skipped over a step in our explanation earlier. In the previous section, we described how a local form of 'currency' might arise in a village if trusted members of the community wrote IOUs, or debt notes, to the benefit of other members, in exchange for labour that wasn't paid for on the spot by barter. Then, we suddenly jumped to talk of a 'standard unit of currency' that 'everyone agreed' was worth about ten hours of a man's farm labour. Where did this standard unit of account come from, and how is it that everyone came to agree on its value?

British woollens traders could not have transferred credits to Portuguese wine merchants without a standardised payment system, a system of transferable IOUs acceptable for doing business between strangers even if they're from different countries. That was crucial for the realisation of their transactions. Similarly, a saddler two days' ride away from Jock's village wouldn't be willing to accept Farmer Brown's IOU to Jock as payment for refurbishing the latter's donkey saddle – Brown's IOU wasn't transferable outside his own village – but the saddler would certainly accept two gold ducats, if he lived in a world where gold coins were a normal part of doing business. But why was that the case?

This is where governments and taxation come into play. A central function of government, without which governance is essentially impossible, is to establish a standard unit of account and a circulating 'currency' which serves as a system of transferable IOUs everywhere within the government's realm.

In centuries past, in Europe, the payments system was composed of standardised metal coins made of relatively rare, hard-to-get metals like gold or silver, generally stamped with the head of a local duke or king. At the end of the day, these coins were still based on a system of recording debts, and of ensuring there would be unpleasant consequences if the debts went unpaid. If one views them from a sufficiently deep historical and functional perspective, one sees that coins were in essence transferable IOU tokens – as are the coins and bank notes we use today.

What medieval debts were involved in turning pieces of shiny metal into transferable IOUs recognised as being so valuable that one could buy sheep or goats or sacks of potatoes with them?

We noted earlier that a farmer in medieval Europe expected several of the local duke's armed henchmen to stop by around the time of the first full-moon after the Winter Solstice (let's say) and demand ten pieces of silver coin with an image of the duke's head stamped on them. The farmer knew the duke's tax collectors would be violently angry with him if he couldn't pay up.

Let's suppose that farmer was Farmer Brown. Brown's annual tax debt to his local duke was at the base of the system for giving metal coins their value. The local duke, in turn, was obliged to provide some of his revenues to the king, as well as to raise an army of local men if his liege-lord called upon him to do so in wartime. If he failed to do so, he would not long remain the local duke. Ultimately, while tradition, custom and common law have always played an important role, coercion through armed force lay at the base of the monetary system, then as now.

In the modern era, the duke's henchmen have been replaced by administrative departments with anodyne names like 'Internal Revenue Service', supported by law courts and uniformed policemen.

But there's more to the story than that.

Anonymising units of debt

The clever innovation at the heart of a banking system backed by duly enforced government laws is that IOUs are no longer issued by individual tradesmen like Farmer Brown, whose reputational strength or weakness determines whether or not his IOU notes are acceptable as means of payment among third parties.

Instead, the credibility of banknotes, coins and electronic bank deposit records is generalised and anonymised. The acceptability of modern bank-issued electronic 'ducats' (euro, dollars, lira, whatever) as means of payment among strangers depends on the reputation and power of the government and the banking system it governs, rather than the credibility of any particular farmer or tradesman.

Modern electronic currency units like dollars or euro are similar in their essential nature to Farmer Brown's debt note to Jock: they're transferable IOUs. But they're a big improvement on Farmer Brown's notes for two reasons: first, modern bank-mediated transferable IOU records (whether they're euro coins, bank notes or electronic 'bank money' records) are easily accepted between complete strangers. Second, it's easy to determine what they're 'worth', because nearly all goods and services are priced in the same government-decreed currency units.

Once medieval kings had established a standard system of coins as monetary tokens, transactants were able to assume that such a coin-based money system would be safe from problems associated with unrepaid debts, since no personalised, tradesman-specific IOU was involved.

In contrast, an issuer-specific loan record, like the IOU note Farmer Brown wrote to Jock in our initial scenario, always carries default risk, since the debtor might not be able or willing to repay.

Brown's written IOU was actually a financial debt, a 'bearer bond'. The bond entitled the bearer to a quantity of agricultural produce grown on Brown's farm, equal in value to two days' farm labour. Final settlement of the debt recorded by the note entailed going to Brown's farm to demand two sacks of potatoes in return for giving the IOU back to the farmer, who would hand over the potatoes and then destroy the note. But if Brown had died or moved away since issuing the IOU to Jock, the bearer of the note was out of luck – it would have become worthless.

In contrast, ducats issued by the king's mint, like euro issued by the ECB, were tradable for valuable goods and services anywhere in the realm, not just at Farmer Brown's farm. The coins themselves, rather than the debt they represented, became the 'means of final settlement'. And the coins ultimately retained their value, they remained in high demand because everyone knew they were in short supply and that the Duke's henchmen might set your hut on fire, drag away your daughter or take you into slavery if you didn't have ten ducats to give them around the time of the Winter Solstice.

Bank deposits are improvements on Farmer Brown's IOU note

Today's money, like Farmer Brown's IOU note, is composed of loan records. These records are created through balance sheet operations in the banking system, such that the total amount of money is always offset by an equal amount of bank debt. Yet despite the fact that 'money in the bank' is really nothing more than records of transferable IOUs, it's widely accepted, including between strangers, in the same way that gold coins were in the past.

The reason strangers accept bank money from each other is that they trust the government to ensure the banks' IOU records are the functional equivalent of gold coins, i.e. they're 'money'. Modern money is contingent on the existence of a powerful government capable of regulating banks and enforcing loan contracts.

Let's think back to when Farmer Brown wrote a local farm labourer named Jock a debt note, or IOU, after Jock had spent two hard days helping with the harvest. The note affirmed that Brown owed Jock an amount of agricultural produce equal in value to two days' farm labour. Brown created a 'credit' in recognition of a 'debt' of equal value. The IOU was Brown's liability and Jock's asset.

In a modern banking system, the nearest equivalent to this exchange occurs when, say, John Doe signs a contract to Deutsche Bank affirming that he now owes €360,000 to Deutsche Bank, to be repaid at 5.2 per cent annual interest over a 20-year period. This contract is legally enforceable, and if he fails to make contractually agreed regular repayments on a timely basis, there will be unpleasant consequences, such as, for example, being forced to move out of the house he purchased with the bank credit he received in exchange for his legally binding promise to repay the 'loan principal' plus interest.

People sometimes say there's 'nothing backing' modern bank money, since there is no fixed weight of gold or silver one can fetch from a central repository in exchange for, say, a €100 note. But really, this is an egregious misunderstanding. There is in fact something very powerful backing modern bank money – namely John Doe's legally binding promise to repay the bank credits he was granted when his mortgage loan was incurred, and millions of other debt contracts like it, coupled to a government-run legal system that will throw John's life into utter turmoil if he fails to honour that contractual debt obligation.

These debt contracts oblige the debtors to do whatever they have to do to go out and get the 'credits', or money, they need in order to keep up with their debt-servicing obligations. This is a much more powerful form of 'backing' for the value of money than a pile of shiny metal somewhere in a vault could ever be.

John can do things like grow food or install solar panels or sew clothes or cook food, and he will do those things in exchange for money, money he needs to acquire in order to be able to keep up his payment obligations. A pile of shiny metal just sits there, looking shiny. Its inherent value is nowhere near as compelling as John's inherent value as a worker. A pile of shiny metal isn't much good to anyone, really. The time, energy and capabilities of a person like John, bound by a debt contract to acquire money, on the other hand, is worth a great deal. The value of our money is actually 'backed' by legally enforceable contractual debt obligations of people like John.

In our medieval village scenario, we began with Farmer Brown's personally issued IOU, which was only transferable locally and only retained its value as long as Farmer Brown was alive and his farm was growing food. Then we considered a system of gold coins issued by the Royal Mint, which were also transferable IOUs, but whose value was recognised anywhere in the king's realm and even in the realms of neighbouring kings (like Portugal). Their value was established in part by the king declaring that each farmer or tradesman had to pay some number of coins to the local duke each year, or face harsh consequences. Taxation was a way of creating an enforceable debt, and hence a strong motivation for citizens to collect gold ducats; in other words, taxation created a 'demand' and a 'value' for those ducats, which functionally made them into transferable IOUs.

Systems of this nature remained in place for centuries. As they became deeply ingrained in the culture, it wasn't even necessary for gold or silver coins to be directly connected to debt-coercive measures like the Duke's henchmen coming by once each year to collect taxes. People valued gold and silver coins because they'd never lived in a world in which people didn't value gold and silver coins. It was part of their cultural context, and they no more questioned that context than fish question water.

And here we are

As modern banking evolved beginning in the early Renaissance era in Italy, and governments grew in administrative sophistication, taxation obligations denominated in gold or silver coins came to be supplemented by the reliable enforcement of property contract laws as a core function of government. This made possible the emergence of bank-mediated transferable IOU records – also known as 'bank credits', or more simply, 'money in the bank'. These credits, too, ultimately became subject to the government's taking a slice of the action, i.e. taxation.

That pretty much brings us into the modern era. It's time to take out our intellectual magnifying glasses and closely inspect just what is going on with those bank spreadsheets, with their columns of assets and liabilities.

The numbers recorded in the rows and columns of double-entry bookkeeping systems in our banks specify the status of each modern human being in terms of the 'debts' or 'credits' recorded in the individual 'accounts' each of us maintains at the particular bank we do business with (some people, of course, remain unbanked, especially poor folks in developing countries). That bank, in turn, maintains just one part of a globally interlinked set of electronic spreadsheets, composed of the spreadsheets of all the world's banks. They're interconnected by myriad financial contracts and by special relationships with top-level banks called 'central banks', which are, in essence, special banks at which only commercial banks and the sovereign government Treasury hold accounts.

Central banks are a means of creating some cohesion for the banking system as a whole; they're a means by which credits and debts recorded by different commercial banks can be netted out between them, or 'settled', at the end of each banking day. They're also a key institutional mechanism channelling the government's powers to raise and spend money.

The balance sheet

Our insight from the stories told in the past few pages is that *someone has to go into debt* in order to create credit that can be put into circulation. Jock has to go spend those 20 hours on Farmer Brown's farm, and trust the farmer to give him some kind of formal token recognising his ensuing debt to Jock. In this case, it's Farmer Brown who has first gone into debt, and whose transferable IOU provides the basis for local transactions denominated in this specialised type of local credit.

Box 2.1 T-account and balances

A T-account is a simple tally sheet, divided down the middle into two offsetting columns, that records receipts and outflows of any category of countable thing. One can set up T-accounts for cash, for bank deposits, for loans, for materials – sacks of potatoes or lumber, for example – or for any other category of countable thing. T-accounts are useful for gaining some insight into the present state, or 'stock', of categories – like how much property one has, offset by how much one owes, both expressed in the same quantity, e.g. dollars or euro. Summing up all the financial T-accounts relevant to a business or household creates what we call a 'balance sheet'.

This shows that in order to have a monetary economy, the creation of 'money' – which is to say, transferable IOUs – must begin by someone extending an initial 'credit' without the credit having been earned by a proper sale. Farmer Brown gave nothing material to Jock after Jock had helped with the harvest – he merely gave Jock an IOU. In our scenario, Jock didn't accept a couple of sacks of potatoes on the spot immediately after working for Brown, because he already had enough food at home and didn't need anything from Brown that particular week.

Instead, Jock accepted Brown's IOU. He was willing to do so because he knew that Brown had an ability to provide something of widely recognised value in the future (food) and that Brown was likely to honour his debt. Moreover, Jock knew that he could probably pass along Brown's transferable IOU to Agnes in exchange for new trousers, because she might well want some potatoes from Brown at some point in the near future.

Without credits, no payments – which are transfers of credits – can be made. This is why payment and credit systems are intertwined. Anyone who wants to talk about money in a modern context, as distinct from a medieval coin-based economy, implicitly also has to talk about debt, because no modern money is created without the simultaneous creation of an equal, offsetting amount of debt.

The idea of debt-free payment systems is based on an understanding of money as a pure means of transaction, like the gold coins of medieval times. This, however, does not even do justice to the historical nature of gold coins, whose value was also ultimately based in debt obligations. Still less does the notion of debt-free payment systems correspond to the nature and requirements of money, credit and debt in a modern market economy.

Getting interested in debt

How shall we talk about debt, then? What mental models and terms of art shall we employ to help deepen our understanding of how it arises, functions and disappears again?

In standard academic macroeconomics, equilibrium models are constructed in which an 'equilibrium interest rate' arises as a function of the demand for money and its available supply. The idea is that there's a rate of interest at which willing 'suppliers of money' (lenders) find enough 'demand for money' (borrowers) and vice versa. The market for money clears when all suppliers and demanders find partners to trade with.

The idea of a 'supply of money' rests on an assumption of scarcity, i.e. money is considered to be just like a scarce resource or commodity – analogous to gold, for example. This model, historically rooted in cultural memories from a time when rare metals were the tokens we used to represent standard units of transferable debt, remains widely accepted in standard academic economics. Unfortunately, it's wrong.

In the following pages we shall see that money is not a commodity, and hence the doctrine that a 'price of money' is the instrument used to clear the market cannot be applied. The interest rate is not an indicator of an overall scarcity of money, as is often asserted – even if individual prospective borrowers are short of it.

Debt begets credit, and credit is money

How can we understand money and credit? We've already gone a long way towards setting up a framework of understanding. Now we'll get into more detail. The following exposition is based on the insight that money (also known as 'bank credit') is debt-based, created through transactions and entries in banks' balance sheets.

Money and credit are not merely commodity-like means of payment to facilitate barter, similar to quantities of gold coins. Money is nothing other than bank credit! Bank credit arises simultaneously with precisely equal amounts of bank debt, which is incurred in the course of specific types of business transactions: firms have credit lines with other firms or with banks; exporters use export credits; households overdraw their deposit accounts and use credit cards to make consumer purchases; people take out mortgages to buy overpriced houses; and so on. Money does not initially arise directly from production or trade – it arises from the willingness of some of the economy's actors to get into debt in relation to other actors.

Balance sheets are at the very heart of the economy

The central bank has a balance sheet. The government also has one, and banks, households and firms have balance sheets too. The methodology we'll be using in the remainder of this text is based on the inspection of simplified balance sheets that are themselves abstractions from legally binding debt contracts and other socially enforceable debts.

This methodology has the advantage of being highly quantitative and hence 'objective', since it focuses on debts and double-entry bookkeeping. It allows us to follow the logic of our economic system by following the transaction records that show us what is actually going on – i.e. the stocks and flows of credits and debts, who owes what to whom, who the creditors are and who the debtors are and how they came to have those roles.

In what follows, we define various equilibria of monetary values as balances of wealth and debt, assets and liabilities, credits and debits. To simplify, we'll use the terms 'assets' and 'liabilities' in the following expositions. These are displayed in balance sheets. The term 'balance sheet' is derived from the Latin 'bilanx', which means weigh-scale or equilibrium.

_____individual_____	
credits (+)	debits (−)
assets (+)	liabilities (−)
wealth (+)	debt (−)

In general, at any given point in time, it is quite unlikely that an individual has assets (the sum of wealth claims) and debts (the sum of liabilities) of the same total value.

Let us assume an individual named Jane has more assets than liabilities. Assets worth 20 are counterposed by liabilities of 10. Jane's assets consist of bank deposits and payments she has received, plus the monetary value of assets she owns, which is the amount of money she could receive if she were to sell those assets. Liabilities are debts, which Jane will have to settle at some time in the future, usually at a pre-agreed time (for any given debt, this agreed repayment time is called the 'maturity' of the debt). Since a balance sheet must, by definition, be balanced, the amount of assets has to match the amount of liabilities. We create equilibrium by inserting the entry 'net wealth' into the liabilities side of the balance sheet. Net wealth corresponds to assets minus liabilities (where liabilities do not include the term 'net wealth' for the purposes of this calculation), in this case $20-10=10$.

Net wealth is always shown on the liability side of the balance sheet, by convention. Theoretically, by the way, it might make more sense to show net wealth on the asset side with an inverted sign, since it is a claim of the owner against the balance sheet. Don't let that worry you – the location of the term 'net wealth' in the balance sheet is merely a matter of accounting convention.

_____Jane_____		
assets	20	liabilities	10
		net wealth	10

A balance sheet allows one to extract information about the net wealth of a person or institution. It is a two-column list of all of Jane's monetary or monetisable assets and liabilities in juxtaposition, with assets shown on the left and liabilities (what Jane owes) on the right.

Individuals, as well as institutions, like the government, the central bank or firms, have assets not only in the form of financial assets like money, stocks and bonds, but also material assets (goods, real estate, etc.) and immaterial assets (patents, trademarks, etc.). If Jane owns a house, for example, its current estimated value may be deemed at €125,000 and recorded at that value in a balance sheet written up on a particular day; in a lively real estate market, Jane's house may be valued at €133,000 only a year later. Jane's house is an example of an asset that is monetisable (she could sell it and get bank credit, or 'money', in return) but not yet monetised (she hasn't sold it yet). In contrast, we'll call assets that have already been monetised, and which are now held in the form of currency units, 'bank deposits' or just deposits. One could also speak of 'credit' or 'money'.

Note also that a balance sheet is a snapshot in time – and an estimate, not a statement of absolute fact. At any given time, one real estate assessor might assign a value of €125,000 to Jane's house, whereas a different assessor, on the same day, might assign the same house a value of €130,000. Six months later, or even a week later, the balance sheet will have changed, not just because some of Jane's monetary balances (money in the bank and financial debts) will have changed, but also because the valuations of her assets will have changed, depending on whether (in this example) the housing market has moved up or down.

Jonathan			
house	200	mortgage	150
shares	30	net wealth	100
deposits	20		

The hypothetical individual, Jonathan, who owns the above balance sheet is relatively wealthy. The value of his assets exceeds the value of his liabilities by 100. (We haven't specified which currency these numbers refer to – it doesn't matter; think of them as being in units of kilo-dollars or kilo-euro, i.e. 200 would mean 200,000 euro, if you will.) In the real world, a surprisingly large percentage of the population isn't so lucky. In Germany, about 28 per cent of the adult population had zero or even negative net wealth in 2012, according to a report in a publication of one of Germany's leading economic research institutes (DIW Wochenbericht 9/2014).

Although balance sheets always balance, they do not always display an accurate picture of reality, and must be treated with caution. As Spaniards and Irish found out after 2007–8, real estate prices are subject to sudden, major downs as well as multi-year sequences of ups. The valuation of the corresponding wealth positions is hence neither objective nor certain. The value of real estate can decline, just like the price of shares, and banks can go insolvent, although the customer's deposits are usually protected up to a certain amount by means of government-mandated deposit insurance schemes.

Assets experience variations in their value over time, liabilities normally do not. A mortgage debt of 150 would stay the same, even if the originating bank goes bankrupt. In this case the mortgage would be sold out of the insolvency estate to another bank, which would then take over the mortgage.

Similarly, even if the bursting of a house-price bubble caused Jonathan's house to drop in value by one-third, his mortgage debt wouldn't change at all –

except in rare situations in which a bank, perhaps under pressure from government in a post-bubble environment, agrees to take a loss by reducing the borrower's debt. If repayment is in danger, the bank might be forced to reduce the mortgage's book value. The loss incurred would reduce the bank's equity, or some other item on the liability side of the bank's balance sheet. Debtors' liabilities can be changed through debt cancellation, but normally not without the consent of the creditor. This happens only very rarely.

The above balance sheet of Jonathan, an individual, contains some uncertainty regarding the value of his assets and hence his net wealth. Not all assets are equally uncertain in value. Bank deposits do not fluctuate in nominal monetary value, as long as the bank is solvent. (Jonathan's bank deposits are liabilities of the bank, i.e. they are credit claims Jonathan has against the bank's balance sheet. If the bank becomes insolvent, and the money it owes depositors cannot be fully repaid even after deposit insurance schemes are invoked – which can occur if a depositor had claims against the bank in excess of the maximum amount specified in the deposit insurance scheme – then some depositors may find themselves unable to fully realise these claims.) On the other hand, bank deposits do fluctuate in value in terms of their purchasing power for goods and services, or in terms of foreign currencies.

Treasury bonds usually are just as safe as bank deposits – indeed, in most countries they're safer, since a government Treasury is much less likely to become insolvent than is a commercial bank, and countries with their own sovereign currency really can't become insolvent at all, unless they rack up excessive debts in a foreign currency.

Corporate shares and real estate, on the other hand, are subject to large changes in financial valuation, and the same goes for prices of goods like gold, oil, copper or grain, or of foreign currencies, including bitcoin. In the following, we'll focus on financial assets like bank deposits, bonds and shares, and for the sake of clarity we'll omit everything else.

Let's assume a stock market crash and a real estate bust have just occurred. In the aftermath, Jonathan's balance sheet might look like this:

Jonathan			
house	100	mortgage	150
shares	10	net wealth	−20
bank deposits	20		

With the house-price correction, Jonathan's net wealth has been reduced from a positive 100 to a negative 20, without his having effected any transaction. The balance sheet must balance, and so the reductions on the asset-side valuations are mirrored by a numerically identical total reduction of net wealth, recorded (by convention, as noted earlier) on the liability side. This leads to an updated view of reality. If Jonathan was living in his house and planned to continue doing so, and had a fixed, regular income such as a pension or a civil service job to pay for food, heating oil and so on, then only small changes of behaviour might follow. If Jonathan had a variable income – for example, if he made a living gigging as a freelance website developer – he might work a bit more and spend a bit less in an effort to bring his 'net worth' back up a bit, or he might not.

If, however, the house was supposed to be sold, and the monetised value from the sale had been earmarked to pay for monthly living expenses because Jonathan is a retiree and his pension doesn't suffice to make ends meet, then this plan is off. He now must react to the new situation by working more – i.e. to abandon retirement and return to the workforce, if possible.

Alternatively, Jonathan might have bought the house as a speculative investment during a rising house-price bubble, hoping to 'flip' it for a profit. If he failed to time the market well and was left holding the mortgage after the bubble burst, he is now faced with working and saving more to keep up with his mortgage payments, in an effort to climb back out of negative equity. Earning more income from work, and saving a bigger share of his income, will be necessary to bring his net wealth back upward. The difference between Jonathan's income and his expenditures must rise if he is to achieve that.

Let's assume Jonathan obtains an annual income of 20. Expenditures of 10 are subtracted. At the end of the year, his savings equal 10. How do we update the balance sheet?

Financial stocks vs. financial flows

We must now differentiate between *stocks* and *flows* of monetary value. Previously, we had only looked at stocks. Here, we don't mean 'stocks' in the sense of company shares – we mean 'stocks' in the sense of a quantity of any countable thing, e.g. a grocery store's 'stock' of rice bags denotes the amount of rice it currently has in its inventory. The value of a house and the value of a corporate share portfolio at a given point in time are *stocks* – they are data points that belong to some particular reporting date.

Income and expenditure, by contrast, are *flows*, because they measure data that cumulate over a period of time. Flow data belong to a span of time, not to a moment in time.

In the following balance sheet, which represents Jonathan's situation one year after the previous (post-crash) balance sheet, a dashed line separates stocks and flows. Above the line we have flows, and below it we have stocks. Savings are defined as income not spent. An increase in bank deposits by 10 is identical to savings of the same amount. The rise in Jonathan's assets represents an increase in his net wealth, which nevertheless is still negative at −10.

		Jonathan		
income	20	expenditure	10	flows (over one year)
		savings	10	
house	100	mortgage	150	stocks (at a point in time)
shares	10	net wealth	−10	
deposits	30			

Jonathan, bent over his year-end spreadsheet, might now want to think about whether the composition of his balance sheet is (still) optimal. Perhaps the interest he has been receiving on his bank deposits is lower than the interest he has been expending on his mortgage. It would then be rational to use available savings deposits to repay part of the mortgage, if that's possible under the terms of his mortgage contract with the bank. A repayment of 10 would change the balance sheet into this:

		individual		
income	20	expenditure	10	flows (over one year)
		savings	10	
house	100	mortgage	140	stocks (at a point in time)
shares	10	net wealth	−10	
deposits	20			

In financial jargon, Jonathan has 'rebalanced his portfolio' of assets somewhat. He could go on to take some more decisions as well. He could sell some stocks and use the proceeds to reduce the mortgage some more.

What Jonathan will end up doing, and what millions of other Jonathans and Janes end up doing in response to changes in the prices of various categories of assets, is a question of perpetual interest to both financial speculators and government economists. Some patterns can be discerned, and people like George Soros have got immensely rich by discerning them and timing movements in the prices of financial assets correctly more often than not. But in general, it's quite difficult to make correct forecasts of the reactions of individuals or institutions to changes.

Some institutions, however, have adopted a fixed set of publicly known goals; hence some operations can be predicted with a fair degree of confidence. It's helpful to have a basic understanding of the core operations of the monetary system (Soros certainly does!).

Four questions about the monetary system

In the following, we focus on four leading questions, which should help us to understand how a modern monetary system in general, and the monetary system of the Eurozone in particular, is supposed to work. The questions are:

1   How are bank deposits created ('deposits' in what follows)?
2   How are central bank deposits created ('reserves')?
3   How are government bonds created (in Germany)?
4   What are the instruments of the ECB?

Answering these questions requires applying the principles of double-entry bookkeeping. The most important of these is that each transaction triggers two balance sheet entries. These two entries are not allowed to cause an imbalance in the balance sheet; assets and liabilities must always balance (i.e. add up to the same number) at every step. In the following, we'll look at stocks in balance sheets, and mostly neglect flows.

3   The creation of bank deposits

First of all, we'll look at the creation of bank deposits – money born in ordinary commercial banks. Commercial banks are banks that work with the private sector. We'll just call them 'banks' from now on.

Central banks, on the other hand, belong to the public sector. They serve as the banks' bank – i.e. they're used for the core transactions between commercial banks, and they safeguard the functioning of the payment system, which is about enabling payments to occur between the spreadsheets of rival banks.

Bank deposits – the deposits you or I or Jonathan or Jane hold at our banks – are not the same thing as 'reserves', which are deposits of a special kind of money that banks hold at the central bank. That's explained in the next section. Bank deposits – the kind you or I hold at our banks – are spreadsheet entries in the balance sheets of banks, which in the Eurozone are denominated in euro, just like physical cash (but bank deposits are not at all the same thing as physical cash, as we'll see).

The central bank does not create the kind of bank deposits that you and I consider 'money in the bank'. It's exclusively commercial banks that create bank deposits. Commercial banks can be privately or publicly owned, by the way – that doesn't have any bearing on the mechanisms by which they create bank deposits.

Banks map the results of their business operations in their accounting systems, using electronic spreadsheet operations. Households see the respective changes in their chequing accounts by looking at their bank statement, in print or electronic form. Let's unpack these to see how bank deposits are created.

The creation of bank deposits can follow from the extension of credit by a bank to a borrower. How much credit banks extend to borrowers in a given time-frame (in a given month or year) depends on the aggregate demand for credit in that time-frame, and on the availability of prospective borrowers banks deem creditworthy. A bank can advertise loans, and indeed a typical commercial bank regularly sends letters to its clients suggesting they come into their local branch to see about getting a consumer loan, but it cannot force people to borrow. The bank can attempt to persuade or coax customers into taking on fresh bank debt, but it is the customer who has to sign the loan contract.

When lending, the bank usually pays attention to the customer's collateral and solvency. The latter consists of a judgement regarding the customer's capability to repay debts using income. Collateral is relevant in case the customer defaults on a loan – i.e. if there's a lasting interruption in the agreed stream of repayments. In that case, the bank takes recourse by exercising its right to take ownership of the posted collateral, and selling it (in most cases) to recover as much as possible of the nominal financial value of the defaulted loan.

Things that have been bought with the loan might count as collateral. This is typical for real estate loans, which in some countries are called 'mortgages'. If the borrower stops making payments on his mortgage, the bank eventually takes possession of the house and usually sells it. If this does not provide the bank with sufficient money to pay off the loan, residual debt might be placed on the borrower by means of a 'lien', requiring him to repay the balance of the debt from his future earnings. Rules vary from country to country.

Bank lending from a balance sheet perspective

What does the extension of bank credit, or 'making a bank loan', look like in the balance sheets of the parties concerned? Ultimately, the transaction is an exchange of promises to pay or, put differently, an exchange of assets. The bank, let's call it Alfa Bank, promises the borrower, let's call him Jonathan, that it will put a defined amount of bank deposits in his account at Alfa Bank. In exchange, Jonathan – the bank's counterparty in this deal – promises to repay the loan by regularly trans- ferring a defined monthly amount of deposits to Alfa Bank, composed partly of a repayment of the nominal value of the loan (the loan 'principal') and partly of interest payments, calculated as a percentage Jonathan must pay annually on the value of the principal. Jonathan's promise to pay this stream of deposits to the bank (if this is a routine bank loan contract) is backed by some durable collateral with an easily estimated financial value, such as real estate (Jonathan's house).

Jonathan's debt to the bank is the bank's asset and Jonathan's liability. In mirror image, the deposits that have been created in favour of Jonathan by the bank's act of entering a number in his deposit account at Alfa Bank are Jonath- an's asset and Alfa Bank's liability. In this sense, Alfa Bank and Jonathan have mutually exchanged assets and liabilities of equal value.

The legal basis for this exchange is a loan contract in written form, which triggers changes in the balance sheets of the concerned parties. The bank's asset (Jonathan's agreement that he is in debt to Alfa Bank for a given amount) and the bank's liability (the deposits the bank 'puts' by spreadsheet entry into Jonathan's bank account) are created simultaneously.

The same is true of the entries in the borrower's balance sheet. Jonathan's balance sheet now has a new asset, which is the amount of bank deposits put into his account at Alfa Bank by spreadsheet entry; and a new liability, which is the amount of the debt he has agreed to take on. Remember, he has contractually promised to pay Alfa on an agreed future schedule.

There's something really important for you to recognise here: loans create new assets and new liabilities, which offset each other. It is not correct to say that banks 'lend out the deposits of savers'. A new bank loan creates new deposits. These deposits are not taken from any other account held by anyone else at Alfa Bank. No other account anywhere in the banking system is decremented in order to incre-ment Jonathan's account when he is granted a loan! The bank is not 'on-lending' some money from some other stash or source to Jonathan. These new deposits are additional deposits – they are not based on savings of other households or firms.

This is why the process of bank 'lending' is called 'credit creation' or 'extending credit' – it really does extend the amount of credit in the monetary system! At the same time, it extends (increases) the amount of bank debt in equal measure.

So far, we have ignored interest rates, so the balance sheets look like this:

bank		household	
loan	100	deposits 100	deposits 100	loan	100

If we include interest, say at 5 per cent, then the balance sheets would look like this (assuming a one-year loan):

bank		household	
loan	105	deposits 100	deposits 100	loan	105
		equity 5		net wealth	−5

As a consequence of the extension of credit, we have an extension of the balance sheets of the two parties: assets and liabilities have increased for both. Net value is not affected, since both sides of the balance sheets of both counterparties have increased by the same amount.

Nevertheless, with each new loan, the instability of the banking system rises slightly, because each loan has a certain positive probability of default. Uncer-tainty has increased. This is an essential property of debt: debt has to be settled in the future. The future, as is well known, cannot be predicted with certainty.

Box 3.1 Why is there an interest rate?

An interest rate is, in principle, not strictly necessary for the functioning of a credit system. An interest rate can be derived from the expectation that some loans will not be repaid. However, not all financial assets carry risk, as we will see later on. A bank usually does not lend to borrowers which it thinks will not repay their debts; however, even in the best of economic times, the circumstances of some individual lives will lead to occasional debt defaults. Interest payments (plus other sources of bank revenues, such as transaction fees) must cover the lender's balance sheet costs caused by such defaults, plus the costs of operations; profits come out of what's left over after these are accounted for.

Typically a loan has some particular 'maturity', meaning that interest and principal must be paid on specific dates, either together or separately. When loans are extended, it is never entirely certain that the payments will actually be made on a timely basis (or at all), which is why the financial system is inherently potentially unstable.

An absolutely stable system could only be achieved if no loans were made. This, however, would not be a financial system – it would at best be a barter system mediated by tokens representing assets that already exist (I'll trade you tokens worth five of my sheep for a token worth one of your cows). Banks have an incentive to take care to ensure their extensions of credit are sound, since otherwise they'll lose money – unrepaid debts are counted against the bank's 'capital', composed of paid-in shareholder money plus retained earnings, and if this falls below some legal minimum of the bank's total liabilities, the bank is counted as 'insolvent' and must either raise new capital or declare bankruptcy. But banks' stability crucially hinges on appropriate and stable future incomes of borrowers. All kinds of macroeconomic shocks can play havoc with those incomes – and also with the value of the collateral, such as real estate, put up by borrowers to cover potential loan defaults.

The whole financial edifice is therefore rather fragile. The 'sustainability' of a financial system, as an idea, is quite hard to pin down, or even to define (see Chapter 7). Since all loans are risky, a 'sustainable' financial system in the strict sense of the term can only be one that features no loans. Then we would have thrown the baby out with the bath water. One has to define the sustainability of the financial system by measuring the likelihood that borrowers will have sufficient income flows to meet their repayment commitments over the time horizon of the debt agreements that have been made.

During an economic crisis with high rates of unemployment, many economic actors encounter problems making timely repayments on their debt obligations. Some households fall behind on their mortgage payments; some may suffer a visit from a bailiff, eviction and a public auction of the property by court order. Some firms find themselves unable to repay their loans because they cannot sell enough of their output or services to generate sufficient income to keep up payments. In good times, the firms might be able to renew the loan, but in bad times this option might not be available.

In this situation, debt can go from being a microeconomic (individual and local) problem to becoming a macroeconomic (systemic) problem. We'll address this issue in more depth later. At this stage, it should be emphasised that a conception of 'financial system stability' built on a notion that uncertainty could somehow be completely removed is not helpful. It's true that banks can never be quite sure if or when loans they've made will be repaid – so there is a degree of inherent instability unavoidably built into the financial system. However, at the same time, by virtue of its function of extending loans in the form of newly created bank deposits, the financial system is an essential factor of stability. Loans create or sustain employment, incomes and purchasing power. By extending credit (purchasing power), contractual agreements to deliver and pay for future deliveries of goods and services can be arranged. The overall effect of having a system of credit creation is that far more goods and services are supplied than would otherwise be possible.

Credits are transferable IOUs, i.e. debt certificates, and debts are inherently about the future. If debts didn't exist, we'd be limited to bartering goods and services in the here-and-now: five of my sheep for one of your cows, here and now. If instead of that here-and-now barter deal, you promise in writing to give me a calf that you think one of your cows will give birth to next year, in exchange for my giving you three of my sheep today, and I agree, then that written promissory note is credit. It's money – I can trade it for something else, perhaps for a plough, and the ploughmaker, in turn, can give it to the publican to pay off his year's tab at the village pub.

Accepting your promissory note is inherently risky, because by next year you or your cows may have died or moved away. I – or the publican – may never get that calf. But probably you'll still be here in the village, and the note will be honoured; our mutually agreed claim on the future will work out. I believe so, in the here-and-now, and because I believe it, we both immediately benefit – you now have three sheep to work with; three sheep I didn't really need because I have more sheep than I really know what to do with, but which you can use to sheer some wool from to make sweaters; I have my new plough; the ploughmaker is back in the good graces of the publican and can start running up a new tab; and the publican is looking forward to some tasty veal to serve his clients come springtime ... all thanks to the magic of debt.

Box 3.2 The neoclassical perspective

In the doctrines of neoclassical economics, an incorrect theory of banking called the 'loanable funds' theory remains ascendant (though perhaps not for much longer, since word is increasingly getting around that it's nonsense). Among others, US economist Paul Krugman and German finance minister Wolfgang Schäuble have made statements indicating they believe that banks lend out the deposits of savers. Bank loans are assumed to be essentially the same as loans of physical cash, only in this case in the form of 'electronic cash': if a saver lends €100 in physical cash to her cousin, she won't have access to that money until her cousin gives it back to her. In neoclassical theory, the bank is merely an intermediary between such loans between private individuals – a way for such loans to be made between people who don't know each other (because they both are known to the bank, and both trust the bank). This, as we have seen, is wrong.

Speculation and bubbles

Let's return to a household that has received a fresh loan – Jonathan's household. Jonathan can now use the deposits that were credited to his account by his bank. He instructs his bank to transfer these deposits to the account of another household – say, Frank's account. For example, the deposits might leave Jonathan's balance sheet when he buys a house from Frank. The house enters Jonathan's balance sheet with the value assigned at the time the transaction is completed. From the perspective of the seller's balance sheet, the mirror image of this transaction is recorded. Frank has a positive net wealth since his balance sheet has assets, but no liabilities.

Jonathan				Frank			
house	100	loan	100	deposits	100	net wealth	100
deposits	0			house	0		

By buying Frank's house, Jonathan could be using the loan he was granted by the bank to speculate on rising real estate prices, or to buy a house for the purpose of owner-occupation. Buying the house might pull up average house prices. This doesn't always happen, and it's decidedly difficult to correctly predict the movement of prices. However, if house prices do indeed move upwards, then Jonathan will feel richer without Frank feeling poorer. The former's net wealth will be larger than it was before he borrowed money to buy Frank's house, if the increase in the house price is reflected in his balance sheet. The following balance sheets illustrate this.

Jonathan				Frank			
house	110	loan	100	deposits	100	net wealth	100
deposits	0	net wealth	10	house	0		

If Jonathan has speculated on rising prices, and now feels validated in his expectation of rising real estate prices, he might now borrow even more. Given that he now has higher collateral – because the market value of his house has increased by 10 per cent – the bank should be willing to increase the amount of its lending to him. Let's assume Jonathan does borrow more, and that the next loan of €110 is invested in buying another house – this time not from Frank, but from some other party we'll call Jane.

Jonathan				Jane			
house	230	loan	210	deposits	110	net wealth	110
deposits	0	net wealth	20	house	0		

Once again, we assume that the purchase of a house leads to a rise in the level of house prices. Jonathan's net wealth increases by another 10, while his liabilities increase as well. This can go on for quite a while – for many years, in fact. There were thousands of real estate speculators like Jonathan in the US, UK, Spain, Ireland and elsewhere in the run-up to 2007–8, a period in which real estate price bubbles inflated for many years in a row.

Our hypothetical example shows how a credit cycle arises, with rising prices leading to more speculation, which leads again to higher prices, and so on. This process can be self-sustaining until debt levels stop rising – perhaps because a wave of defaults on mortgage debts makes banks realise their borrowers have become over-leveraged, or borrowers start noticing that prices have become so insanely high (measured as a multiple of annual household income) that they're unlikely to rise much further, at which point fewer people keep engaging in competitively bidding up the prices of housing, house prices level off or fall, and the game stops, with large numbers of people suddenly faced with 'negative equity' in the houses they've bought with too much borrowed money.

A rising credit cycle is often called a 'bubble', but the term is difficult to define. There is no 'equilibrium' or 'fundamental' price of houses or other assets, since these are financed with credit, which by definition goes hand in hand with uncertainty. A useful gauge of whether housing prices are reasonable or inflated might be to look at ratios like the ratio of house price to median annual income in a regional housing market, or the ratio of the house price to the expected annual rental income from the house (what it would bear in a rental market, regardless of whether it's actually rented out or not), and compare these ratios to historical data from other housing markets – including markets which were, in retrospect, clearly in a bubble, and others which were not.

Box 3.3 Accountancy rules and procyclicality

It's clear that accounting rules have a powerful influence on the extension of credit. Depending on whether current market value or price at time of purchase are used in the balance sheet, the same collateral can be used for different amounts of borrowing. A rise in prices leads to a rise in the potentially available amount of credit. This can create a self-sustaining cycle – both in the upswing and the downswing. This is called 'procyclicality'.

The American economist Hyman Minsky, who was active from the 1960s through the 1990s, described the way private sector firms (or households borrowing to buy a house) finance their activities by dividing financing deals into three categories. *Hedge finance* was his label for financial terms under which firms are able to repay both interest and principal, using their cash flow. Deals that only allow firms to keep up with interest payments, but are unable to generate the revenues necessary to repay the principal, fall in the category of *speculative finance*. As the name implies, the firms hope that in the future they will be able to repay the principal – perhaps through a rise in the value of their assets, or some other change in market conditions – and are hence speculating on their future success in a way that isn't entirely justified by the internal terms of the deal itself. Those firms that are so optimistic that they make deals to buy assets that are able to repay neither principal nor interest are engaged in what Minsky labelled *Ponzi finance*. Firms using speculative or Ponzi finance need to 'roll over' (refinance) their debts, and are hence dependent on financial markets' willingness to keep extending them fresh credit.

The way the private sector uses external debt has an influence on asset prices across the board. Another influence is that of market dealers, who make markets in different financial and non-financial assets. Since these often use credit to finance their books, in times of crisis these markets might break down one after the other, as the appetite for risk is replaced by a race to liquidity. Dealers in declining markets can become either unwilling or unable to sustain their books, and the subsequent sell-off depresses prices in all market segments. The fact that asset prices fell in almost any asset class and in many places simultaneously can be explained this way. Once markets turn, an abundance of actors engaged in speculative or Ponzi finance implies that financial decline will become contagious and self-reinforcing.

The monetary circuit

Historically, German firms used debt extensively to finance themselves over the course of the twentieth century – using, in Minsky's terms, a 'hedge finance' model. Private investments were financed not only through accumulated earnings, but also through borrowing. A firm usually negotiated a credit line with a bank that allowed it to purchase raw materials and capital goods. Raw materials and capital goods (real estate and machines) served as collateral for the bank. Earnings from the sale of output were intended to suffice to repay the loans as well as cover operating costs (especially labour costs).

After a loan is granted, a young firm may use the bank deposits it has been granted (remember, that's new money!) to acquire labour services, among other things. Let us look at the balance sheets of a simple three-player economy, consisting of a bank, a firm and households who are also the firm's employees, after the loan contract has been signed

bank				firm	
loan	100	deposits	100	deposits	100	loan	100

The firm now purchases labour services. To keep matters simple, we assume the firm produces services by using only labour. The firm transfers its deposits to households, who in return supply labour. The services created in this way are recognised in the balance sheet with a value of 100. Nothing changes in the balance sheet of the bank (note: for simplicity, we're assuming the firm and the households maintain accounts at the same bank); however, the deposits have changed their owner.

households				firm	
deposits	100	net wealth	100	services	100	loan	100

This is how deposits find their way into the hands of employees. These are thus enabled to buy the output (services) of the firm by transferring deposits back to the firm. In the latter's balance sheet, services have been replaced by deposits.

households				firm	
services	100	net wealth	100	deposits	100	loan	100

The firm has recovered its deposits and can now repay the loan. After repayment the balance sheets return to the original state:

bank				firm		
loan	0	deposits	0	deposits	0	loan	0

The loan and the deposits have now been destroyed in the same way they were created. We've gone from balance sheets composed of zeros before a debt was incurred, into offsetting positive and negative values after the debt was incurred (and credit in the amount of the debt was extended), back to a balance sheet composed only of zeros.

Why expend all this effort if the balance sheet returns to the original state? The answer lies outside of the balance sheet. The firm's production, in this case consisting wholly of services, was supplied and consumed. This is the purpose of a monetary economy: it facilitates the supply of goods and services and their subsequent consumption by households.

Additional deposits circulate in the economy after credit has been extended by a bank, i.e. after a bank 'makes a loan' (see Figure 3.1). After all, enabling expenditure of these deposits is the reason for the borrowing. Hardly anyone borrows and then leaves the deposits at the bank.

The main cause of borrowing in much of the developed world (comprising the majority of all bank loans by total financial volume) is a desire by households to

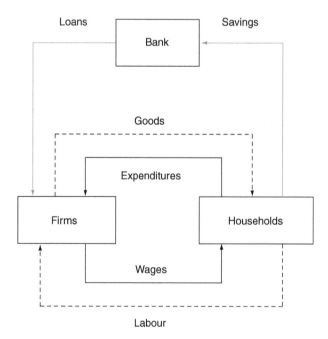

Figure 3.1 Simple monetary circuit.

finance the purchase of a house or apartment. However, in regards to production activities, the cause of borrowing is often a firm that expects additional demand for their goods and services and wants to pre-finance production. The monetary circuit hence starts with expected demand, which leads firms to pre-finance their production. Firms pay employees by a transfer of deposits at the bank. These employees demand goods and services, and at least partly validate the expectations of demand held by the entrepreneurs. The deposits of the firms will be replenished by the spending of households. Our simple three-sector model scales up to the economy as a whole when one considers the bank, firm and household to represent sectors rather than a single bank, firm and single-firm group of households.

Box 3.4 The Keynesian textbook story of demand for money

In his *General Theory* book of 1936, John Maynard Keynes postulated an equality of money supply and money demand. Demand for money depends mostly on income and liquidity preference. Liquidity preference describes at what rate of interest savers are willing to give up their liquidity and hold an illiquid asset – like a sovereign bond – instead. An increase in the monetary supply creates an expansionary effect for the economy, increasing incomes until the additional money supply has been absorbed. Income adjusts until supply and demand for money match. This idea of an equality of demand with a fixed supply is an essential difference with this book.

When does this credit circulation end? It ends when the owner of the deposits decides to use them to repay an outstanding loan. Another possibility is that the owner of deposits is satisfied with holding and not spending the credits, leaving them sitting idle at the bank. He or she might transfer them to a savings account, or a certificate of deposit or something similar. He or she could also use the deposits to pay taxes or fees of the state – you may be surprised to learn that this would also destroy the deposits and remove them from circulation permanently. We will look at this process in more detail later.

Hoarding deposits above and beyond one's immediate expected need is quite rational. Not every indispensable expense can be planned. Many households and firms therefore will want to hold a buffer balance at their bank. However, with the emergence of overdraft mechanisms at banks for clients with good credit ratings, this hoarding of deposits may have decreased somewhat in a historical perspective (though in recent years, some large firms like Apple have held huge reserves of unspent bank deposits – why they've done so is an interesting question, but it's beyond the scope of this text). Firms often have set credit lines at their home bank, which they can draw on up to a specified limit. It's obvious that once such an arrangement is in place, an increase in credit depends only on the demand side, that is, on the actions of the entrepreneur.

In regards to the monetary circuit and its main purpose, which is to facilitate production and consumption, there is a serious problem associated with hoarding, also called precautionary saving. The problem stems from the fact that the afflu-ent, which include successful entrepreneurs and capital owners, save relatively more than average or poor households.

To illustrate, let's assume that an entrepreneur borrows one million euro and produces some quantity of output by paying employees four-fifths of one million in wages. The output is supposed to bring in revenue of one million euro, but the entrepreneur would like to keep the €200,000 not expended, not to finance his own consumption, but rather as savings. Where could the purchasing power come from to close the gap of €200,000? The entrepreneur does not want to save in the form of keeping a part of the production as inventory. He or she wants to hold deposits at the bank.

For this to work out, additional demand would have to be created. As we will see later, this demand normally comes from the state (though it could also come from his employees borrowing money from the bank, in the form of consumer loans). By spending more than it takes in, in the form of taxes, the government adds deposits to bank accounts of firms and households. In so far as public spending closes the gap in demand, the corresponding deposits held by house-holds and firms make the accumulation of desired savings possible. This is an interesting point to ponder for businessmen who dislike government deficits.

The implication of this is that there's a macroeconomic requirement to run public deficits, founded on a demand gap that arises from households and firms wanting to set aside savings in the form of money. In other words: because some households do not spend all of their income and some businesses have positive profits, and this overcompensates any households or firms with deficits, we have a problem of a lack of demand. This demand gap cannot be closed but by an increase in government spending and hence debt.

Private debt could close it only temporarily since it cannot rise forever. Household debt to GDP ratios have risen substantially in many countries over the last decades, but it is almost impossible for the ratio to rise for a much longer period of time. People will not accept mortgage payments in the range of 50–100 per cent of their disposable income. This is an empirical observation coupled with psychological speculation rather than an equilibrium outcome of any sort, but sometimes it is better to be roughly right than precisely wrong.

The existence of this demand gap in economically good as well as bad times explains why the government budget balance is almost always in the red. A per-manent public deficit is not a pathological symptom, but a macroeconomic necessity in order for private households to be in a position to save money. If governments were to balance their budgets, or worse, run surpluses, then as the relatively wealthy continue to set aside some of their income in savings, the quantity of circulating money would gradually decrease – and so would effective demand. Firms would not be able to sell all of their production. Subsequently, output would be reduced or grow less strongly, leading to lower rates of eco-nomic activity and higher unemployment.

The interest rate

So far we have abstracted from interest payments. Interest payments are the source of income for traditional banks. To ensure profitability of a bank, interest earned on its assets must surpass interest paid on its liabilities (we'll ignore other sources of bank revenues for now, like transaction fees or profits from trading financial papers). That's why interest rates on deposits tend to be relatively low. Let's look at the balance sheets of a bank and a firm just after the extension of a loan.

bank				firm		
loan	100	deposits	100	deposits	100	loan	100

The bank will demand an interest rate on the loan higher than the interest rate it pays on deposits of clients. In the next section we'll have a look at how banks set interbank interest rates when they need reserves for 'clearing', or settling accounts between consecutive business days, in the interbank market.

For now, we'll focus on the firm's side of the debt contract. The company will only agree to pay an interest rate if it expects to generate sufficient income to cover all its costs, including interest payments, over the coming time horizon. This becomes obvious if we think about what happens over the time horizon of the debt contract. Let's have a look at the balance sheet at the time the loan comes due. We'll assume the interest rate on the loan was 5 per cent and the interest rate paid by the bank on the deposit was 0 per cent.

bank				firm			
loan	100	deposits	100	deposits	110	loan	100
interest	5	equity	5			equity	5
						interest	5

Here, the balance sheet indicates the firm incurred production costs of 100, and paid 5 in interest, but was able to sell the goods or services produced for 110. At the time of maturity of the loan, the firm will thus have additional deposits of 5. This is mirrored by an increase in equity of 5.

The bank books the interest rate payment of the firm as an asset, which rises above liabilities. Again, the adjustment works via equity on the liability side. A positive equity says that there are some assets without corresponding liabilities. Equity is not a liability in the normal sense, but a pure balance sheet construction. Equity designates the amount of money that would be available at liquidation of the firm, after assets have been sold and all liabilities have been settled. After the loan is repaid the balance sheets look like this:

bank				firm			
~~loan~~	~~100~~	~~deposits~~	~~100~~	~~deposits~~	~~100~~	~~loan~~	~~100~~
~~interest~~	~~5~~	deposits	5	deposits	5	equity	5
reserves	10	equity	5				

What is especially interesting is that in order to repay the loan, more deposits are needed than are circulating at that time. The bank extended a loan, through which deposits of 100 have been created. The firm, however, has to transfer deposits worth 105 in order to repay the loan. If only 100 in deposits have been created through lending, where will the deposits come from that will allow the firm to repay the loan?

Box 3.5 Maximisation of profits and minimisation of debts

It is usually assumed that firms maximise profits. However, in a context of financial crisis, firms might switch their top priority to debt minimisation. The repayment of debt destroys deposits, which slows down the monetary circuit. Had the deposits remained in circulation, they might have been used to finance investment, which would have led to more demand, more income and more growth.

The additional deposits have been created, among other things, by other banks, and the owners of these deposits have transferred them to the firm. Alternatively, a bank might have bought something from the private sector by creating new deposits in the account of the seller. It might have been a house or a share of a firm. Naturally, the repayment of loans is easier when the amount of loans is growing strongly, since then more deposits are circulating in the economy. The creation of additional deposits from the public sector's deficit spending or lower taxes might also be easing the pressure.

The unit of currency and the acceptance of money

So far, we haven't looked at the denominations of the deposits in balance sheets of banks, firms and households. In principle, banks would be able to create deposits in all kinds of possible units: euro, dollar, lira or claims on bushels of fresh apples. Why do so many banks in Europe choose the euro?

Bank deposits are created in the euro denomination because this is the accepted currency in the Eurozone. It is often said that we accept a particular means of payment because other people accept it. While this might be true today, it doesn't explain how it came to be that way. Before what we consider 'money' was generally accepted as a means of payment, someone must have got the ball rolling by being willing to accept it.

In most countries, the most important reason people prefer to do business in a particular currency is probably that the state uses its powers of law-making to fix that currency as the only accepted means of payment that discharges tax liabilities and payments for fines and fees. This automatically creates an important category of demand for the state-specified means of payment, which is why people will accept it as their common currency for other uses as well. The connection between a currency's value and taxes is as follows:

1 Government debits the private sector with taxes and fees, and fixes a compulsory and exclusive means of payment (a state monopoly), accepted by the state for citizens to discharge these liabilities, in units like euro or pound sterling (the state currency).
2 Government demands some goods and services, or labour services, and pays with the same form of money that it has decreed is the only form with which citizens are able to discharge their tax liabilities.
3 To avoid difficulties, taxpayers have an incentive to produce and trade using that same currency, in order to acquire money with which to pay fees and taxes to the government.
4 The state money paid out in return for goods and services or labour functions, in effect, as 'tax vouchers', so from the government's point of view, money denominated in the currency specified by the state as the only means citizens' taxes may be paid is a liability to the government. The government's liability consists in freeing the taxpayer from his tax liability if the taxpayer transfers the required amounts of money to the government. This is why cash and central bank deposits are shown as liabilities on the balance sheets of central banks and governments. Conversely, they are booked as assets in private sector balance sheets.

If the whole game seems a bit circular, that's as it should be. It is circular! That's why we call it 'the monetary circuit'. The monetary system is a scorekeeping system for debts and credits (i.e. transferable IOUs), managed by double-entry bookkeeping conventions whose parameters are decided by government laws.

Before the euro was introduced, taxes were paid in national currency, such as Deutschmarks (DM) in Germany. Since the introduction of the euro, taxes have been paid in euro. Tax payments in other currencies are not accepted. Not every country has its own currency, but those that do have one usually accept only their own currency for tax payments.

The simplified balance sheets of household and Treasury look like this before the payment of taxes (we assume the Treasury and central bank, both of which are government institutions, are unified into a single entity we call 'Treasury' here, i.e. their balance sheets are combined):

Treasury			households		
taxes	100	money 200	money	200	taxes 100
		net wealth −100			net wealth 100

The households know their taxes will come due at the end of the year. Nowadays, most people have income taxes deducted at source from monthly or biweekly salary payments, but let's consider the situation of entrepreneurs or freelance workers. They have an incentive to accumulate deposits in the banks over the year, because they'll be needed for their tax payment at the end of the fiscal year. When taxes are paid, households transfer deposits to the state, leaving the balance sheets like this:

_____Treasury_____			_____households_____		
taxes	0	money 100	money	100	taxes 0
		net wealth −100			net wealth 100

In the simplified balance sheets above, which lack a banking system, it is evident that taxes are money that returns to the government to extinguish tax liabilities. Net wealth of the private sector and perhaps working hours will be changed because of the tax collection. The debt of one sector corresponds with the wealth of another. A tax cut would also provide the households with more deposits, at least relatively, and would correspondingly increase the deficit of the government.

Taxes effectively serve as a tool to reduce the purchasing power of the private sector through removal of deposits from private sector bank accounts. If a firm or household pays taxes, then deposits are transferred to the state that otherwise could have been spent on goods and services.

The state, intent on making sure there's 'room' in the economy to exercise its own claims on a society's ability to produce goods and services (in total, government spending accounts for around 40–50 per cent of total GDP in many advanced industrial economies), uses taxation to limit total consumer demand from the private sector to keep inflation in check.

If aggregate demand – including that of private and public sectors added together – were to surpass the productive capacities of the economy, inflation would result. Government should then respond by increasing taxes and fees, in order to restore price-level stability. Alternatively, a higher rate of interest would reduce 'borrowing' (new credit creation) for investment, thus reducing the purchasing power of the private sector.

As we will see later, in principle, the government does not need tax revenues to finance its spending, since government is able to create money. Taxes merely help government to spend without causing inflation. However, stability in the value of money is an important economic and social goal. Hence, it would be wrong to say that in a modern monetary economy, tax payments are not necessary for government spending.

The monetary pyramid

In everyday life, we don't distinguish between euro denominated in physical cash and euro in our bank deposits. We take it for granted that each euro recorded in our deposit account at the bank can be exchanged into one euro in physical cash, either at a branch of our bank, or at an ATM (automated teller machine). The deposit guarantee scheme in Germany protects individual deposits up to €100,000, as it currently stands, which puts some institutional flesh on the theoretical bones.

Moreover, politicians recognise the importance of the citizenry's maintaining faith that the financial system is a safe place to park their savings. German chancellor Angela Merkel (Christian Democrat, CDU) and finance minister Peer

Steinbrück (Social Democrat, SPD) gave a promise to German savers in October 2008, a few weeks after Lehman Brothers failed, that all their savings were safe. Lehman Brothers was one of the biggest financial firms on Wall Street. Its insolvency put the solvency and stability of the global financial system in question, because the balance sheets of global banks are interlinked via millions of debt contracts and speculative bets. No one knew at the time what Lehman's reneging on its contracts would mean for the system as a whole. Peer Steinbrück literally said: 'I would like to underline that we feel a shared responsibility to assure you that German savers do not have to fear losing one single euro of their deposits.' In practical terms, these sums would never have to be reimbursed, but theoretically, he claimed, it was possible to reimburse everyone. This, although it seems fantastic, is true. The state can 'bail-out' not only banks, but also households.

Show me the money ... cash money!

Money in the form of bank deposits is a promise to pay cash. So, if you have a deposit with a nominal value of €500 in your bank account, this is the bank's promise to you to supply €500 in physical cash to you if and when you demand it. This works like an exchange rate between two currencies – 'bank deposits' and 'physical cash' – at an exchange ratio of one to one. Deposits and physical cash are therefore said to be at 'par value'.

Box 3.6 Some lessons of the French Revolution

The time immediately after the French Revolution provides a historical case study to highlight the necessity of tax payments to fight inflation. Unpopular taxes had been one of the causes of the revolution, and after it succeeded, these taxes were consequently scrapped. The state had to keep financing its spending, however, so it did that by emitting government 'bonds', or promises to pay. As a result, more and more bonds circulated on financial markets over time. Therefore, the bonds gradually lost their value – i.e. there was a high 'inflation rate'. This was not due to the flimsiness of paper money, but due to the inability of government to reign in inflation through higher taxes.

But what is physical cash, exactly? And what are bank deposits if they are really, in technical terms, a claim on a bank to be paid money, rather than 'real money' in the sense that physical cash is real money, i.e. the 'means of final settlement' of debts or promises to pay?

It turns out that there is more than one kind of money in the system. Bank deposits aren't the means of final settlement – they're depositors' claims on being paid out the means of final settlement in the form of cash. Physical cash is one of two forms the means of final settlement can take. The other is a special form of electronic deposits called 'reserves' which only exist in deposit accounts kept at the central bank. Only the Treasury and commercial banks are allowed to have deposit accounts at the central bank, and 'reserves', which are sometimes called 'high-powered money', can never leave the accounts at the central bank – except by being traded for physical cash, as we'll see.

Ordinary deposit accounts held by households or businesses in commercial banks aren't 'reserves', nor are they means of final settlement. Again, they're merely the depositor's claim on being paid out some quantity of the means of final settlement, on demand – or on the bank's using some of the reserves it holds in its reserve deposit account at the central bank to settle a debt on the depositor's behalf that the latter has incurred with another depositor whose account is at a different bank.

Since a commercial bank can go bankrupt, bank deposits held by clients in commercial banks are somewhat more vulnerable to losing their value than are bank reserves or physical cash (although, again, a deposit insurance scheme exists to compensate the bulk of the money in commercial bank deposit accounts in the event of a bank's insolvency or failure). Central banks cannot go bankrupt, though they can fail if people lose faith in a particular currency during a national crisis, e.g. if the state whose laws and coercive powers underlie a currency system disintegrates or ceases to exist as a result of war or revolution. So, the safety of central bank 'reserve money' is contingent only on the continuity and institutional integrity of the state. Moreover, banks settle claims between each other at the end of each business day by means of interbank transfers of 'reserves', not by transferring commercial bank deposits. In contrast, non-bank firms and households generally settle debts with each other by means of transfers from and to commercial bank deposits (or in cash, for small payments).

For these reasons, we can speak of a 'monetary pyramid' with central bank reserve money and government bonds at the top, bank deposits in the middle and various promises to pay between non-bank private sector firms or households at the bottom.

Figure 3.2 shows the monetary pyramid. At the top are 'reserves' and 't-bonds' (Treasury bonds). 'Reserves' are electronic money deposits at the central bank held by banks, plus physical cash held by the private sector. Central bank deposits can be exchanged into cash and vice versa. Government bonds are a government's promises to pay some amount of money at a specific future date, and to pay some defined annual amount of interest to the bondholder in the meantime. Bondholders purchase government bonds from the government. In effect, these are loans of money made to the government by investors.

What bonds promise to bondholders is the delivery of a specific amount of 'reserves', the 'face value' of the bond, at a defined future date, the 'maturity date', as well as (normally) a schedule of annual interest payments calculated as a percentage of the face value, in the meantime. Government bonds are equally as safe as reserves in most monetary systems.

In contrast, retail bank deposits are a promise to deliver cash on demand – i.e. if you go to your bank and ask for cash in exchange for a decrement of your deposit account, you will receive it, unless the bank turns out to be insolvent and undergoing bankruptcy procedures on that day.

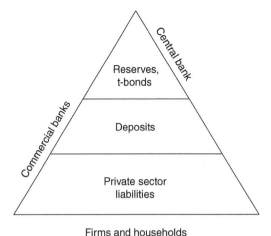

Figure 3.2 The monetary pyramid.

Private sector liabilities, such as a contractual agreement to pay an invoice to a freelance computer programmer for services rendered to a software firm, arise from business activities of the private sector. They're promises to deliver some amount of bank deposits (usually by a particular day, in exchange for satisfactory delivery of specified services), and hence indirectly, a promise to deliver cash (more precisely, they represent transfers of claims on a bank's promise to deliver cash in exchange for decrementing the balances in bank deposit accounts).

Box 3.7 What government is meant by 'government' in this text?

Here, we mean the central government of the state, often the federal government. Only it can issue bonds without limit. Governments of sub-federal states (or provinces, etc.) are in most countries required by law to run a balanced budget. They have less privileged relationships with their country's central bank compared to the central government.

The pyramid illustrates that debt is always cleared by the transfer of means of the payment of the next higher level. These means of payment are liabilities of the institutions of the upper level against those of the next lower level. The private sector uses commercial bank deposits, which are banks' liabilities, for payment and debt repayment purposes, both vis-à-vis banks and other private sector parties. Commercial banks, on the other hand, use reserve deposits at the central bank, which represent the central bank's liability vis-à-vis commercial banks, in order to pay debts among themselves.

On the same level as central bank reserves, we have government bonds. They are quite similar to central bank deposits, but typically have a time limitation and also an interest rate. In the next subsection, we examine the role of cash and central bank deposits in the monetary system.

Another aspect of the money pyramid is that each asset – read: each promise to pay – that's acceptable as a means of payment can be considered to be 'money'. The economist Hyman Minsky wrote about this phenomenon:

> Anyone can create money; the problem is in getting it accepted.

Box 3.8 Casino chips and Disney dollars

The pyramid of money can be extended downwards in various ways. Casino chips, for instance, are promises to deliver local currency. In a similar way, Disney dollars are promises to deliver US dollars. Disney customers expect that these two currencies can be exchanged without cost in both directions, in unlimited amounts and at a ratio of one to one.

In a modern monetary system, only state money can be used to extinguish tax liabilities. Private money – bank deposits – is not accepted. Even though it looks like households pay taxes by transferring deposits, what's going on in the background is that the banks transfer state money to the government's account at the central bank. It is therefore not bank deposits that people pay their taxes with, but state money in the form of central bank deposits. Since the state can choose what it wants to accept in payment of taxes, it inherently has more power than banks (see Chapter 6).

Conclusion

In the first section of this chapter, we saw that money is always debt (money is essentially anything that functions as a transferable IOU), that its creation requires an appropriate transaction, and that banks can create money apparently 'from nothing' (*ex nihilo*) – or more accurately, from the contractually agreed, legally enforceable promise of a debtor that he will repay the money, and also pay interest on his debt in the meantime. Assets and liabilities are created at the same time for both lender and borrower. In a perfect world, the monetary circuit stimulates production and consumption (rather than house price inflation or other asset price bubbles). Repaying loans or paying taxes destroys deposits. The state, as we have seen, sets the currency unit in which taxes must be paid, thereby institutionalising society-wide demand for its form of currency.

Until now, we've only looked at bank deposits, which are assets of the private sector held at banks. The next section deals with the question of how bank deposits can be exchanged into cash. We've mentioned that banks promise to exchange deposits into cash one-for-one. How does this work in practice?

4 The creation of central bank deposits

In most of today's monetary systems, the monopoly for production of cash lies with the state. As we've seen above, in a pure credit economy there's no need for cash. Even though today we handle the bulk of our transactions through transfers of bank deposits, we still expect banks to deliver cash to the full extent of our deposits, whenever we go and demand cash in exchange for a decrement of our deposit account. Since we do not get our cash directly from the central bank, the mechanism must be more complicated than is normally assumed.

There are three essential mechanisms by which commercial banks can increase the amount of cash or deposits at the central bank. First, banks can increase their holdings of cash by borrowing directly from the central bank. Second, the central bank can influence the amount of central bank deposits held by banks through 'open market operations', i.e. by buying (or selling) illiquid assets and hence providing banks with more (or fewer) central bank deposits. The central bank usually does this in order to change the short-term interest rate. Or third, central bank deposits increase following an increase in fiscal spending. In this section we focus on the first two possibilities; the third is covered in the following section. Let's have a more detailed look at the creation of bank deposits first.

bank				firm	
loan	100	deposits	100	deposits	100	loan	100

The bank gave a loan to the firm, based on a debt contract between the two parties (i.e. between the bank and the firm). The bank creates deposits in its accounting software, which shows that the firm owns 100 in deposits. At the same time, the loan will be booked as an asset for the bank. Nowhere in the system are deposits reduced by 100; this makes it obvious that banks do not lend out other people's money (deposits), nor do they lend out central bank money. We also see that the bank does not have any cash before making the loan. How does it acquire cash then, if the firm demands physical cash for the deposits that it holds? We have no cash in the balance sheet of the bank (yet).

The main refinancing instrument of the central bank

The answer is simple but ingenious. Banks borrow central bank money, usually called 'central bank reserves' or simply 'reserves', from the central bank, which requires banks to put up collateral to secure these loans. The collateral has to be high-quality, low-risk and of equal value to the loan. Often, government bonds in the possession of a bank will be used as collateral for such loans of 'reserves'.

Banks' 'reserve account' deposits can be exchanged into physical cash at the nearest branches of the central bank. Indeed, cash plus the electronic deposits banks maintain in their 'reserve accounts' at the central bank, taken together, are considered to be equivalent; both are forms of 'central bank money' or 'reserves', and sometimes they're called 'high-powered money'.

Note that neither reserves nor physical cash are quite the same thing as the claims you have against a bank in the form of deposit records in your name in a retail account at your bank. That's because reserves and physical cash, by law, are 'means of final settlement', whereas the numbers in your bank account aren't. We'll explain this in more detail later.

Banks have electronic 'reserve accounts' at the national central bank, which – in the Eurozone – are denominated in euro.

Eurozone commercial banks can build up stocks of central bank deposits in their reserve accounts at ECB by borrowing them from the central bank at some rate of interest. This normally happens through the main refinancing instrument, with interest charged at the 'base rate', also called 'bank rate', which is set by the central bank. The loan usually is short-term and does not exceed a one-month maturity, though often it's shorter. Here are the relevant simplified balance sheets, in which a bank borrows reserves from the central bank:

central bank				bank		
loan (bank)	100	reserves	100	loan (ps)	100	deposits	100
				reserves	100	loan (CB)	100

The central bank offers to lend reserves against collateral at regular intervals. Given that the commercial bank has extended loans to households or firms (the private sector – ps), its balance sheet changes. The loan of the central bank to the commercial bank is booked as a liability of the commercial bank, which promises to pay when the loan comes due.

At the same time this loan, backed up with collateral, is an asset to the central bank. This way, the central bank ensures that in the case of default its balance sheet is not overly burdened. It has the possibility of recovering up to 100 per cent of the loan by selling the underlying collateral, so the central bank can be operated risk-free, at least theoretically. As matters stand in the real world, this is generally not the case: the collateral often does entail some risk of its market value not being worth 100 per cent of the value of the corresponding reserve loan.

In the scenario discussed above, the collateral for the loan from the central bank was the loan of the bank made to the firm. Since the balance sheet of the bank does not have any other items, the loan is the only possible collateral. The central bank, in this case the ECB, accepts collateral or not depending on the rating assigned to the collateral by rating agencies, which are private sector firms. The minimum has been a BBB– by Fitch or Standard&Poor's, Baa3 by Moody's or BBB by DBRS.

Only when the collateral satisfies the minimum requirements does the ECB extend a loan to the bank up to the amount of the collateral. The ECB sets the minimum required rating and can change it if it wants to. If the frictionless functioning of the payment system is in danger, the central bank can then accept collateral of lesser quality to keep credits flowing through the monetary system.

The commercial bank thus acquires a reserve deposit in its account at the central bank by using a loan to the private sector as collateral. Other ways for the bank to increase its holdings of reserves are the sale (or repo'ing) of assets and getting a loan from another bank. The account at the central bank is called the reserves account. Only banks and the Treasury own accounts at the ECB and have direct access to reserves. No firms and no households have an account at the central bank, although some firms own banks that do have a central bank account. The government, represented by the Treasury, usually has an account at the central bank, but in the Eurozone this is arranged somewhat indirectly. The account of the German government, for instance, is operated by the German central bank (*Bundesbank*), which fulfils instructions given by the Treasury, on whose behalf it executes transactions.

From the perspective of the central bank, reserves are liabilities. In the same way that commercial banks making loans to borrowers create deposits in those borrowers' accounts, so that those deposits are liabilities from the point of view of the loan-making banks, central banks carry their deposits on the liability side. Reserves are booked as liabilities at the institution creating them.

Box 4.1 The end of the Bretton Woods system

In the global currency system of Bretton Woods (1945–71), the US dollar was fixed to gold. The US government promised that the bearer of coins or bank notes totalling $35 in nominal value could exchange these for an ounce of gold on demand, by presenting the notes and coins at the central bank. Since the other participating currencies in the Bretton Woods currency-board system were fixed against the US dollar, they were indirectly fixed to gold. In 1971 US president Richard Nixon suspended the dollar's gold convertibility. Despite widespread fears, no hyperinflation resulted.

Decades ago, gold at least partially backed up reserves, but fortunately this is not the case today. If it were so, the requirement for central banks to compete with each other for 'possession' of a limited supply of gold would massively distort the global financial system, present a constant threat of deflationary catastrophes due to gold shortages, and artificially privilege whichever country happened to have accumulated a lot of gold, leading to exchange rate distortions.

In the Eurozone, the central bank uses *repurchase agreements* (shorter: *repo*) to supply banks with reserves. This means that banks cede collateral for some specified amount of time, and are bound to buy it back for an amount agreed when the contract was signed. The price is calculated by looking at the central bank's base rate and the quality of the collateral.

Let's look at the balance sheet of a firm after it has received cash from its bank. The bank has exchanged central bank deposits for cash at the local branch of the central bank. This trade works in both directions: cash can also be paid in at the central bank by a commercial bank, and the bank's account at the central bank marked up with the corresponding amount of reserves.

	bank			firm	
loan (F)	100	~~deposits~~ ~~100~~	~~deposits~~ ~~100~~	loan	100
~~cash~~	~~100~~	loan (CB) 100	cash	100	

As we can see, the disbursement of deposits leads to an asset swap at the firm: an asset held against the bank (deposits) is swapped into an asset held against the central bank (cash). The net wealth of the firm doesn't change, only its composition. The bank, on the other hand, has lost its liability of deposits, but at the same time has lost assets of the same value (cash). What remain are the loan from the central bank as a liability and the loan to the firm as an asset. Equity does not change.

As long as the interest rate the firm pays to its bank is higher than the interest rate the bank has to pay the central bank, the bank is profitable. This is one reason why the interest rates banks charge for making loans to the private sector are almost always above the base rate set by the central bank.

Money as a scoring system

Whereas banks take the initiative when it comes to borrowing from the central bank, the latter can also change the amount of reserves in the system on its own initiative – for instance through the purchase of bonds by crediting the seller's account. These electronic transactions are analogous to bank loans; they don't require the central bank to 'save' any money first, and no third-party deposits are decremented when the central bank buys bonds from (for example) pension funds or investment banks. Whereas goods, services, raw materials and labour can be scarce, any scarcity of deposits and reserves is man-made. If scarcity of reserves is a problem, then additional reserves can easily be created.

In the same way, any scarcity of bank deposits can be cured by the creation of additional bank deposits. The question is which institution is entitled to do that, and which rules shape the process.

The whole setup resembles the scorekeeping system of a football game. In a modern stadium, the digital scoreboard can display an unlimited amount of digits. Even a score in the triple digits would be easy to show. On the other hand, the existence of a digital scoreboard does not increase the number of goals just because it is easier to display them! The result of the game is independent from the nature of the display.

A central bank is like the warden of the game-score; the monetary system is a scorekeeping system for credits and debts (or assets and liabilities), nothing else and nothing more. On its spreadsheet, the central bank can theoretically grant unlimited deposits, but in practice this is not allowed. The problem of deflation, for instance, is not generated by a central bank 'running out of money'. Neither the amount of printed bank notes and minted coins nor the amount of virtual money in the form of bank deposits is limited in any physical way. What is limited are the available or retrievable resources, available labour-hours and achievable supplies of products and services in a given time-frame.

The mere statement that banks and central banks can create unlimited amounts of deposits does not mean that they should aim at unlimited credit creation or tolerate it. Likewise, it is not useful to demand the repayment or reduction of all debts. The monetary system fulfils a particular purpose: it facilitates the production of goods and services and their distribution. To reach this goal, it's reasonable to establish intermediate goals for monetary ratios, flows and aggregates, but these should not be cast in stone.

A low rate of inflation, for instance, can be sensible, but it does not have to be the highest priority aim under all circumstances. Likewise, keeping the government's annual budget deficit small is a goal that often cannot be aligned with the highest ranking goals of the financial system – a high level of production, low unemployment, a low level of inflation – and it should therefore not be used as an intermediate goal. Instead, the size of the budget deficit should be accepted as an outcome rather than as a driver of economic policies.

Physical limitations play no role in the process of creation of money at central banks (reserves) or in banks (deposits). However, limits to the production capacity in the real physical world means that an increase in deposits can, under some circumstances, lead to a rise in the rate of CPI, or inflation in the price of financial assets or houses (or of all of these things). An important indicator for a currency is its purchasing power per unit, and the change in that value in a given time period, which is represented by the inflation rate. But the most important issue for a society is production and distribution.

The possible relationships between production, on the one hand, and deposits or broader measures of monetary aggregates, on the other hand, are quite complicated. Figure 4.1 shows changes in the monetary aggregates M1, M2, M3, and Figure 4.2 shows CPI for the US. A clear correlation cannot be found for the period from 1980 to 2006. The inflation rate is quite stable at around 3 per cent, even as monetary aggregates move sometimes up, sometimes down.

Data for M3 is only available until 2006, since after that year the US central bank was no longer satisfied with its definition, and stopped reporting it. Among other things, this was due to the rise of derivatives, which are notoriously difficult to measure, but had very high liquidity before the crisis. The relative 'liquidity' of a financial asset refers to the relative ease of transforming those financial assets into money (deposits or reserves) without delay, costs or a drop in the price.

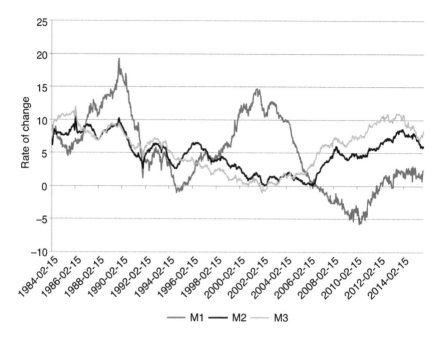

Figure 4.1 Rates of change of US monetary aggregates M1, M2, M3 (source: Federal
Reserve Economic Data, FRB of St. Louis (M1, M2, M3)).

Box 4.2 Goals of a central bank

The primary objective of the ECB, according to the Treaty on the Functioning of
the European Union's Paragraph §127(1), is to maintain price stability. The ECB
defines this as a medium-term inflation rate of close to but less than 2.0 per cent.
The ECB is also supposed to support the economic policies of the European Union,
in so far as this does not endanger price stability. Other central banks, e.g. the US
Federal Reserve, have been assigned additional primary objectives apart from
maintaining low levels of inflation, such as supporting economic growth and
employment.

The definitions of the different monetary aggregates depend on the maturity
of the relevant deposits, with M0 – the monetary base – containing only cash
and central bank deposits, and M3 containing relatively long-term financial
assets. M3 subsumes M2, M2 subsumes M1, and M1 subsumes M0 (see Table
4.1). There is no empirical evidence that links changes in these monetary aggregates to the rate of inflation. An exact prediction of future inflation rates or of
monetary aggregates, or of any ratios between them, is just as impossible as the

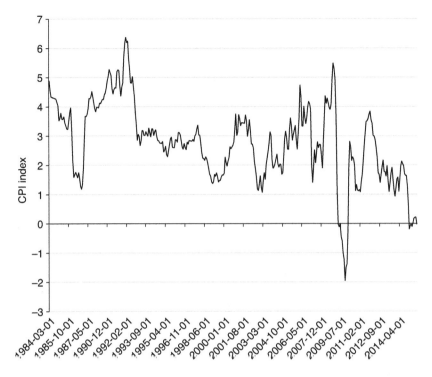

Figure 4.2 Rate of change of US consumer price index (source: Federal Reserve Economic Data, FRB of St. Louis (CPIAUCSL)).

Table 4.1 Definitions of monetary aggregates (*Bundesbank*)

Aggregate	Definition
M0	Cash and central bank deposits (also: *monetary base*)
M1	M0 + overnight deposits of non-banks held at monetary financial institutions in the euro area
M2	M1 + deposits with an agreed maturity of up to and including two years, and deposits redeemable at notice of up to and including three months.
M3	M2 + repurchase agreements, money market fund shares and debt securities with a maturity of up to and including two years

Source: www.bundesbank.de/Navigation/EN/Service/Glossary/Functions/glossary.html?lv2=129536 &lv3=162818#162818.

prediction of exchange rates. It's important to know the limits of one's discipline – in this case, monetary economics.

Since we know that banks cannot lend out reserves to firms and households, the monetary base has lost much of the significance that has often been attributed to it in the past. Its recent huge increase has triggered warnings of sustained high

inflation lately, but these are fading as the ECB's massive bond-buying programme ('extended asset purchase programme', often called 'quantitative
easing' or QE in the financial press) of more than €60 billion per month, in progress since March 2015, continues apace (inflating the quantity of reserves held
by financial institutions as a result) and CPI remains stuck in a narrow band of
±0.3 per cent. Slowly, those who had warned stridently of the hyperinflationary
consequences of QE have gone rather quiet, and a few of them may even have
taken the trouble to inform themselves sufficiently about the workings of the
banking system to realise why their concerns were misplaced.

Open market operations of the central bank

In the example above, we had increased the amount of reserves because a bank
with sufficient collateral asked for a loan from the central bank. The initiative
for this transaction came from the commercial bank, while the central bank
played a passive role. According to European law, the ECB has to provide
reserves at its base interest rate, up to the value of collateral pledged by the
bank requesting reserves. There is no leeway in decision-making on the part of
the central bank. This is intended to provide a level playing field. The central
bank cannot deny credit when a bank provides eligible collateral. The implication is that – contrary to popular belief – the central bank does not control the
monetary supply.

However, the central bank can actively change the amount of reserves in the
system. ECB can add reserves to her balance sheet by buying assets from a commercial bank. This transaction, a so-called open market operation, adds reserves
to the commercial bank's account, which increases the amount of reserves in the
system. Why the central bank would want to do that we will see later. The
central bank creates reserves by keystroke at a computer, marking up the reserve
accounts of banks that sell financial assets (for example, sovereign bonds) to the
central bank. Let's assume that the commercial bank owns a Treasury bond that
the central bank wants to buy. For pedagogical reasons, we show the transactions
in two steps rather than one.

_____central bank_____		_____bank_____			
reserves	100	reserves	100	t-bond	100	deposits	100
				loan (f)	100	loan (CB)	100

The central bank first announces that it wants to buy a Treasury bond (t-bond).
Next, the central bank and a commercial bank now have to agree on a price.
The central bank finds a bank with the balance sheet above. The central bank's
purchase of t-bonds from a commercial bank is actually more like a swap,
where one views reserves as just another financial asset. The balance sheets
below show what happens after the transaction. (In reality, the central bank
will have marked up the reserve account of the bank without granting itself
reserves.)

	central bank				bank		
t-bond	100	reserves	100	reserves	100	deposits	100
				loan (f)	100	loan (CB)	100

Since the bank has additional reserves, the total amount of reserves must have risen. Is it correct, then, that a rise in the inflation rate will follow? The answer is no, and that's not even open to dispute. From a balance sheet perspective, there is no such causality. Why not?

Box 4.3 The long-term refinancing operations (LTROs) of the ECB

In auctions taking place in late December 2011 and again in late February 2012, the ECB lent out more than €1,000 billion in total. Some economists argued that the rise in the money supply would lead to inflation. It didn't, and we are now able to understand why it didn't. Deposits of the banks at the central bank cannot flow into the private sector and cause an increase in the inflation rate. Banks cannot lend out reserves to the private sector at all!

As we have seen above, the extension of a loan by a bank to a household or firm does not require a pool of third-party savings into which the bank dips to get money to on-lend. It doesn't require a pool of savings of any kind. Banks are not intermediaries who on-lend deposits of savers to borrowers; rather, they create deposits by lending.

An increase in reserves does not increase the inflation rate per se, since the amount of loans made to households or firms is not affected by an increase in reserves. The reserve position of a bank is quite irrelevant for the extension of credit by that bank. There is no mechanism that would lead from a rise in reserves to a rise in demand for cash or loans. Even if a borrower from a bank were to transfer his deposits elsewhere, the bank does not rely on any excess supply of reserves when settling its interbank debts. As we have already seen, the bank can borrow more reserves any time it wants, as long as it has sufficient collateral. An increase in reserves does not facilitate bank lending. There is no role for it in the process of credit creation.

The real motivation behind open market operations is the central bank's interest-rate-setting process. Before we turn to this issue, we must examine further where demand for reserves comes from. A part of this demand comes from the private sector's demand for cash. Another part comes from the bank's settlement process. These procedures will be described by balance sheet transactions in the next subsection.

The settlement of the banks (interbank market)

Banks create deposits of commercial bank credit ('bank money') for their customers. In turn, banks hold reserve deposits at the central bank, which they can exchange into cash. When a customer of a bank makes a payment to another at the same bank, the accounting is quite easy. Customer A's deposits are reduced by the amount X and customer B's account is credited. There is no effect on the bank's reserve position at the central bank.

But what happens in the accounts when customer B is not a client of the same bank as customer A?

In this case, the two banks have to settle their accounts at the end of the business day. Let's assume that customer A is at bank A and customer B at bank B. During the business day, the two banks' customers execute multiple payments. At the end of the business day, the two banks look at all the payments in both directions, and determine the net amount that the bank in deficit owes to the bank in surplus. If customers of bank A transferred €1,000 to those of bank B but vice versa the amount is only €950, then bank A has to make a transfer of €50 to bank B.

For simplicity, in what follows we'll assume that the only business done on this particular business day between banks A and B is that household A transferred some deposits to household B:

bank A			bank B		
loan	100	deposits	loan	100	deposits 150
		household A 50	deposits at		
		bank B 50	bank A	50	

household A			household B		
deposits	50	loan 100	deposits 150	loan	100
		net wealth −50		net wealth	50

The resulting balance sheets could look like the ones above. Household A loses €50 in deposits, household B gains €50. The deposits of bank A stay at the same level, but the distribution changes. Bank B now has an account with bank A with €50 in deposits. The increase in assets is balanced by an increase in liabilities since the account of household B was credited with €50.

However, while the foregoing scenario is technically possible, settlement cannot take the form of a credit in an account operated by bank A and owned by bank B. Why not? Because the banks are competitors they try to compete each other out of the market. Therefore, it would be problematic to entrust the safety of the payments system – a public purpose – to private banks, which are entangled in competition. After all, bank B would have to write-down some of its assets if bank A were go bankrupt, and this could trigger an unwanted chain reaction in the banking system.

Instead, the settlement of accounts between banks runs through the central bank. The net difference in the flow of payments over a business day can be transferred in reserves, which are subtracted from the account of banks in deficit and credited to the accounts of banks in surplus. While this is not what banks actually do at the end of each day, it is instructive to see how this plays out.

We'll assume that bank A borrows €50 in reserves from the central bank at the end of the day, based on the private loan to its client, which it submits as collateral. Bank A transfers these reserves to bank B, whose account is hence marked up. The actual balance sheets are balanced before as well as after the transaction, as can be seen below.

_____bank A_____				_____bank B_____			
loan	100	deposits	50	loan	100	deposits	150
reserves	+50	loan (CB)	+50				
reserves	−50			reserves	+50		

_____household A_____				_____household B_____			
deposits	50	loan	100	deposits	150	loan	100
		net wealth	−50			net wealth	50

An interesting observation is that actual settlement between banks only redistributes reserves in the banking system. Settlement does not lead to a change in the amount of reserves; what one bank loses in reserves, another gains. This opens up an alternative route to gain the required reserves. Banks that end up with excess reserves after end-of-day settlement could lend those reserves to those banks that are short of reserves (the lending takes the form of overnight loans for which a modest interest rate is charged).

In that case, there is no increase in reserves in the balance sheet of bank B, but instead an interbank loan to bank A (loan IB) removes the necessity to settle instantly. A loan moves a payment into the future to avoid a payment today. The price to pay is the interest rate. In this way, a rise in demand for reserves and a consequent rise in the interbank market interest rate are prevented.

_____bank A_____				_____bank B_____			
loan	100	deposits	50	loan	100	deposits	150
		loan (IB)	50	loan (IB)	50		

_____household A_____				_____household B_____			
deposits	50	loan	100	deposits	150	loan	100
		net wealth	−50			net wealth	50

An interbank loan defers settlement. Bank A still has to pay reserves to bank B, but only when the loan granted by bank B matures. Bank B receives an interest rate for postponing settlement. This interest rate is determined on the interbank market. Since banks can borrow from the central bank at the going base rate, the interbank market rate will be lower than that, but will not deviate too far from it.

This interbank reserve lending market is also called the 'money market', since money in the form of deposits at the central bank is what's being traded. These reserves can be swapped for cash at the local central bank branch. The market dealing in deposits at commercial banks (bank money), by contrast, is called the 'capital market'. On both markets, the respective deposits can be lent for shorter or longer maturities.

The reference rates on the European money market are the euro versions of the *London Interbank Offered Rate* (LIBOR). They're called the *Euro Interbank Offered Rate* (EURIBOR) and the *Euro OverNight Index Average* (EONIA). LIBOR and EURIBOR are collected through phone-in surveys of several major banks during daily conference calls between the representatives of those banks – which leaves these rates vulnerable to manipulation, i.e. the money market traders participating in these calls can (and, it turns out, have) misreported rates in order to gain trading advantages. EONIA, by contrast, is computed by taking the arithmetic mean of interbank transactions; this is what the ECB uses for its statistics.

The interest rate on the money market is not determined by supply and demand, although both exist. In the next chapter we'll look at central banks and the instruments they use to ensure that interest rates do not deviate from the rates that the central bank sets, which in the past were short-term rates, but nowadays the ECB also intervenes in financial markets to influence long-term rates.

The way European banks handle their settlement today involves the use of net debt positions. Banks do not settle at the end of the day; rather, they record their positions vis-à-vis other banks at the end of each business day. If they are net debtors they pay overnight interest, and if they are net creditors they receive interest. Usually what is paid is the base rate. Over time, settlement balances should net out, since on some days net flows will favour bank A, on others bank B, depending on random actions taken by the banks' many clients.

If the settlement balances show a pattern over time, and fail to net out – i.e. if there's a consistent trend towards more payments going from bank A to bank B than vice versa – then bank B will at some point decline to roll over any balances owed and demand settlement. Banks that are net debtors would then search for longer-term financing options on the interbank market, as was described above.

Conclusion

Contrary to popular opinion, the central bank does not control the monetary aggregate (the total amount of money in cash, deposit accounts or savings accounts).

Cash is created on a demand-driven basis when banks swap some central bank deposits for it. Reserves are created when banks borrow from the central bank, or sell Treasury securities to the central bank. Repurchase agreements (repos) also create reserves. At the time of repo creation, the time of destruction is set, because banks promise to repay the reserves at some fixed date.

Banks have access to central bank reserves via 'standing facilities' and 'open market operations'. Among themselves, they also trade reserves, and that trading constitutes the interbank market.

A last but not least possibility for banks to get reserves is via private sector customers. Banks in need of reserves can raise their interest rate so that they lend less and attract more deposits from customers. Since customers either 'pay in' cash or transfer credit (bank money) from other banks, the incoming bank will have its reserve account marked up. Conversely, if a bank has excess reserves, it can decrease its interest rate so that more customers take out loans and less keep their deposits at the bank.

Box 4.4 Money and capital market – who is who?

Originally banks used 'reserves', i.e. deposits at the central bank, for settling interbank accounts at the end of each business day. In the last few years before the financial crisis, banks switched to a new practice: they postponed settlements by granting overnight loans to each other. The borrowers promised payment of reserves in the future, backed up by collateral from the capital market. Functionally, money markets (trade in reserves) and capital markets (trade in deposits) merged.

The demand for reserves arises from two contingencies: from the private sector demanding cash, and from banks demanding central bank deposits for interbank settlement. Banks promise their customers that their deposits can always be swapped into cash without loss. Excess circulating private sector cash will reflux to banks, which mark-up clients' bank balances in exchange for paid-in cash. In turn, a bank gives cash received from clients who have 'deposited cash in their account', as the public thinks of this process, back to the central bank in exchange for reserves credited to the bank's reserve account at the central bank. Given some level of demand, these additional reserves could lead to a fall in the interbank market interest rate, unless the central bank takes action to defend its target short-term base rate – which it usually does.

Central banks have a monetary tool-kit with different instruments at their disposal that they can use to influence short-term interest rates (in particular, interbank lending rates). Let's take a look at these instruments.

5 The instruments of a central bank

Central banks commonly make use of three distinct instruments to manipulate short-term rates. The ECB offers two different interest rates at which commercial banks can borrow reserves, and yet another interest rate which it offers banks for parking excess reserves in their reserve accounts at the central bank.

Standing facilities

As we've noted, commercial banks are allowed to borrow reserves from the central bank on short-dated loans if they submit appropriate collateral. The central bank sets the interest rates at which banks can borrow reserves. When the act of borrowing reserves is made, reserves are first added to the reserve deposit accounts the banks hold at the central bank.

Marginal lending facility

When a bank needs reserves urgently, either to settle interbank balances or to finance the paying-out of physical cash to customers, it can borrow reserves overnight against collateral temporarily given to the central bank. This is the so-called *marginal lending facility*.

Conversely, commercial banks that have excess reserves can park these in their accounts at the central bank. This generally yields a low positive interest rate. At the time of writing, however, the interest rate on excess reserves held by banks in their reserve accounts at ECB is actually negative.

As Figure 5.1 shows, the interest rate charged by the central bank's marginal lending facility is higher than the central bank's other interest rates. The marginal lending facility's interest rate is the price banks pay for borrowing from the ECB up until 30 minutes after markets have closed.

A key purpose of the marginal lending facility is to allow banks that realise only very late that they are short of reserves for settlement to borrow them at the last minute. This is reasonable, since insufficient reserves would mean that transfers of deposits from one bank to another would not be executed. The customers of the bank would lose confidence in the banking system if their transfers fell through merely for technical reasons. As we've noted, ensuring the functioning

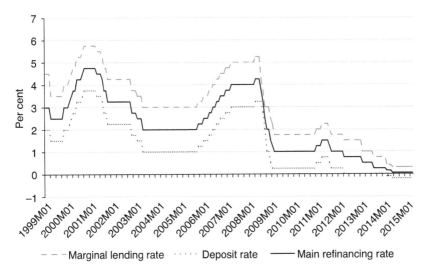

Figure 5.1 Interest rates in the Eurozone (source: www.ecb.europa.eu/stats/monetary/rates/html/index.en.html).

of the payment system is the most important task of a central bank, next to monetary policy.

Main refinancing operations

The second way to borrow reserves directly from the central bank is by making use of *main refinancing operations* (MROs). Under MROs, too, the ECB sets an interest rate at which it permits banks to borrow reserves from it, and banks borrow as many reserves as they need, always against sufficient collateral. MRO maturity is not overnight, but rather days, weeks, months or even years. The long-term loans made to banks by the ECB between late 2011 and early 2012 had a maturity of three years and were exceptionally long-dated. Given that some banks had problems with the quality of their collateral, some were quite willing to borrow for a longer period in case of a further deterioration of its assets. This would make future access to reserves complicated and costly.

Deposit facility

So banks in need of reserves are offered the option of borrowing them from the central bank. Conversely, the ECB doesn't neglect banks with excess reserves either. The central bank has made a standing offer to borrow excess reserves from Eurozone commercial banks and then pay an interest rate. This *deposit facility* of the ECB is always open to banks that want to park their excess reserves.

However, the central bank doesn't actually need the reserves for anything. It's a bit like the checking and savings accounts a retail client might hold at a commercial bank. Banks hold a fraction of their reserves in an account at the central bank, and a fraction in cash. They can move the balance of their excess reserves into the deposits facility, which is like a savings account.

As of this writing, in 2016, Eurozone banks have to deposit excess reserves – those above the reserves needed to comply with the required reserve ratio – in the deposit facility, which at present carries a *negative* interest rate. The idea seems to be to force banks to lend out more reserves to other banks and financial market participants. Since banks do not need reserves to make loans, this policy is not going to succeed.

However, unlike in the case of your money when it's put in a regular savings account, banks' reserves aren't 'tied up' or inaccessible to them as a result of their being parked in the ECB's deposit facility. Banks continue to have their reserves at their daily disposal without any limit. The only limitation is that transactions must be announced to the ECB no later than 15 minutes before closing time of the TARGET2 settlement system – otherwise, the negative interest rate is imposed on reserves left in the bank's deposit facility account after that time. During other times, the interest rate is positive.

In 2015, the ECB reduced the deposit rate to a negative value. At the time of writing, its value is –0.4 per cent per year. Since the interest accrues overnight, it is calculated as 1/350 times the deposit rate, which imposes a sort of 'excess reserves parking fee' of roughly −0.00057 per cent per night on Eurozone banks. A negative interest rate means that a Eurozone bank pays to have reserves in its 'deposit facility' account at the ECB.

Box 5.1 Can a central bank set interest rates on commercial bank reserve deposits at negative values?

Yes. The ECB's deposit rate at the time of writing is −0.4 per cent. The deposit rate of the Danish central bank was negative from mid-2012 until spring 2014. Conversely, in 2015, Sweden's central bank set its repo rate at a negative value. Therefore, banks borrowing overnight money from Sweden's central bank repay less the next day than they borrowed.

Interbank lending and borrowing

Having gained some knowledge about the marginal lending facility, the main refinancing facility and the deposit facility, we can now turn to the determination of the short-term interest rate on the interbank market. We have just examined the case of bank A borrowing reserves from the central bank in order to go into settlement with bank B. Let's examine the balance sheets again, this time with interest rates added.

Box 5.2 Central bank deposits and capital flows

Reserves are deposits at the central bank and can only be held by affiliated banks. Foreign banks can hold reserves via subsidiaries or other banks. Reserves thus always stay inside the country. When banks sell US dollar denominated reserves, they are transferred to other banks' accounts at the Fed. Reserves cannot 'flow out of the country' or 'take flight'. That's only possible with cash.

Suppose that if bank A borrows from the central bank it pays an annualised interest rate of 0.3 per cent. Bank B does not get paid any interest rate until the reserves it's owed by A are moved into B's deposit facility account, or lent by B to other banks.

_____bank A_____		_____bank B_____	
loan	100 deposits 50	loan	100 deposits 150
	loan (CB 0.3%)50	reserves (0%) 50	

At this point there is a possibility for both parties to improve their situation. Bank A, instead of borrowing reserves from the central bank, might as well borrow them from bank B. If an interest rate of 0.2 per cent can be agreed upon, then both parties would be better off. Bank A pays a reduced interest rate of 0.2 per cent, and bank B gets 0.2 per cent instead of the –0.4 per cent it would be charged if its excess reserves were parked in the deposit facility.

_____bank A_____		_____bank B_____	
loan	100 deposits 50	loan	100 deposits 150
	loan (IB 0.2%) 50	loan (IB 0.2%) 50	

As long as the risk of bankruptcy for bank A is negligible, banks will use the interbank market and the central bank need not intervene. Since all parties are better off, this is what happens most of the time, provided the solvency of banks is not in doubt.

What would happen if bank A would like to borrow some reserves on the interbank market, but other banks are not willing to lend to A? (It is assumed that the bank does not try to attract more deposits from depositors of other banks to increase its holdings of reserves.)

The interbank market interest rate

If bank A cannot borrow reserves at 0.2 per cent from other banks, then the usual market mechanism sets in when something is in short supply: bank A pays a higher price, in this case a higher interest rate. Offers will be increased in small steps until a deal is reached. Maybe bank A can come to an agreement with bank C at an interest rate of 0.24 per cent, since bank C has some reserves on hand it does not need, and bank A avoids the expense of having to borrow from the ECB overnight at 0.3 per cent. This leads to a rise in the interbank market rate.

Box 5.3 The manipulation of the LIBOR

The interest rate on the interbank market LIBOR is calculated through a survey of participating banks, in a daily conference call. Representatives of the banks are expected to report honestly about the interest rates at which they would lend reserves to each other. In 2012 Barclays Bank disclosed that the rates reported in this daily survey had been manipulated by the participating bankers over many years in order to gain trading advantages. The EU Commission imposed penalties of €1.7 billion against several European banks.

The rise in the interest rate is limited because banks can always borrow reserves from the central bank, rather than each other, when it comes to short- and medium-term loans. In our example, no bank would be willing to pay an interbank interest rate of more than 0.3 per cent, since this is what they have the option to pay to the central bank when borrowing overnight. On the other side of the trade, a floor is introduced since no bank would lend at an interest rate lower than the deposit rate.

Setting interest rates on the marginal lending facility and the deposit facility is almost all a central bank needs to do to anchor the interbank market interest rate and keep it bounded within a tight corridor.

An alternative route for the central bank to influence interest rates is intervention via open market operations, as described previously. Illiquid assets (such as sovereign bonds) can be bought from banks with fresh central bank created reserves, in order to increase the amount of reserves and lower the interbank market interest rate. Conversely, to raise the interest rate, the central bank can sell illiquid assets to banks.

The fact that the central bank can change the level of reserves does not mean that the central bank controls the quantity of reserves. On the initiative of commercial banks, reserves can be parked in the deposit facility or borrowed in the marginal lending facility. Since the latter is possible up until half an hour after the closure of the interbank market, banks have the last word. The central bank does not determine the quantity of reserves.

Emergency liquidity assistance

Yet another option in times of crisis is emergency liquidity assistance (ELA). Through ELA, national central banks (NCBs) can provide reserves or other assistance that may lead to an increase in central bank money channelled to solvent financial institutions facing liquidity problems. Under ELA, the ECB determines the interest rate an NCB charges its member banks, but the NCB can accept collateral that would be unacceptable to the ECB – for example, sovereign bonds from a government whose solvency is in question, like Greece. However, the NCB would have to shoulder any losses resulting from ELA. The ECB is very powerful in this relationship, because it can interfere with NCBs' process of granting commercial banks access to ELA:

> In the event of the overall volume of the ELA operations envisaged for a given financial institution or given group of financial institutions exceeding a threshold of €500 million, the NCB(s) involved must inform the ECB as early as possible prior to the extension of the intended assistance. In the event of the overall volume of the ELA operations envisaged for a given financial institution or given group of financial institutions exceeding a threshold of €2 billion, the Governing Council will consider whether there is a risk that the ELA involved may interfere with the objectives and tasks of the Eurosystem. Upon the request of the NCB(s) concerned, the Governing Council may decide to set a threshold and not to object to intended ELA operations that are below that threshold and conducted within a pre-specified short period of time. Such a threshold may also refer to several financial institutions and/or several groups of financial institutions at the same time.
>
> (www.ecb.europa.eu/pub/pdf/other/201402_elaprocedures.en.pdf)

Interest rate changes

Getting back to normal monetary policy, we'll note that the central bank can change the interest rates as it wishes, though subject to the arithmetical logic of the system. Obviously it's advisable for the ECB to keep the interest rate it charges under its MRO above those for central bank reserve deposits, since otherwise banks could borrow reserves and then deposit them at a higher interest rate. This would constitute a gift to the banks.

Banks will generally pass on changes in the base rate to customers. However, a certain asymmetry exists. Reductions in the interest rate are usually passed on with some delay, whereas rate rises are passed on instantly: the bank increases interest rates for consumer loans, mortgages, etc. Interest rates of existing loan contracts adjust contingently, since loans often include variable interest rates.

It's conventional for households and businesses who borrow from banks to pay an interest rate calculated as a mark-up on an interbank market interest rate like EURIBOR or LIBOR. This reduces interest rate risk for the bank. If interest rates on the asset side of a bank's balance sheet (i.e. interest rate charged to its own borrowers) adjust to reflect any increase in the base rate, then from the bank's point of view, base rate increases are nothing to worry about.

What are the limits of credit creation by banks?

We can summarise that banks can theoretically create unlimited quantities of deposits. This holds for banks that create deposits for households and firms, as well as for central banks that create deposits for banks. If this possibility exists, why is credit to the private sector not expanding without limit, in conjunction with an unlimited expansion of reserves at the central bank? What stops the institutional players from grossly over-lending? Will this system not end in hyperinflation?

We have to distinguish the theoretical possibility of the total system from the actual behaviour of the individual players. Not every action that is technically feasible is always in the interest of all the actors who would need to participate in the action in order to make it happen.

So, what is it that stops a single bank from extending virtually unlimited credit? After all, the spread between interest charged for loans and interest paid on deposits and reserves constitutes profit, so the bank should be interested in extending as much credit as it can, should it not?

Let's have a closer look. What if bank A extends more credit than bank B? Customers of bank A will consequently transfer more deposits to customers of bank B than vice versa when they spend their deposits, and as a result bank A will have some additional demand for reserves. The following balance sheets illustrate this:

bank A				bank B		
loan	1,000	deposits	750	loan	100	deposits	350
		loan (IB)	250	loan (IB)	250		

A bank with a loan portfolio that grows markedly stronger than that of the competition will over time accumulate a deficit in reserves, which will have to be offset by loans from other banks or from the central bank. An interbank market loan is marked loan (IB). One bank has a claim on another; accordingly, the loan is a liability for the debtor bank.

As long as the portfolio of loans granted by a bank to households and firms is eligible as collateral at the central bank, refinancing can be secured, albeit at the price of paying higher interest rates than other banks. Furthermore, the bank is at the mercy of the central bank's decisions regarding hikes in interest rates. Refinancing on the interbank market instead would lower costs, but the transfer of interest improves the financial results of the other banks.

The bigger loan portfolio held by a bank that's a relatively more active lender will give that bank more interest rate income, but its risk will rise correspondingly. The other banks receive interest on the interbank market, which is lower. Admittedly their risk is also lower when they make interbank loans rather than loans to non-bank clients.

For a bank that extends much more credit than other banks, a rise in interest rates can put it into a position in which it loses money and the other banks don't. Other banks might not have to borrow reserves at all since they are net suppliers, but a bank that has had huge outflows of reserves is a net borrower. The interest rate on the interbank market is a cost to the bank that extended relatively many loans, so a rising interest rate will lead to losses at some point. Other banks will see their profits increase since they are lending on the interbank market at a higher interest rate. The bank that has extended relatively many loans might try to increase revenues by charging higher interest rates to its customers, but these are free to take out loans from other banks that offer better rates.

If all banks lose money, they will band together to defend their balance sheets. To sum up, it can be said that the incentives in play tend to lead banks to expand loan portfolios in lockstep.

Quite another matter is the fall in quality of bank A's loan portfolio over time. Let's assume that the loans made by bank A have financed customers' purchases of real estate. Now, suppose that due to a fall in the price of real estate, some borrowers cannot pay off their loans. The bank has to partially 'write down' their loans, which has a negative effect on equity – because the rules of bank accounting stipulate that when banks book losses, the losses are charged against bank equity.

Let's assume that equity of bank A is €50. Equity is, by definition, the excess of assets over liabilities. We'll further assume that bank A has built up equity in the past, and that this equity has been invested in Treasury bonds. This is what the balance sheets look like:

_____bank A_____			_____bank B_____		
loan	1,000	deposits	750	loan	100	deposits	350
t-bonds	50	loan (IB)	250	loan (IB)	250		
		equity	50				

Box 5.4 Greece's banking crisis

When Greek sovereign bonds were downgraded by Standard&Poor's in February 2012, the ECB decided not to accept these anymore as collateral for loans of reserves. Since Greek banks held many Greek government bonds, they ran into trouble with liquidity. Their balance sheets were not problematic in terms of debt overhang, but they were threatened by a risk of running out of reserves. A month later, Greek sovereign bonds could be exchanged into more secure paper at the bail-out fund European Financial Stability Facility (EFSF), which could be used as collateral at the ECB.

The fall in real estate prices puts the loan portfolio under pressure. A complete repayment is not on the cards anymore. Assuming that the rating of the loan portfolio sinks below the limit regarding the required quality of collateral set by the ECB, then the bank cannot get additional reserves from the central bank – so now its liquidity fully depends on obtaining loans on the interbank market.

If the bank cannot borrow more reserves, it will be unable to pay out cash or execute transfers to other banks. Such a situation is called illiquidity. An illiquid bank cannot execute any more transactions, and is often judged to be insolvent.

Insolvency by over-indebtedness is quite similar to this. Consider: a bank's assets are composed of everything else it owns, i.e. financial papers, buildings and, above all, its loan book (the money owed to it by borrowers). A bank's liabilities are, by accounting convention, composed of what it owes its creditors (including the amounts in its depositors' accounts) plus equity capital, i.e. paid-in shareholder capital plus retained earnings.

Suppose the value of the bank's assets falls below the value of total liabilities. Since the balance sheet has to balance, the bank's equity capital must now adjust by an appropriate negative value. In other words, the 'retained earnings plus paid-in shareholder capital' line item takes a loss when the bank has to recognise a reduction in the value of its loan portfolio.

A permanent fall in the value of the loan portfolio of bank A from €1,000 to €900 would lead to insolvency, as the following balance sheet shows.

_____bank A_____				_____bank B_____		
loan	900	deposits	750	loan	100	deposits	350
t-bonds	50	loan (IB)	250	loan (IB)	250		
		equity	−50				

The reduction in the value of assets first wipes out existing equity, then turns it negative. Selling all assets, if it were possible, would bring some €950. Existing liabilities are €1,000. Here, the banking system's regulators have to intervene and close the bank's doors, denying its depositors access to their accounts and protecting the bank from actions by its other creditors until things are sorted out. If they were to refrain from doing so, a bank run might result. Bank B would issue payment request after payment request to bank A, even as the latter's customers queue up in front of ATMs and in the bank's branches. Depositors and creditors would know that the quantity of reserves is not sufficient to discharge all liabilities, even if bank A can sell its entire loan book for the market price, or use the loans as collateral at the central bank.

When this situation arises, the regulator then gives the insolvent bank an opportunity to try to restore solvency by raising fresh capital from shareholders (until it has once again attained or exceeded the regulatory required minimum 'capital ratio' – the ratio between the size of the bank's loan book and the sum of its paid-in capital plus retained earnings). Alternatively, or in addition, the bank can try to come to some arrangement with creditors, such as a partial write-down of their debt claims – again aiming at restoration of the required capital ratio (or better).

Shareholders lose their money if banks make lending mistakes or go insolvent. That's why reputable banks should see it as being in their own interest to avoid extending proportionally more loans than competitors, and why it's advisable to avoid entering loss-making or illegal credit arrangements.

A systemic risk across the banking system can arise if many banks (or a few very large banks) engage in dubious lending activities. During times of credit frenzy, during a credit bubble's rapid expansion phase, with asset prices rising across the board (in particular, real estate prices), all banks increase their loan portfolio because no bank wants to be left behind in this short-term situation of enormous potential profits. At such times, loans are extended come hell or high water, and conventional standards fly out the window. Herd behaviour overrides the usual market mechanisms and sober risk assessment practices.

Such events don't change the fact that banks' theoretically unlimited collective ability to extend loans does not lead, in practice, to unlimited lending, just as little as the invention of fire-making didn't lead to ubiquitous arson. However, the law-maker has to try to ensure that it doesn't pay to break the rules, and that's a very difficult thing to ensure.

We'll conclude this section with a general observation: if it is correct to say that the creation of deposits, be it at banks or at the central bank, is basically unlimited, then it is obviously nonsense to speak of scarcity of money. There can no more be an inherent scarcity of money in an economy than there can be a shortage of points to tally up the result of a basketball game. The monetary system is just a scorekeeping system for keeping track of quantities of transferable IOUs.

What's at issue in an economy is not any supposed scarcity of money, but rather its proper distribution. A loan default – of banks in terms of obligations to other banks, counted in central bank reserve currency, or of households and firms counted in bank deposits – does not arise from any general scarcity of money. Rather, problems arise when a borrower does not command a proper quantity of the means of payment to redeem his or her debts on a timely basis.

Until now, we've been examining the central bank, commercial banks and the private sector. Government spending and taxation have been omitted from the analysis. How does (the German) government spend? What happens to tax revenues? How does the government go into debt? What is the function of government in the monetary system? These questions are addressed in the next section.

Conclusion

In a modern monetary system, banks extend loans. They're supplied with cash by the central bank if they're able to offer 'collateral' in exchange. Banks hold deposits called 'reserves' at the central bank, and these can be transformed into physical cash. Firms and households do not have accounts at the central bank. Rather, they own claims on commercial banks in the form of 'deposits' in bank accounts at commercial banks. These deposits are the principal means of payment for the private sector, whereas banks use deposits at the central bank (reserves) or promises to deliver reserves in the future for settling accounts between banks. By postponing settlement, the connection between deposits (quantity of credit) and reserves (quantity of money) is broken. Whereas additional bank deposits can increase demand in the real economy and under certain circumstance might cause inflation, this is not possible for the reserves that banks hold in their accounts at the central bank.

Table 5.1 Deposits in central banks and banks

	Deposits in...	
	Central banks	*Banks*
Name	Reserves	(Bank) deposits
Means of payment for	Banks	Private sector
Interest rate	Interbank market	Capital market interest rate
Insolvency, illiquidity	Impossible	Possible

Owing to the fact that reserves as well as bank deposits are created on a spreadsheet in a computer, neither reserves not bank deposits are limited by any physical boundary. This does not mean that deposits can grow without limit. Central banks cannot change the amount of reserves very much without moving the interbank market interest rate. Moreover, central banks only lend against collateral, which is in limited supply. In principle, a central bank could also lend reserves without requiring collateral, although this is impossible in practice, given the legal constraints governing central banks.

Nor will banks tend to expand their loan creation excessively compared to other banks, since otherwise reserves will be drained and the bank will become dependent on the interbank market. Borrowing reserves incurs costs and this reduces bank profitability.

A rise in the quantity of credit usually leads to higher risk of default. When the quality of loans deteriorates, a bank finds it more difficult to gain access to reserves. If things go badly, a bank ends up depending on the liquidity provision of the central bank; if the sum of liabilities exceeds the sum of assets and the situation cannot be quickly rectified with an injection of fresh shareholder investment capital, the bank must be closed and liquidated.

Box 5.5 J.P. Morgan paid $13 billion in a settlement with the Department of Justice

In November 2013 the bank J.P. Morgan and the US Department of Justice agreed on a fine of over $13 billion to settle charges of wrongdoing. At issue were asset-backed securities which lost a lot of their value during the real estate crisis. J.P. Morgan admitted having lied to investors by misrepresenting the quality of the assets.

Alan Greenspan, former chairman of the board of the Federal Reserve System from 1987 to 2006, did not think it necessary to regulate banks rigorously, since he presumed that banks would have a self-interest to avoid insolvency. Since retiring, Greenspan, who was a disciple of libertarian guru Ayn Rand in his twenties, has lost some of his belief in the perfection of unregulated markets. In front of a congressional committee in October 2008 he said: 'Those of us who have looked to the self-interest of lending institutions to protect shareholders' equity, myself included, are in a state of shocked disbelief.'

As we've learned, not all banks take into account the protection of their proprietors or stockholders. Management might be tempted to get rich quickly through short-term profits (i.e. bonus payments) that in the long run bankrupt the bank, which is a collateral damage managers may be willing to accept. After all, following the last financial crisis in the US, only one investment banker was sent to prison, even though bankers broke the laws on a massive scale and banks were required to pay fines totalling many billions of dollars.

6 The creation of sovereign securities

Public institutions vary from country to country. Just as constitutions define different rights and duties, as well as institutions to enforce and protect these, central banks are not identical to each other. The model central bank we'll work with in this section is not *the* central bank; it is *a* central bank.

In the following, we describe a central bank that's cooperating with a Treasury, which implies that the government cannot go bankrupt: the central bank is allowed to grant unlimited credit to the government. Moreover, both short- and long-term interest rates stay at a very low level even in the case of supposed debt overhang crises. This can be seen today in countries like the US, Japan, the UK, Sweden and many more.

The regime explained in the following does not fully apply to the Eurozone, where originally the possibility of bankruptcy of Eurozone members' national governments was allowed for, even though European institutions have moved away from that principle somewhat recently.

Where the government gets its money

A government needs access to goods and services, and a means to employ workers to implement its programmes. The sovereignty of a nation is defined, among other things, by the ability of parliament to vote for a budget without any foreign interference, which is subsequently executed without any arbitrary budgetary boundaries. This only works when the government commands its own currency, or (alternatively) is part of a currency area in which government access to reserves via the central bank is granted in all cases. According to this definition, the nation-states in the Eurozone are not sovereign *de jure*.

In most Western countries, a constellation has emerged in which sovereign securities act as a riskless asset. The yield of this asset is a benchmark to which a mark-up is added, with the size of the mark-up depending on whatever other financial asset is being priced. We see such a set-up in the US, the UK, Japan, China and Sweden. The Eurozone does not have such a set-up, because sovereign securities (Eurozone member government bonds) are not necessarily riskless. The reason is that member governments – at least individually – cannot control ECB policy, and have no legally assured recourse to the support of the central bank if they run into trouble selling their bonds to private institutional investors at an affordable rate of interest.

The euro monetary system is unique in that respect, or, more precisely, it used to be: after a crisis emerged in sovereign bond markets affecting several countries in the Eurozone, including Greece, Italy, Ireland and Spain, in 2013 the ECB reacted by promising that it would use *outright monetary transactions* (OMTs) to prevent the insolvency of national governments that are members of the Eurozone. This move was very controversial, and opposed – inappropriately, in the author's view – by a number of senior German policy-makers, including the head of the Bundesbank.

Sovereign monetary systems

The following description refers to a monetary system in which the central bank can buy unlimited amounts of Treasury securities. This is possible in Canada, for instance, where the central bank is required to provide reserves for government securities. What does a government security look like?

As a thought experiment, let's suppose Canada issues an IOU ('I owe you' note) on 1 January 2016. An IOU is a documented financial obligation. It is a liability that the issuer has declared it will honour. It could look like this:

> Herewith the Treasury of the Government of Canada promises to pay the holder of this IOU the amount of (Canadian) $100 plus interest of $5 on 31 December 2016.

The government could try to pay suppliers or workers with this IOU. If they have trust in the government's financial instrument, they might accept it as a means of payment. However, such a promise might not be sufficient. This is where the central bank comes in. The government contacts the central bank and proposes the following deal. The government delivers the IOU promising $100 plus $5 interest to the central bank, which in turn credits the government's account with $100. This is done electronically with the help of a computer. As we've seen, reserves are central bank money, which can be owned by banks or government, but not by households or firms. Reserves can be exchanged into cash at central bank branches nationwide, and the reverse is also possible. Firms and households can obtain cash only via the banking system.

Now that the Canadian government has received $100 in central bank reserves, it's ready to spend. This might look a little odd at first sight, since the government has presented an IOU to the central bank and in return received an (electronic) central bank IOU, both with a face value of $100. The reason why we call the government's IOU a 'sovereign security' and that of the central bank 'reserve money' is historical; among other things, the market value (measured in Canadian dollars) of the government's securities fluctuate as they're traded, whereas 'reserve money' doesn't. The balance sheets of the two institutions are shown below.

central bank				government			
t-bonds	100	reserves	100	reserves	100	t-bonds	100

On the left-hand side of each balance sheet, we have assets, and on the right side, liabilities. The government owes the central bank repayment of the amount promised by its sovereign security; the central bank owes the government the corresponding value of reserves. Since both the central bank and government Treasury are part of the public sector, there is no change in net debt. The government owes the central bank $100 (sovereign security), the central bank owes the government $100 (reserves, in the form of a deposit in the Treasury's account at the central bank).

Two arms of the public sector have produced mutual debts among themselves, but the private sector is not affected yet. This changes when the government spends the reserves.

Let's assume the government pays an invoice arising from a delivery of goods – apples from a Quebec farmer for the Treasury's in-house cafeteria in Ottawa – worth $100. Normally, the farmer won't be paid in cash, although it would be possible to do so, since reserves could be exchanged into cash. The farmer is paid by bank transfer instead.

Let's display this transaction in a balance sheet. As an intermediate step, we have the government transfer reserves to a commercial bank in return for bank money deposits credited to the Treasury's account at that bank.

bank				government			
reserves	100	deposits	100	deposits	100	t-bonds	100

In the next step, the government transfers these bank money deposits to the apple farmer, and thus pays for the goods delivery. The farmer is the new owner of the deposits.

bank				household			
reserves	100	deposits	100	deposits	100	net wealth	100
				apples	0		

As we can see, the household is now wealthy. Its savings – by definition this is equal to income not spent – of $100 are not neutralised by any liabilities. To close the hole in the balance sheet (again, the two sides of all balance sheets have to balance, that's a basic accounting rule in double-entry bookkeeping), we introduce 'net wealth', which corresponds to the difference between assets and liabilities.

The bank has liabilities of $100, but also holds $100 worth of reserves. There is no net wealth or equity, which is a simplification.

The bank pays an interest rate on deposits, which in normal times could be something like 2 per cent. Reserves do not yield any interest. This is a crucial difference in comparison with other financial assets.

Another is that deposits at the central bank can be exchanged into cash, which is an accepted means of payment in the general population. Cash is liquid, whereas other financial assets have to be sold first ('liquidated') so that the cash obtained through the asset sale can be used to buy something or pay debts.

Whereas the purchasing power of other financial assets depends on their market price, this is not the case with cash. The nominal value of cash is fixed; there are no fluctuations as there are with shares. To move from nominal value to purchasing power, however, some information about the price level is needed. We will return to this issue later.

As it stands, the balance sheet above has the bank bearing losses. Therefore, the bank's reserves should be lent out or used to buy financial assets, so that the bank acquires a stream of interest income. At a minimum, this stream of income should exceed paid-out interest costs plus cover the expenses of running the bank.

A fundamental requirement is that the bank must stay liquid all the time. The household could spontaneously withdraw its deposits. Let us assume that the household does not plan to do that, and that the bank knows it. Perhaps the customer is interested in saving and 2 per cent is enough. Now the bank seeks to invest its reserves of $100. Most macroeconomics textbooks argue that the bank can lend out the $100 in reserves by giving loans to households or firms. This story, as we have already seen, is wrong.

Calling to mind what the balance sheet of the bank looks like, we find that its assets include deposits at the central bank, which are called reserves. Private firms or households hold their deposits at commercial banks, not at the central bank. An increase in reserves in the banking system will not create additional loans to the private sector, since banks do not and cannot lend reserves to non-banks – and they also do not lend out cash, although they could get cash in exchange for their reserves. Banks make loans independent from the quantity of reserves they hold at any given time, since they can borrow reserves when they are needed from other banks or the central bank later on.

Banks can lend out excess reserves to other banks that have a proportionate demand. Banks need reserves for settlement with other banks whenever their own customers have transferred deposits to customers of another bank.

Let's assume that the bank with excess reserves does not find another bank willing to borrow these reserves at 5 per cent plus a risk premium. One alternative use of its reserves would be to purchase Treasury securities. We'll assume that the central bank sells them at par, which is $100. After the transaction has taken place, the bank expects to receive 5 per cent interest, yet it must pay only 2 per cent to savers. The spread is the bank's gross profit.

The balance sheets of the four institutions are shown below. The government's net wealth is negative because it has issued a Treasury bond and spent the reserves.

central bank				government			
t-bonds	100	reserves	100	reserves	0	t-bonds	100
						net wealth	−100

	bank				household		
reserves	100	deposits	100	deposits	100	net wealth	100

Box 6.1 Standard&Poor's chief economist loses his cool

In a publication of 13 August 2013 the rating agency Standard&Poor's joined the debate on the (non-)inflationary consequences of an increase in the reserves of banks following some central bank operations with a paper entitled 'Repeat After Me: Banks Cannot and Do Not "Lend Out" Reserves'. Apparently S&P's chief economist was fed up with the recurring incantation that a rise in the supply of central bank reserves must lead to inflation, as many commentators had been hysterically and incorrectly insisting. This example reminds us that even if many people parrot something with great conviction and vehemence, that doesn't necessarily imply that what they're saying is correct.

Let's summarise what the issuance of Treasury securities has led to. The central bank created additional reserves, which belonged first to the government, then to a commercial bank, and at the end flowed back to the central bank. The quantity of reserves is the same as before.

Reserves that are owned by the central bank can be removed from the central bank's balance sheet. Here's why this is the case (even if the following description of the situation is legally imprecise, it's valid): an IOU securitises a claim that its owner holds against the IOU's issuer. When such an IOU reverts to its issuer, the issuer would owe himself the amount fixed in the IOU. The issuer now has a choice: destroy the IOU, or put it back in circulation by transferring it to another person. The latter action would be the same as issuing a new IOU.

The following two balance sheets are identical in terms of net wealth. However, only the right-hand side is technically correct. In its balance sheet, the central bank does not recognise reserves or cash that it owns. For didactic reasons, I show the left-hand side balance sheet as an intermediate step.

	central bank				central bank		
reserves	100	reserves	100	reserves	0	reserves	0

The government has incurred debts. Households have obtained additional incomes and accumulated net wealth through the acquisition of bank deposits, which are indirectly backed up by claims on the government. It is obvious that this wealth would not have come about without the government incurring additional debt. This is due to double-entry bookkeeping: the asset of one party always corresponds to the liability of another (its counterparty). Without government bonds, there would be neither government debt nor private net wealth in the form of government securities. Also, the amount of deposits in the banking system would be lower.

Wealth and debt

The connection between public debt and private wealth is a consequence of the fact that debt and wealth are inseparable. When government moves into debt, it allows households to build up wealth in the shape of a riskless asset. Government securities are wealth, because they are a claim on the government.

By implication, a reduction in government debt is equal to a reduction of household wealth. Wealth management funds have invested a significant part of their money in government securities, and when government reduces its debt, fewer government securities will be available in the market. After all, the government has reduced the amount of deposits held by the private sector when it spends less or increases taxation.

Does the government debt burden future generations?

Government bonds usually have a limited maturity. Often it is between some months and 10, 20 or even 30 years. The existence of long-dated debt has led to a widespread idea that an increase in government debt burdens future generations – but this is based on faulty reasoning. The private sector holds government securities, which from the point of view of those who hold those securities are assets, not liabilities. Therefore, the payment of interest out of taxes to the owners of government securities redistributes income not across generations but within them. Taxpayers lose deposits and bondholders gain them. No taxes paid by generations of the past or the future are used to support these redistributive interest payments. Hence public debt leads to a redistribution that is strictly intragenerational and not intergenerational.

If the result of a large debt burden is that an unacceptably large transfer of wealth from taxpayers to bondholders occurs within a particular generation, then that generation's voters are free to elect politicians who will change the tax code in ways that will restore an acceptable balance – for example, by levying a redistributive tax on private wealth or on high incomes, while reducing taxes on those with low incomes.

The government can reduce its debt by increasing its revenues from taxation or by lowering government spending. This, however, will have negative feedback effects on the economy, as the case of excessive restraint in public spending imposed during the recent recession in Europe has shown. GDP and employment declined due to constraints on government spending ('austerity' policies), and those reductions in GDP and employment, in turn, resulted in lower tax income. This is an important macroeconomic issue we'll look at more closely later.

Can a state or government go 'bankrupt'?

It's often claimed that a state or a government can go 'bankrupt'. In December 2009, for example, US president Barack Obama said that without reform of the healthcare system, the US would go bankrupt. However, a modern state with sovereign money cannot go bankrupt – unless political barriers have been erected to prevent the monetisation of sovereign debt using the balance sheet of the central bank. The possibility of sovereign default is a deliberate political choice, not inevitability.

Even where rules against sovereign debt monetisation are in place, the institutional barriers against changing those rules are not insurmountable. Even the constitution can be changed if a qualified political majority that's in control of the relevant legislature is in favour of changing it.

Financial systems are different from one another, and we have only looked at one with sovereign money. Let's look at the balance sheets of such a system again.

_____central bank_____				_____government_____		
t-bonds	0	reserves	0	reserves	0	t-bonds	100
						net wealth	−100

_____bank_____				_____household_____		
t-bonds	100	deposits	100	deposits	100	net wealth	100

A currency is 'sovereign' when the government that controls it cannot go bankrupt.

Any institution other than a currency-controlling government (and its central bank), by contrast, can fall into bankruptcy. This can occur in two different ways. First, insolvency can result if liabilities exceed assets. Second, the institution might find itself unable to pay its current bills, even though it owns assets whose value exceeds that of its liabilities. This is called 'illiquidity'.

Nearly all sovereign countries have an accumulated national debt, created by decades of running up annual public deficits in their own currency, but we do not talk about public 'insolvency'. Insolvency is not possible since the government that has a sovereign currency has no externally constrained balance sheet. A state is neither a household nor a firm; it does not need to obtain financing from anywhere. A state insolvency, let me repeat, is not possible as long as the government does not have excessive debts denominated in a foreign currency.

This is among the great accomplishments of the Enlightenment, because in the previous era, during the time of absolute monarchies, rulers actually depended on loans and money from the rich. If before adopting a budget, a government has to ask its citizens for money, the government is not truly sovereign. A group of wealthy households can thwart the budget by refusing to finance it. Since today's governments are legitimised by democracy, such a veto power in the hands of a plutocratic class would be a severe blow to democracy.

Given that there can be no state insolvency in the state's own currency, we now examine the possibility of illiquidity. Imagine that a sovereign bond matures, and the government does not own any assets, but has to pay back the bondholder. This would constitute a big problem for a private debtor.

For the Canadian government, which provides a wonderful example for the working of a modern monetary system, it's no problem at all. The procedure to 'raise the money' needed to pay out the bondholder is quite simple. If money taken in through tax receipts is momentarily insufficient to meet currently maturing bond obligations along with current expenditures, the government asks the Treasury to issue a fresh sovereign security – i.e. a fresh bond. The bond will be issued in the currency of the sovereign state – in this case, Canadian dollars.

The nominal value of the bond is its face value plus an annual interest rate of, for instance, 5 per cent (totalling C$105 if we're talking about a one-year maturity bond). The central bank is required by law to credit the government's account. It can't say no. The balance sheets look like this:

_____central bank_____				_____government_____			
t-bonds	105	reserves	105	reserves	105	t-bonds	205
						net wealth	−100

The Treasury bond was accepted in payment by the central bank, and the government's account at the central bank was credited with C$105. These deposits are at the disposition of the government. They are used to pay out C$105 to the holder of the t-bond, with a principal of C$100 and an interest rate of 5 per cent. The government thus moves its deposits from the central bank to the bank of the owner of the Treasury bond. The bank gets C$105 in reserves, and credits the account of the bondholder with the same amount.

_____central bank_____				_____government_____			
t-bonds	105	reserves	105	reserves	0	t-bonds	105
						net wealth	−105

At first sight this process of the government 'borrowing' from the central bank might seem surprising, since the transaction is neither 'real' debt nor is the 'free market' involved. A debt is usually created between two parties, with one party becoming the debtor and the other the creditor. This often happens in conditions of voluntariness and not coercion. However, the central bank and government both belong to the state. In this sense, the word 'debt' is misplaced in this context. One cannot be indebted to oneself.

In a modern monetary system with a sovereign currency, the government has access to unlimited amounts of reserves via the central bank. Illiquidity, which is possible in the private sector, is impossible for governments with sovereign currency (as long as they have not issued excessive liabilities denominated in a foreign currency). What remains to be understood is whether central banks are limited in the creation of reserves.

The arrangement that has been described so far has evolved historically and is not the only possibility of financing government spending, nor is it the best. Theoretically, the Treasury could issue currency directly and thereby render a central bank redundant. Monetary policy would, like fiscal policy, obviously be a government affair.

Another option would be to ban credit creation by banks, and instead endow the private sector with accounts at the central bank. Or, central bankers could be democratically elected. These alternatives could also be discussed with the help of balance sheets to examine advantages and disadvantages.

In order to repay its debt – the old t-bond – the government borrows by issuing a new t-bond. It is subsequently 'sold' to the central bank. The balance sheets look like this:

_____central bank_____					_____government_____		
t-bonds	105	reserves	105	reserves	105	t-bonds	205
						net wealth	−100

The new Treasury bond was accepted in payment by the central bank, and the government's account at the central bank was credited with C$105. These deposits are now at the disposition of the government. At maturity of the old Treasury bond, the owner can be paid C$105. This increases government debt by C$5:

_____central bank_____					_____government_____		
t-bonds	105	reserves	105	reserves	0	t-bonds	105
						net wealth	−105

Box 6.2 The default of Argentina's government

During the Argentinean debt crisis of 2001/2, the government's ability to pay out maturing dollar-denominated bonds was in danger. Like many other governments of developing and emerging countries, the Argentinean government had incurred debts in US dollars. Since the Argentinean government is unable to create US dollars, it was forced to acquire them through taxation or coercion, or roll over the loans. In the end, in 2005 old Argentinean government securities were exchanged for new ones, with creditors taking a loss ('haircut') of 75 per cent of the bonds' nominal value.

What remains to be understood is whether central banks are limited in the creation of reserves.

Box 6.3 Do taxpayers have to repay the national debt?

No. As long as the government incurs debts in its own currency and the central bank provides additional reserves in exchange for Treasury securities, a government is not forced to finance itself through taxes. There is scarce historical evidence of countries that reduced the quantity of sovereign securities back to zero by increasing taxation to the required level. One example of 'successful' debt repayment is the US, which did so once and shortly afterward plunged into the economic crisis of 1834. Soon afterward, the possibility of running up public debts was used again.

Can a central bank go 'bankrupt'?

The short answer to this question is: no. This is true without reservation, given that the central banks have not been given such an option by the legislators. It would be possible to set up a central bank using legislation that specifies conditions under which it would be considered 'bankrupt', but to date it hasn't been done (because there's no good reason to do it, and lots of good reasons not to). Even though 'debt brakes' exist for governments, none exist for central banks. In essence, the balance sheets of central banks are infinitely flexible.

I use quotation marks around 'debt brakes' to avoid some confusion. The reality is that introduction of 'debt brakes' has often led to a *rise* in cumulated debt, so the name is actually misleading. A more proper term would be 'annual sovereign debt increase limit'.

Modern Western central banks are not hampered by debt limits. They can credit the accounts of banks and government entries in the payment system at their discretion, subject to the legal framework they operate within.

Should the central bank want to increase the quantity of reserves on the asset side of their own balance sheets, it can do so in a way that creates deposits owned by itself. The balance sheet would look something like this after the central bank has given itself $100 worth of reserves.

central bank		
Treasury bonds 105	reserves	205
reserves	100	

Box 6.4 Who prints bank notes, who mints coins?

The printing of bank notes and minting of coins was often a responsibility of the public sector. Today it's private companies that provide these services. Obviously, the central bank doesn't pay the supplier €100 for a bank note of €100; it pays only the price which the printing company has negotiated. If that is too high, the order can be placed with a cheaper provider. The printing plates are designed by the central bank or Treasury and remain a property of the state. Of course, the provider of coins or bank notes has to sell these exclusively to the central bank (notes) or Treasury (coins), but not at face value!

The central bank's balance sheet will be extended by this entry. It can spend the reserves right away. However, only the instruments introduced above are available to it. The central bank cannot exchange reserves into cash and 'go shopping'. It can buy financial assets from banks, sometimes only temporarily (i.e. it is likely to sell them back to the private financial sector again later). The central bank is not allowed to speculate or intervene in the market in order to maximise profits.

The central bank, despite its nominal independence, is an institution of the state. The state controls the central bank. In the case of most central banks, the Treasury owns the capital of the central bank.

The central bank can create reserves without limit. Ben Bernanke, who was then chairman of the US central bank, the Federal Reserve, was asked by CBS where the central bank got the money that it spent during the crisis to support the commercial banks. Bernanke answered:

> It's not tax money. The banks have accounts with the Fed, much the same way that you have an account in a commercial bank. So, to lend to a bank, we simply use the computer to mark up the size of the account that they have with the Fed. It's much more akin to printing money than it is to borrowing.
>
> (www.cbsnews.com/news/ben-bernankes-greatest-challenge/2/)

Bernanke confirmed that the central bank does not draw on taxes, but instead simply credits the accounts that banks have with the central bank when it extends loans to these banks or buys assets from them. He said that this is 'much more akin to printing money than it is to borrowing'.

As was discussed above, we cannot divide the creation of money and credit from the creation of bookkeeping entries. Bernanke emphasised that the creation of additional reserves, which are credited to banks when the central bank buys some of their assets, is comparable to a purchase with money (in this case, money created by the buyer).

This is why the intermediate step we showed in the central bank's balance sheet, with the creation of new reserves as asset and liability for the central bank, is more a didactic tool than an exact representation of reality. The central bank doesn't first create some reserves, and then use them to buy financial assets from private financial institutions (commercial banks) that have accounts at the central bank. In reality, the reserves are created in the act of buying those financial

---

Box 6.5 What is seigniorage?

Central banks can create reserves and use them to acquire assets. Since deposits held by commercial banks in the accounts they hold at the central bank usually pay interest at a rate below that paid by assets the central bank has purchased, the central bank makes a profit. This profit is called 'seignorage'.

Seignorage also applies to the central bank's ability to trade reserves for physical cash. However, production of physical cash is costly, which reduces the profit of the central bank. According to the Money Museum in Kansas City, which belongs to the Federal Reserve Bank of Kansas City, it costs 6.2 cents (US) to produce any bank note. Having said this, the central bank is not allowed to spend this note. Additional bank notes enter circulation only when they are exchanged against reserves held by commercial banks at the central bank.

assets. The central bank essentially creates an IOU in the amount of a quantity of reserves and gives these to a commercial bank in exchange for a financial asset deemed equal in value.

Entering numbers into a spreadsheet creates money in the form of deposits in the accounts of banks at the central bank with the help of a computer. It has nothing to do with 'printing money' in the sense of turning on a money-printing press. A central bank can print cash (or more precisely, order cash from the company that runs the government's money-printing press), but it only supplies banks with cash when these demand it and can pay for it with reserves. Commercial banks order stocks of cash in anticipation of demand for cash from their clients (holders of deposit accounts at commercial banks).

Quantitative easing: long-term open market operations

A central bank controls the overnight interest rate on the money market by setting its interest rates. The overnight rate is the interest that a bank pays when borrowing overnight. For the private customer, the overnight rate is the interest he or she pays when borrowing deposits (and possibly, indirectly borrowing reserves) overnight.

A bank might not need to hold additional reserves sufficient to cover possible customer withdrawals in a given time period, if the customer keeps his money in a savings account – thereby implicitly promising neither to demand cash nor transfer the money elsewhere.

Commercial banks can borrow or lend out reserves in the 'money market'. Reserves are transferred among banks during settlement of accounts between them at the end of the business day. In the end, some banks end up with more reserves than they need. Others have fewer reserves than they need. A market for reserves is created which is called the 'interbank market'. It is a zero-sum game as long as banks transfer reserves only among each other. Reserves are lent out for days, sometimes weeks or even months. Banks can also borrow

---

Box 6.6 What determines the yield curve?

The bedrock of the yield curve normally is the risk-free asset, the sovereign security (sovereign bond). Its yield is displayed for different maturities. These range from weeks or months to years. The latter usually pay interest, the former do not. Since they are not always traded at the issue price (also called 'face value' or 'nominal value'), the yield varies. Investors looking for a two-year investment period can buy two one-year Treasury bonds consecutively, or a two-year Treasury bond. If the price of the two-year Treasury bond is very low, and hence its implied yield is higher, it makes sense to buy it instead of two one-year Treasury bonds. This arbitrage shifts demand to those bonds that are relatively cheap, which leads to a convergence of yields. Expectations about the future play a large role in this.

reserves from the central bank if they wish. These transactions influence short-term interest rates.

If the central bank wants to manipulate long-term interest rates, it does so via quantitative easing (QE). Let's look at how long-term interest rates are determined.

As we've seen, the short-term interest rate is determined by the set of interest rates the central bank sets, and by open market operations. An important link exists between the 'base rate' or interbank market rate and bond yields. The interest rate banks pay other private financial institutions to get additional over-night reserves is determined on the interbank market. It never falls below the overnight deposit rate the central bank would pay to banks that have parked reserves in their deposit accounts at the central bank, since banks won't be willing to lend each other reserves at a rate below the rate they can get by holding reserves in their own deposit accounts.

Banks holding reserves can buy sovereign bonds. The yield of sovereign bonds is determined by arbitrage. Arbitrage is a general term used for all kinds of financial trades that exploit price differences. In the case under discussion, we have differences in interest rates. The interest rate is the cost of holding financial assets for some period. Banks will seek to borrow assets for which they pay a low interest rate, and use those assets to acquire and hold assets, which pay a higher interest rate. That's what successful arbitrage means in this context.

A bank interested in buying sovereign securities will consider the following possible alternatives. On the one hand, it can borrow reserves for a certain time on the interbank market, i.e. from some other bank that has excess reserves that it doesn't currently need. The bank pays an interest rate for the privilege of holding those reserves, and so its balance sheet looks like this:

_____commercial bank_____		
reserves	100	loan (IB) 100

The bank will make a loss, since it does not get any interest on its holdings of reserves, whereas it has to pay interest on the loan. So it won't be satisfied with this trade.

However, the bank is allowed to make use of the reserves it's holding until the loan matures and must be repaid. In the meantime, the reserves could be lent out to some other entity against interest. This only makes sense if the bank can borrow reserves at a cheaper rate than it lends. Depending on the bank's assess-ment of counterparty risk, i.e. its assessment of the creditworthiness of a pro-spective borrower, this can be a profitable endeavour.

Another possibility for the bank is to use the central bank's deposit facility, i.e. to deposit the reserves it's holding there. Since the interest rate paid by the central bank to commercial banks holding reserves in the deposit facility is below the interbank market rate, this will not yield any profit.

Certainly there are many other possible trades the bank could engage in with the reserves it's holding. It could engage in speculation and buy assets, like shares, real estate, corporate bonds or any number of other financial assets. This is risky, of course; banks can be brought to ruin by traders making bad calls, or caught holding assets that drop in value as a result of sudden economic shocks, perhaps caused by the failure of a major counterparty bank or a war involving petrostates. If such a shock happens, and as a consequence the assets that had previously been purchased fall in value by half, the balance sheet would look like this:

commercial bank		
'toxic waste' 50	loan (IB)	100
	equity	−50

This bank is insolvent, as it cannot repay the loan. Selling the toxic asset would yield 50 in reserves, which is not enough to settle the liability.

So in general, banks should confine themselves to purchasing risk-free assets. What makes an asset risk-free? In most modern monetary systems, sovereign bonds can be considered risk-free, since the central bank directly or indirectly guarantees that it will swap sovereign bonds for reserves at the market price. Hence banks would be interested in investing borrowed reserves in sovereign securities whenever their yield lies above the interest rate the banks pay on the interbank market. If this is the case, a bank will use reserves it's holding to buy sovereign bonds.

commercial bank	
sovereign bonds 100	loan (IB) 100

This deal is lucrative as long as the bond yield remains above the interbank interest rate. Maturities should coincide to exclude any risk associated with refinancing. Sovereign securities with a maturity of three months should be financed with interbank loans of the same maturity. If the maturity of the latter is shorter than the former, the bank carries the risk of rising interest rates in the interbank market. In the worst case, the interbank rate might rise above the sovereign securities' yield, and the bank will lose money on the trade.

Opportunities for risk-free arbitrage only exist when sovereign securities are perceived as risk-free. Depending on institutional arrangements, this may or may not be the case. The matter is complicated, because the yield of a sovereign bond does not necessarily correspond with its nominal interest rate. A sovereign security carries the following information at issuance:

1   statement of currency that the owner will be paid at maturity;
2   statement of the sum to be paid, the 'face value' or 'nominal value' of the bond;
3   statement of interest to be paid (if applicable); and
4   statement of the bond's maturity date.

The interest rate of a sovereign security, if there is any, is fixed, and is calculated as an annual payment on the face value of the bond. The price of the security on bond-trading markets, however, is flexible. A $100 US Treasury bond with an interest rate of 0 per cent and a one-year maturity can be traded at higher or lower prices than its face value. This can lead to a yield that diverges from zero, even though there is no interest paid by the bond issuer (here, the US Treasury). So, assume the bond was purchased at $90 at the time of issuance, for instance. Given the expected payout of $100 one year later, a profit of $10 can be expected. The corresponding yield is more than 11 per cent, i.e. $10 divided by the amount invested, $90.

The yield of risk-free sovereign bonds forms the basis for calculating the interest rates paid under a great many loan contracts. For example, if a construction firm wants to take out a loan for five years, the interest is often calculated by using the interbank market interest rate (like LIBOR). Since loans to construction firms are not risk-free, some mark-up will be added to the interbank market interest rate.

Many medium- to long-term financial contracts, including the issuance of corporate bonds or other instruments, are based on the yield of sovereign securities with the same or similar maturity. This yield depends on the securities' market price. Central banks make use of this link when they engage in QE. The following balance sheets show the situation before QE.

central bank				Treasury			
reserves	100	reserves	100	reserves	0	t-bonds	200
						net wealth	−200

bank				household			
t-bonds	200	deposits	300	deposits	300	mortgage	100
mortgage	100			real estate	200	net wealth	400

Here, the central bank has increased the amount of reserves in its balance sheet. It buys sovereign securities from the banks. The price of these is determined on the market. The additional demand for long-term sovereign securities leads to an increase in their price; and the higher the price, the lower the yield. For example, a $100 Treasury bond with an interest rate paid by the issuer (the Treasury) on the face value of 4 per cent might be traded at $101. The implied yield would be about 3 per cent.

The central bank's strategy when it buys long-term Treasury bonds under QE programmes is to keep buying them until their yield has reached the desired level.

central bank				Treasury			
reserves	50	reserves	100	reserves	0	t-bonds	200
t-bonds	50					net wealth	−200

bank				household		
t-bonds	150	deposits	300	deposits	300	mortgage	100
mortgage	100			real estate	200	net wealth	400
reserves	50						

Banks receive additional reserves when selling Treasury bonds. They can lend these reserves out on the interbank market, which pushes the interest rate down until the central bank intervenes. Alternatively, they can park the reserves in their account with the central bank's deposit facility. However, they cannot lend out the reserves to the private sector, since firms and households have no accounts at the central bank. Reserves can only be transferred between accounts at the central bank, and such accounts may be held exclusively by commercial banks and by the government Treasury.

Some Treasury bonds are owned not by banks, but rather by banks' customers – albeit indirectly, for example through their ownership of shares in a pension fund. In that case, if a central bank buys Treasury bonds from a pension fund, for example, then households would hold more deposits as a result of QE. In our example, they rise from 200 to 250, while holdings of pension fund shares are reduced from 100 to 50.

The following balance sheets show the situation after the central bank has engaged in a round of QE. The household gains 50 in deposits and loses 50 in pension fund shares, of which it originally held 100.

central bank				Treasury		
reserves	50	reserves	100	reserves	0	t-bonds	200
t-bonds	50					net wealth	–200

bank				household		
t-bonds	150	deposits	250	deposits	350	mortgage	100
mortgage	100	pension fund	50	real estate	100	net wealth	400
reserves	50			pension fund	50		

This way, more deposits in the private sector are created. There are good reasons to believe that the owners of these deposits will not spend them on consumption or investment goods. They probably would still like to save, and hence buy shares, bonds or real estate. This is why it is not surprising that one of the side effects of QE is an across-the-board rise in the price of financial assets, as reserves flow into investment managers' accounts as deposits, and large amounts of additional demand for investible secondary market financial assets drive their prices up. This is not without consequences for the distribution of wealth.

Central banks can influence long-term interest rates by means of QE. Why are they motivated to do that? The reason is that many major investments require long maturities to be profitable or reach the cumulative sales volume needed to repay the initial investment. A factory might turn profitable only after 10 years, a power plant after 20, infrastructure after 50. Adequate long-term financing has to be secured. The norm is: the longer the maturity of a loan, the higher the interest rate.

Entrepreneurs look at medium- to long-term interest rates, which usually are not controlled by the central bank. With QE, the central bank can push down these interest rates, which are relevant for entrepreneurs in the context of long-term investments. The hope is that by making long-term financing cheaper, entrepreneurs will undertake more projects, because cheaper long-term financing makes more projects profitable on a net basis, calculated after financing costs.

However, there are other criteria that entrepreneurs have when considering making investments, apart from low interest rates. The existence of sufficient demand can increase the quantity of investment, the lack thereof lower it. If entrepreneurs perceive a widespread lack of effective demand – let's say, if the factories they already own are not producing at full capacity because of a lack of customers – then bringing down long-term interest rates by means of QE will be without effect. There's not much point in expanding production capacity if there's insufficient customer demand so that existing production facilities are not going at full capacity. This seems to be the case in the Eurozone today.

Government securities in Germany

The German government's account (*Zentralkonto des Bundes*) is run by the German central bank (*Bundesbank*) on behalf of the Treasury (*Finanzministerium*), which acts for the government. Because Article 123 of the Lisbon Treaty on European Union institutions specifies that the central bank is prohibited from funding governments or public investment agencies, the German central bank is not allowed to buy sovereign securities of the German government (Bunds) directly from the issuer; instead, it may only buy Bunds on the secondary market. For this reason, the process of increasing government spending is a bit different from what has been described so far. If the Treasury has an insufficient amount of reserves in its account to meet its desired spending targets, it asks the German Finance Agency (*Deutsche Finanzagentur*) to issue new securities. These are sold to private institutional investors in the primary bond market.

On the buying side of the primary market, the members of the officially licensed bidding group (*Bietergruppe Bundesemissionen*) enter the stage. At the time of writing, this bidding group consisted of 37 banks from the European Union, the US, the UK and Japan (or their European subsidiaries). These banks purchase sovereign securities directly from the German Finance Agency. From a balance sheet perspective, it looks like banks buy the government's securities, which increases the amount of deposits the German Finance Agency has at the central bank. Where did those banks get the reserves they needed in order to purchase these financial instruments?

In a monetary system in which the government gets its deposits at the central bank from the central bank itself, the government first spends additional reserves into the private sector. These reflux into the banking system and thus increase the amount of reserves. Banks look for an interest-bearing investment opportunity and buy the sovereign securities that the central bank holds.

In the Eurozone, however, banks effectively make advance payments. Banks in the Eurozone are structurally indebted vis-à-vis the ECB. They borrow reserves against collateral, which they then use to purchase sovereign securities. Banks have lots of collateral, since they hold assets worth trillions of euro on their combined balance sheet. Borrowing a couple of billion euro to finance the purchase of government bonds is not a problem at all for the banking sector.

We'll start our examination of the relevant balance sheets with a loan from the central bank. The base rate is essential, since it influences the overnight interest rate of reserves. In a perfect world, the maturity of a loan from the central bank to a commercial bank would match that of the sovereign security the commercial bank then buys with those reserves.

central bank				Treasury			
loan	100	reserves	100	reserves	0	t-bonds	0
						net wealth	0

bank				household			
t-bonds	0	deposits	0	deposits	0	net wealth	0
reserves	100	loan (CB)	100				

Now banks are able to purchase sovereign securities offered by the government. The reserves are transferred to the account of the government at the central bank, and the sovereign securities are transferred to the banks.

central bank				Treasury			
loan	100	reserves	100	reserves	100	t-bonds	100
						net wealth	0

bank				household			
t-bonds	100	deposits	0	deposits	0	net wealth	0
reserves	0	loan (CB)	100				

Banks purchase Treasury bonds on the primary market without any involvement of the central bank. It is possible, at a given time, for there to be no demand for sovereign securities at all if banks do not want to buy any just then. The reason for insufficient demand might be that sovereign securities of particular Eurozone governments are perceived as not being risk-free.

The *no bail-out clause* in the Treaty of Lisbon does not allow members of the Eurozone to assume the debts of another. Since the ECB is not allowed to directly finance a government, that is to say that it is forbidden to purchase sovereign securities on the primary market, it might come to pass that there is no demand for sovereign securities of a particular Eurozone state, particularly a state which is seen as being at risk of insolvency, and the issuance fails. But sometimes, even states that are unquestionably solvent find their auctions of bonds failing to find sufficient buyers – though that's very rare.

Box 6.7 A failed auction: German government bonds in November 2011

In November 2011, German sovereign bonds with a maturity of ten years were to be auctioned in the primary market. However, there had been few bids and banks only bought €3.644 billion of the issue. The German central bank took over the remaining issue of €2.345 billion, with the intention of selling it later. Even though the financial press went mad at the time – Bloomberg titled *German Auction 'Disaster' Stirs Crisis Concern* – in the following months German sovereign securities were perceived as a good investment and prices increased significantly.

If issuance succeeds, the central bank deposits belonging to the government eventually flow back to the banks. Government pays the private sector – households and firms – for work or goods and services provided. From the balance sheet perspective, it is of no further consequence whether the government pays public employees or private sector firms.

Let's assume the government transfers funds to a household. The household sees the quantity of deposits in its bank account increase, while the bank gets reserves from the government. The latter debits its account at the national central bank.

_____central bank_____			_____Treasury_____			
loan	100	reserves 100	reserves	0	t-bonds	100
					net wealth	−100

_____bank_____			_____household_____			
t-bonds	100	deposits 100	deposits	100	net wealth	100
reserves	100	loan (CB) 100				

The central bank money that banks initially transferred to the government has refluxed to the banks. They can use the reserves to repay their loans from the central bank (i.e. to pay down their debt to the ECB). By transferring reserves to the ECB, the loan is eliminated from the liability side of banks' balance sheets. Both loans and reserves are eliminated from the ECB's balance sheet.

	central bank				Treasury		
loan	0	reserves	0	reserves	0	t-bonds	100
						net wealth	−100

	bank				household		
t-bonds	100	deposits	100	deposits	100	net wealth	100
reserves	0	loan (CB)	0				

Just like in a monetary system where the central bank buys sovereign securities in the primary market, the quantity of reserves is not increased directly when the government spends. This would only happen if households demanded more cash because of the higher income they have. The additional demand for money would not be caused by an increase in government spending per se, but by higher incomes. Private investments financed by loans would also increase incomes, and hence increase the level of demand for cash to spend.

In the Eurozone, like anywhere else, an increase in European public debt leads to an increase in private sector wealth. After some additional government spending has occurred, households hold additional deposits and banks hold additional government bonds. No increase in liabilities of firms or households compensates this. The additional incomes will probably be spent on consumption or investment, since the monetary circuit has been replenished with additional deposits.

TARGET2: the Eurozone's payment system

The Eurozone has a payment system which processes the transactions of participating banks. Payments in central bank money (reserves) are transferred back and forth. The system is named TARGET2, as it is the second iteration of the *Trans-European Automated Real-time Gross settlement Express Transfer system*. Banks use this payment system among other things for settlement of interbank debts and credits, and the central bank uses it for its instruments. When it is lending to banks or buying/selling, the account of the counterparty of the ECB is credited and debited via TARGET2. So-called TARGET2 'imbalances' have received quite a lot of media attention lately, so we'll take a look at their creation. But first, we'll describe the TARGET2 system.

Again, TARGET2 is a settlement system used by banks. Interbank 'settlement' of accounts is necessary if customers transfer deposits to and from accounts held at different banks. Both participating banks have to 'settle' their accounts by netting out the flow of credits and debits that occurred as a result of interbank payments between their clients. Settlement occurs at the end of each business day.

If both banks are located in the same country, then TARGET2 balances will not change. In the following example, it's assumed that one bank is located in

Spain (Banco) and the other in Germany (Bank). The Spanish bank has an account with Banco de España, the German bank with Bundesbank.

Let's assume that Spanish customers transfer more deposits to Germany than vice versa. The reason might be that Spaniards buy more German goods and services than Germans buy Spanish goods and services. Another reason might be that a Spanish household has decided to transfer the bulk of its savings deposits from the Spanish banking system to the German banking system. Perhaps Spanish banks are not deemed trustworthy, because of a fear that banks may be at risk of insolvency in the aftermath of Spain's real estate bubble having burst.

The balance sheets look like this before any transaction takes place.

ECB	
0	0

Banco de España				Bundesbank		
loans	200	reserves	200	loans	200	reserves	200

Banco				Bank		
reserves	200	deposits	200	reserves	200	deposits	200

household				household		
deposits	100	net wealth	100	deposits	100	net wealth	100

We assume that Banco has enough reserves to close the transaction. Banco reduces the deposits held by the Spanish household by €100 to execute a transfer to the German household. In order to achieve this, it transfers €100 in reserves to Bank via TARGET2. This transfer of reserves from Banco to Bank is all that actually takes place. The changes in the balance sheets of the ECB and the NCBs concerned are purely passive entries. The amount of reserves held by Banco de España is reduced and that of Bundesbank is increased.

A settlement between central banks at the ECB is constructed to make this happen, but it is a fiction, since the balances of the central banks are unlimited. They can 'borrow' as much reserves as they need. This is necessary because of the Eurozone's commitment to free capital flows. Everybody is free to transfer deposits from A to B without limits. If the Spanish central bank were to run out of reserves, than deposits could not be shifted anymore from Spanish to German banks. This would render the idea of free capital flows obsolete.

ECB			
T2 (BdE)	100	T2 (Buba)	100

Banco de España				Bundesbank		
loans	200	reserves	100	loans	200	reserves	300
		T2 debts	100	T2 assets	100		

_____Banco_____			_____Bank_____		
reserves	100	deposits 100	reserves	300	deposits	300

_____household_____			_____household_____		
deposits	0	net wealth 0	deposits	200	net wealth	200

As a result of this transaction, ECB would report a positive increment in the TARGET2 balance for the Bundesbank and a decrement for Banco de España's TARGET2 balance. What are the consequences for the central banks? None. They do not have to act, since the TARGET2 balances are mere statistics. Solely a breakdown of the euro monetary system would transform them into something of higher information value, but the same numbers could also be distilled from the European banks' balance sheets.

While banks go into settlement and cause TARGET2 imbalances, the NCBs do not do that. In the pyramid of money, there is hence no third monetary circulation above central bank deposits in which NCBs would go into settlement.

The Spanish household's transaction has been completed, but that does not necessarily mean that we are finished. The German bookkeeping entries are the mirror image of the Spanish ones; they end with additional deposits for central bank, bank and household. In the balance sheets above, we can see that Bank holds additional reserves. These do not carry an interest rate, whereas Bank pays some small interest on the additional deposits of its customer. It would hence be useful to invest or lend out the additional reserves. Since Banco has fewer reserves than before, it might be interested in obtaining an interbank market loan from Bank. Banco could borrow reserves from Bank at the going interbank market interest rate. The balance sheets would look like this:

_____ECB_____		
T2 (BdE)	0	T2 (Buba) 0

_____Banco de España_____			_____Bundesbank_____		
loans	200	reserves 200	loans	200	reserves	200

_____Banco_____			_____Bank_____		
reserves	200	deposits 100	reserves	200	deposits	300
		loan (Bank) 100	loan (Banco) 100			

_____household_____			_____household_____		
deposits	0	net wealth 0	deposits	200	net wealth	200

Banco has received a loan from Bank and returned the quantity of reserves to the previous level. The profit of Banco is reduced, that of Bank is increased. The

TARGET2 balances are not changed by the transaction. How, then, do permanent changes in TARGET2 balances come about?

In the prior step, we had non-zero TARGET2 balances before Bank lent back its excess reserves to Banco. If Bank would instead decide not to lend to Banco and park its reserves in its account in the deposit facility of ECB instead, we would have permanent TARGET2 imbalances.

Banks do not lend out reserves to other banks if they fear insolvency of the counter party. In this case, the excess reserves accumulated by Bank would not be returned, or not fully, as this cannot be compensated by a high interest rate.

In another step, let's look at what happens if Banco does not possess the necessary quantity of reserves. Now Banco borrows directly from the authorised national central bank, Banco de España. After the transaction, TARGET2 imbalances persist. The bookkeeping fiction assumes that banks hold their reserves not at Banco de España but at Bundesbank. This way, €100 in reserves at Banco de España are replaced by liabilities in the TARGET2 system, whereas Bundesbank's account is credited. This is analogous to settlement of banks at the central bank. However, the ECB normally gives unlimited credit to its affiliated NCBs. After the dust settles, all balances balance.

ECB			
T2 (BdE)	100	T2 (Buba)	100

Banco de España			
loans	200	reserves	100
		T2 debts	100

Bundesbank			
loans	200	reserves	300
T2 assets	100		

Banco			
reserves	200	deposits	100
		loan (BdE)	100

Bank			
reserves	300	deposits	300

household			
deposits	0	net wealth	0

household			
deposits	200	net wealth	200

TARGET2 imbalances arise when payment transactions lead to a situation in which banks with excess reserves refuse to lend them out to banks with a deficiency of reserves, perhaps because of trouble with the latter's balance sheets. TARGET2 imbalances are a mirror image of debt in the Eurozone's banking system, accounted as debt vis-à-vis the central bank rather than other banks, and totted up according to the national affiliation of each bank.

These imbalances will become relevant in a practical, consequential sense only if the Eurozone breaks up. At that point, potential losses would be caused by the devaluation of relevant (new) currencies being booked in the balance sheets of newly independent central banks as well as the ECB. In contrast to the claims of alarmist voices, central banks are able to compensate these losses without further ado, by means of balance sheet operations. There would be no danger for the payment system.

However, a break up of the Eurozone is quite unlikely now that ECB president Mario Draghi has promised to do 'whatever it takes' in order to save the euro. Given that he has not been stopped by lawsuits at the European Court of Justice, he will be able to successfully protect the euro by making appropriately flexible use of the ECB's balance sheet.

Draghi's 'whatever it takes' vow from July 2012 was followed by the inauguration of the *European Stability Mechanism* (ESM), which in case of emergency lends directly to Eurozone national governments to ensure their liquidity. The use of this mechanism would remove any risk of default. Since 2012 we thus have had the euro 2.0, and the fundamental (and misguided) innovation of the Eurozone – which had limited governments to borrowing only from commercial banks or financial investors, and hence be subject to the whims of bond markets and thereby subjected to a risk of default – is history. The Eurozone, after the introduction of the ESM, now looks quite a lot like other modern monetary systems.

Nevertheless, the threat of austerity policies that are imposed on those nations who need access to the ESM is a big hurdle. Politically, it probably is inadvisable for a government in budgetary trouble and facing high interest rates in bond markets to turn to the ESM and, in accordance with the conditions under which Europe makes ESM loans, submit to austerity. In case of emergency, though, it might be the only option available (and predecessor versions of the ESM have indeed been used by several countries since 2011, including Greece, Portugal and Ireland). So how does the ESM work exactly?

The ESM is a financial vehicle with a balance sheet just like any other institution. It borrows reserves against interest from banks in the money market and uses these reserves to buy sovereign securities of the participating countries on the secondary market. Huge losses are ruled out since interest rates on the money market are quite close to the yield of the sovereign securities and possibly even lower during times of crisis. The ESM operates with an equity of €80 billion. Its balance sheet looks like this, if we assume that the purchase of sovereign securities is financed exclusively through money market loans:

ESM			
bonds	100	loans (IB)	100
reserves	100	equity	100

As long as ESM buys sovereign securities at nominal price or a little bit below there is no risk of default for the sovereign securities of Eurozone members.

This does not imply that governments can increase public debt without limit, because national debt brakes or the European fiscal pact still exist. Since a government has no direct control over its deficit, the reasonableness of such regulations must be doubted. After all, estimations of tax income with the required precision are not possible, because they depend on the position of the business cycle. The same goes for government spending, which to a large extent depends on the business cycle as well – if a lot of people are unemployed, government spending has to go up in order to pay unemployment benefits, for example.

7 The sustainability of the financial system

In recent years the term 'sustainability' has often been used in conjunction with financial markets, banks or government debt. Interest and compound interest would lead to debt loads that are not sustainable, some say. The Merriam-Webster dictionary connects sustainability to ecology, to 'methods that do not use up or destroy natural resources'. Given the description of money and credit above, it seems problematic to transfer the concept of sustainability into the realm of money and credit, debt and financial markets. Here's why:

Sustainability implies that (natural) resources or goods are limited, and with that comes the responsibility to not reduce the stock of natural resources too quickly, or to stabilise the stock if it is a renewable resource. However, money in the form of central bank deposits, cash or bank deposits is potentially available in any quantity. Deposits in all forms are created by keystroke. There can be no talk of sustainability, since money that is spent by economic units is not 'used up' – it remains in the monetary circuit, more or less active depending on the balance of hoarding or spending, until the underlying bank debt that gave rise to a given tranche of money is paid off. Also, entering a number has no limiting effect on the ability to enter another one. The 'consumption of numbers' in balance sheets has no negative effects due to scarcity, and this is why there is no need to limit the use of numbers (more or less) voluntarily.

Another problem of the use of the 'sustainability' concept in the context of debt is the fact that debt is often limited in time. A loan is not created to last forever – quite to the contrary: a typical loan is amortised in a series of instalments, and ultimately the loan is gone. This is intended, since nobody wants to pay off debt forever!

How can we usefully employ the concept of 'sustainability' in conjunction with financial markets? Some economists see a problem in compound interest, which they worry will ultimately lead to a breakdown of the credit system. We have seen above that this cannot happen to public actors with sovereign currency. However, private actors – households and firms – could indeed suffer from rising interest rates. The crucial issue is the distribution of income and net income. As long as debts can be amortised, they are 'sustainable'.

Interest rates on loans for the private sector always include a risk premium, because the borrower could become insolvent or illiquid. The loan could be defaulted upon, and the bank would have to write-down part of the loan. If, for instance, a household were to fail to repay a mortgage, perhaps due to income reductions caused by unemployment, then the value of the mortgage would be adjusted. How that works exactly depends on the respective national laws.

Let's take a closer look at this. We'll assume here that the value is reduced by half in order to allow the household to pay off the remaining value of the mortgage. Compared to the status quo ante situation, we'll say the price of houses has fallen from 200 to 100, and the household has spent its deposits. The bank has some equity, which is the mirror of a surplus of assets over liabilities.

_____commercial bank_____				_____household_____			
bonds	200	deposits	200	deposits	0	mortgages	100
mortgages	100	equity	100	houses	100	net wealth	0

The bank's accountants have recognised the value of houses owned by the household at 100 (it could be more or less in reality, i.e. in terms of what the house would currently sell for in the housing market if it were put up for sale). A write-down leads to the following balance sheets:

_____commercial bank_____				_____household_____			
bonds	200	deposits	200	deposits	0	mortgages	50
mortgages	50	equity	50	houses	100	net wealth	50

The bank has reduced its mortgage holdings on the asset side by 50. Perhaps there was some refinancing, with the old mortgage being replaced by a new one. Equity is also reduced by 50.

It should be noted that the amount of deposits is not adjusted. The mortgage originally led to the creation of deposits worth 100, and these continue to exist after the refinancing, even though the value of the mortgage was reduced by half.

On the other side, the household is better off, at least on paper. The mortgage was reduced by 50, and because of double-entry bookkeeping this must lead to a rise in net wealth of the same amount. The household has returned to positive net wealth, since the value of assets surpasses the value of liabilities.

One problem of debt is that not all debts are reduced to zero. However, rising debt or rising interest payments are not fundamental problems. The fundamental problem is the inability to repay debts. As long as income or net income grows faster than repayment, there is no problem with the absolute rise in debt caused by rising interest rates. However, distribution also matters, since incomes and profits do not grow uniformly.

The government as the 'deleverager' of the private sector

Government plays a central role when it comes to the reasonableness or 'sustainability' of private sector debt. It can create additional deposits in the private sector by spending more, which in turn allows the private sector to service a larger pile of debt. This is conveyed by the relevant balance sheets:

central bank			Treasury		
reserves	100	reserves 100	reserves	0	t-bonds 100
					net wealth −100

bank			household		
t-bonds	100	deposits 200	deposits	200	loan 100
loans	100		house	50	net wealth 150

The government has issued additional Treasury bonds, which led to additional central bank deposits for the government, which it spent on labour, goods and services of the private sector. This is how government creates more deposits for households and firms via the banking system. If private sector debt was a problem, now it is less of a problem. The private sector can use the additional deposits to decrease its liabilities. In the following, it is assumed that the household repays half of the loan. The balance sheets mirror this transaction.

central bank			Treasury		
reserves	100	reserves 100	reserves	0	t-bonds 100
					net wealth −100

bank			household		
t-bonds	100	deposits 150	deposits	150	loan 50
loans	50		house	50	net wealth 150

The additional public debt allows the private sector to more quickly reduce its debt. The additional deposits can be used to repay loans, and this reduces risk in the banking system. There are fewer loans outstanding, and since each loan is a risk, the risk of default is lower than before.

This is an exclusively financial view of the rise in government spending. A reduction of tax burdens would have the same effect, although the distributional consequences would differ. Under a tax-cut scenario, loans would now be repaid, but without any direct creation of jobs. Instead of earning the fresh deposits, the private sector essentially get them for free, in terms of work effort and production (the work has already been done to earn the private revenues from which taxes – at whatever level – are subsequently deducted by government; no new work is done).

If government invests in useful projects, this can increase aggregate social production over the medium to long term. This is due to supply-side effects of better infrastructure, better-educated and -skilled workers or other results. At the same time, there is a demand-side effect through the creation of additional deposits in the balance sheets of the private sector. The latter has something to do with debt, whereas the change in the real economy brought about by the government will have an effect on the potential output of the economy. These issues have to be distinguished. Problems with the performance of the economy should be approached from the supply side, and problems with insufficient demand for goods and services (insufficient to enable full use of existing productive capacity, as demonstrated by idle factories or involuntary unemployment) should be approached from the demand side.

Banking regulation: reserve and capital requirements

Money and credit are social constructions that are unthinkable without regulation. Without property rights and enforceable contracts, neither money nor credit would exist to the extent that we see today. Without a central bank there would be no state money (cash and reserves), and without taxes, no destruction of state money. The construction of a central bank that lends to commercial banks against collateral enables banks to develop an extensive portfolio of loans. As has been stated above, there are some brakes to loan creation:

1   The interest rate limits demand for loans.
2   As more loans are issued, the risk rises that some borrowers will prove unable to repay.
3   If a bank extends more loans than other banks, it will have to pay more interest, since more reserves will flow out from that bank than will flow in, over time. This reduces relative profits.
4   If a bank extends more loans than other banks, it will be dependent on other banks or the central bank to keep lending reserves to it, which presents a solvency risk if they decide to stop doing so.

Apart from these systemic brakes, there are additional factors that limit aggregate lending. The essential banking regulations of the last decades in this respect were reserve requirements and capital requirements. Whereas the latter probably have some effect, the former are rather ineffective. Reserve requirements

Table 7.1 Reserve and capital requirements

	Reserve requirements	*Capital requirements*
Rules	National (central bank)	International (Basle III)
Application	Quantity of deposits (liabilities)	Quantity and quality of assets
Buffer	Reserves (assets)	Equity (liabilities)
Quantity	ECB: 1 per cent	Risk-weighted

are concerned with the liability side of a bank, whereas capital requirements are concerned with the asset side. Both are explained in detail in the following.

Minimum reserve requirements

Reserve requirements refer to the deposits of a bank. Whether only sight deposits are affected, or time and savings deposits as well, depends on national regulation. Here's how they work: for every €100 in deposits, exactly €x must be held by the bank in required reserves, stashed in the bank's reserve deposit account at the central bank. In the Eurozone, x used to be 2 per cent, but it was lowered to 1 per cent in January 2012. The deposits with a maturity of up to two years multiplied with the reserve requirement ratio yield the minimum required reserves. Let's assume that a bank has the following balance sheet:

commercial bank			
t-bonds	100	deposits	700
loans	800	equity	200
reserves	100	loan (IB)	100

The value of minimum reserves can be calculated as the sum of deposits multiplied by the required reserve ratio. In this case, it would be €800 multiplied by 1 per cent, which is €8. The bank would have to hold at least €8 in reserves at the central bank. According to the balance sheet, the bank holds €100 in its reserve deposit account, and hence complies with the regulation. Of the €100, €8 are required reserves and the other €92 can be used to cover an increase in customers' demand for cash, or for increased transfers or loans to other banks.

Minimum reserves cannot be lent out. However, the ECB pays an interest rate equal to the base rate on required reserves. Some central banks do not pay an interest on required reserves. Other central banks do not have a minimum reserve requirement at all (among these the central banks of Canada, the UK and Sweden).

What are the consequences of a reserve requirement? Let's look at a bank that just extended a loan. Apart from deposits worth €100 and the €100 loan, its balance sheet is empty. The bank has to meet the regulation regarding the reserve requirements and needs to come up with €1. Where will this €1 come from?

commercial bank			
loans	100	deposits	100

The bank can borrow reserves from the central bank or from other banks. The rating of the collateral it submits in order to do this is crucial. The bank could take the first instalment of the loan it has made to a client, and ask a rating agency for an opinion on its creditworthiness. If the loan is amortised in 100 instalments of €1, the default risk on the first instalment is quite low. Some rating agency will surely offer the highest rating to a claim on the first instalment of this loan. The ECB would then accept this collateral, as would other banks.

The bank would therefore borrow €1 in reserves on the interbank market from another bank. Its balance sheets would look like this:

_____commercial bank_____			
loans	100	deposits	100
reserves	1	loan (IB)	1

Box 7.1 Minimum reserve requirements in China and Brazil

Some central banks continue to use minimum reserve requirements to the present day. In Brazil, different rates are applied to different deposits, and in China reserve ratios stood at about 20 per cent for deposits. However, the increase in the ratio over recent years has not stopped the burgeoning increase in net credit (and bank debt) in China. This is hardly surprising given the weak effect a reserve ratio has on balance sheets.

Alternatively, the bank can use other assets as collateral. This example shows that reserve requirements do not limit the extension of credit. Banks can borrow reserves after extending a loan to a client, and do not have to wait until they have enough reserves (and hence cash) before they can extend a loan. This is also the reason why many central banks have abolished reserve requirements or reduced the ratio to extremely low levels. Before central banks started to pay interest on required reserves, they acted like a tax on banks. Required reserves could not be lent out and no interest rate was paid, which led to a fall in profit, which merely harmed the financial viability of the bank. Yet the reserve requirement had essentially no consequences for the volume of bank loans extended. It served no useful purpose.

That said, an increase in the required reserve ratio at an interest-rate-setting central bank is not without effects. Assuming that the central bank increases the required reserves ratio, the banks will demand more reserves on the interbank market. This will drive up the short-term interest rate until the borrowing rate for overnight loans offered to banks by the central bank is reached. Banks can borrow from the central bank against collateral, and hence will not be willing to bid up the interbank market interest rate above the rate of the marginal lending facility. If they were to do so regardless, the central bank would have to intervene, since the interbank market rate is used as a policy instrument. The central bank can use open market operations to actively increase the amount of reserves held in the banking system, so that the (short-term) interest rate on the interbank market falls back to the desired level.

Originally, reserve requirements were intended to ensure a certain stock of liquidity at the participating banks. This way, a bank's ability to honour demands for cash and for transfers to other banks was secured, since reserves are needed for both purposes. A higher quantity of reserves, it was thought, would increase the safety of the banking system and improve the quantity of loans that can be supplied by banks.

However, reserve requirements have to be fulfilled *ex post*, not before lending. Given the structure of today's banking systems, the logic in favour of reserve requirements is obsolete. If loans can partially be used as collateral for central bank loans, then a bank is not limited by the quantity of required reserves.

Minimum capital requirements

Capital requirements, by contrast, connect to the other side of a bank's balance sheet. The bank is forced to back up its risky assets with an equity cushion. This should strengthen the bank's ability to survive losses.

Capital requirements are developed internationally through the so-called Basel Accords, and then transformed into national law (although the adoption of this set of rules – we are at 'Basel III' now – is not compulsory). In the following example, we assume that loans are backed up by equity at 10 per cent of the original (nominal) value of the loan book. The balance sheet looks as follows:

commercial bank			
t-bonds	100	deposits	700
loans	800	equity	200
reserves	100	loan (IB)	100

The bank has to have €80 in equity, since it has extended loans worth €800 to the private sector. Holdings of sovereign securities or reserves need not be backed up by equity, since both are usually deemed risk-free. The Eurozone is the only major example of a currency without risk-free sovereign securities. However, for reasons explained in the previous section, it seems that today even the sovereign securities of the Eurozone's economically weaker, most heavily indebted member nations are perceived as essentially risk-free.

Equity can be raised through paying-in of money by investors or accumulated through retained earnings. If the bank wants to extend more loans, it must hold more equity. One way to increase equity is to issue shares. The bank of the purchaser of these shares will transfer additional reserves to the issuing bank in return for the shares.

Box 7.2 The money multiplier in macroeconomics textbooks

Surprisingly, most macroeconomics textbooks still tell a story in which a central bank lends reserves to commercial banks which then lend out the reserves to the private sector. The quantity of loans divided by the quantity of reserves equals the money multiplier. Since neither firms nor households have accounts at the central bank and loans are not paid out in cash, this view turns out to be completely unfounded. There is no interface between accounts at the central bank and accounts at banks, which is why banks cannot transfer their deposits at the central bank to households and firms.

bank 1					bank 2	
t-bonds	100	deposits	700	loans	500	deposits	550
loans	800	equity	300	reserves	50	equity	100
reserves	200	loans (IB)	100	shares	100		

The share-issuing bank would see equity and reserves increase by €100, whereas the bank whose client is investing in the shares would have €100 in reserves less, but shares worth €100 would be added (for simplicity, we've assumed bank 2 buys newly issued shares from bank 1 on bank 2's own account, rather than on behalf of one of its clients). The share-issuing bank can use its newly acquired reserves as it sees fit. Its now higher equity allows it to absorb bigger losses than before.

Let's assume that the share-issuing bank's loan portfolio was re-evaluated. The new value is €150 lower than before.

commercial bank			
t-bonds	100	deposits	800
loans	650	equity	50
reserves	200	loan (IB)	100

The asset side is reduced to €950, so the liability side must be adjusted accordingly. It used to sum up to €1,100, but since equity is the difference between assets and other liabilities, equity is now reduced by €150. We are left with equity of €50. If equity had been €100, then equity now would be negative and the bank would be insolvent. Equity protects the bank from insolvency.

However, in some cases increases in equity are not necessarily the best way for a bank to stay within the bounds of the regulatory established minimum capital requirement. There is an alternative: if banks find themselves holding too little capital to meet the requirement, they can also comply with the minimum capital requirement by selling parts of their assets that require capital (in general this means selling part of their loan book to some other financial institution), thus reducing their need for capital. If, however, many banks use this strategy, then a fall in asset prices can follow that has offsetting effects, making it harder to meet their capital ratio requirements by reducing the value of their assets.

The Basel III Accords are a main instrument of today's banking regulation as applied in most countries. The Basel Committee on Banking Supervision, which is located at the Bank for International Settlements (BIS) in Basel, Switzerland, develops and issues these regulatory standards. The BIS, which is a public and not a private institution, is something like a consultant to central banks.

8   Inflation and deflation

Inflation and deflation describe changes in the level of prices, which feed back on the level of economic activity. Because they change the purchasing power of deposits and cash, they change the distribution of income and wealth. Most central banks have an inflation target, set to prevent both too low or negative consumer price level inflation rates (deflation) and too high inflation rates. What are the consequences of inflation and deflation for the actors in the economy?

Inflation is defined as the rise in the price of a basket of consumer goods over a certain amount of time. The basket consists of a selection of specific goods and services, established according to some economic agency's definition. The CPI contains mostly consumption goods. It can be visualised as a shopping trolley containing typical goods of consumption, but also services like haircuts and visits to the dentist. The value of these goods and services is weighted according to their typical share in a typical family's total consumption spending. The result is the price of the basket of goods and services in the shopping trolley. If the contents increase in price after 30 days, we speak of inflation; if it falls, we speak of deflation.

Theories of inflation

While most people almost instinctively believe that an increase in the monetary supply – however that is defined – leads to inflation, the reality is more complicated. The correlation between different measures of monetary aggregates and CPI is weak. While an increase in deposits caused by an increase in private sector borrowing can potentially lead to a higher rate of inflation, there may be several slips between the cup and the lip.

Generally speaking, an increase in the amount of deposits held by the private sector can be inflationary if any resulting increase in spending drives up either wages or the prices of goods. The first is called demand-pull inflation, and the second is cost-push inflation.

Imagine a rise in the price of oil. That alone does not change the inflation rate, since it is just one price among many inputs affecting the final price of consumer goods and services in the shopping trolley. However, if companies react to a rise in their costs of production – after all, oil is now more expensive – by increasing prices of final consumer goods they produce, the overall consumer price level might shift upwards. This is more likely to happen as companies approach their maximum capacity utilisation.

Similarly, increases in wages can lead to higher inflation if companies decide to roll over the increase in costs by increasing the price of the goods or services they produce (note, however, that if they're operating in competitive markets, they may find it difficult to get away with this). This is also called wage-push inflation. The perpetual fight over the distribution of income sits in the background of inflation rate changes. If unions are weak or unemployment is high, or both, wages tend to grow slowly. They even might grow less than productivity. That will tend to drive prices down – but it will also drive purchasing power down, since workers' incomes are also the main wellspring of aggregate consumer demand in an economy.

Demand-pull inflation arises if and when growth in aggregate demand increases faster than growth in aggregate production. The additional demand might come from higher net debt of the private, public or external sector. All these are able to inject deposits into the economy by increasing their spending. There is no magical power possessed by deposits created by government debt that would lead to an increase in the inflation rate, while the private sector can borrow as much as it wants without ever creating inflation. The same goes for exports. If the rest of the world demands more goods and exports rise, then the inflation rate might pick up.

On the other hand, think back to our discussion of economies of scale early on in this book. As demand for any particular good increases, companies tend to invest in scaling up production of that good. As they do so, they achieve improved economies of scale. In a competitive market, there will be constant pressure to drive down prices. Over time, then, increased demand actually drives unit prices down, not up!

Another route to inflation is through a depreciation or devaluation of the currency. This results in higher import prices, causing the domestic consumer price level to increase. Domestic firms might react by increasing their own prices to adjust to the foreign competition and pocket so-called windfall profits.

Wild swings in exchange rates can have serious consequences for small and open economies. If inflation increases unexpectedly, households might prefer to save in foreign currency. To do this, they would sell domestic currency, thus driving down its value. This is a self-fulfilling prophecy that leads to an unwanted drop of the exchange rate, and thus a higher level of prices that erodes the purchasing power of consumers. If these react by demanding higher wages, a potential upward spiral of ever-increasing inflation rates might result. Wage indexation – tying wage increases automatically to price increases – is very likely behind the very high inflation rates of the 1970s and should be avoided.

Inflation, deflation and balance sheets

Let's assume that we used to have an inflation rate of 0 per cent, but now it has risen to 10 per cent. What is the effect on profits of a production company financed by bank loans? What is the effect on the bank's profits?

	bank				firm	
loan	100	deposits 100	deposits	100	loan	100

The firm has financed its operations by borrowing from its principal bank. The deposits were used to buy raw materials and labour.

	bank				firm	
loan	100	deposits 100	raw materials 50		loan	100
			labour	50		

After production, which we'll assume takes a year, the firm's output is worth €110. This is somewhat higher than the value of raw materials and labour used in the process. The market price is not exclusively derived from costs (although prices of goods are very often set by firms as a mark-up over their all-in unit production costs); it is also determined by wage setting, costs of inputs and the level of competition. Current wages will be determined mainly by the level of wages and incomes of the recent past.

	bank				firm	
loan	100	deposits 100	production	110	loan	100
					equity	10

The goods produced are then sold, and the firm's incoming deposits after it sells what it has produced are used, first of all, to repay the loan it took up a year ago. We assume that the interest rate on the loan was 5 per cent. The bank makes a profit of €5 since it gets 5 per cent on the €100 loan. The firm also makes a profit of €5, which increases its equity if these earnings are retained, or alternatively, the earnings may be distributed to the firm's owners (or to the workers if the firm is a profit-sharing cooperative), or some combination of these things. After repayment of the bank loan, the balance sheets look like this:

	bank				firm	
~~loan~~	~~100~~	~~deposits 100~~	~~deposits~~	~~110~~	~~loan~~	~~100~~
reserves	10	deposits 5	deposits	5	equity	5
		equity 5				

The bank has gained €10 in reserves, since customers of other banks have transferred €10 net to the firm. The firm keeps €5 from the €10, and the bank also keeps €5 for itself; the carry-over is counted as increased equity of the bank. The firm keeps €5 on its balance at the bank and has no corresponding liabilities. In the balance sheet above, these €5 are also booked as equity for the firm (the money is kept as retained earnings; it isn't distributed as dividends or whatever). The original loan and the deposits that had been created have been cancelled, since by transferring its deposits the firm has amortised the loan.

Now, what would happen if the inflation rate jumped suddenly and unexpectedly to 10 per cent? We assume that raw materials and labour were bought at the beginning of the period under consideration, on 1 January. Costs of €100 were incurred. The loan is still enough to finance production. However, the nominal value of the output has risen by 10 per cent during the ensuing year, and after the rise in the price level over the course of the year, the value of the firm's output when the production process is finished now stands at €121.

bank			firm	
loan	100	deposits 100	production 121	loan	100
				equity	21

This has changed the distribution of profits, especially when it comes to purchasing power. After repayment of the loan, the firm has a profit of €16, while the profit of the bank is the same as before. However, the purchasing power of the bank's profit has decreased, since €5 have only 90.9 per cent of the purchasing power they did a year ago. After all, consumer goods prices have increased by 10 per cent. This also affects the firm, but the purchasing power of €16 after compensating for an inflation of 10 per cent is still higher than that of €5 with an inflation rate of zero.

bank				firm	
~~loan~~	~~100~~	~~deposits 100~~	~~deposits 110~~	~~loan~~	~~100~~
reserves	21	deposits 16	deposits 16	equity	16
		equity 5			

It can easily be verified that the firm has made some unexpected profits. At the same time, the purchasing power of deposits is reduced, which worsens the bank's situation. It can also be seen that households lose out because of the higher price level. Instead of €110, buying the firm's output now costs consumers €121, and if households have purchased the entirety of the output, either their assets have decreased by €11 or their debt increased by the same amount.

We see that price level inflation has differing consequences for banks, households and firms. Firms would like to increase their production, since they have higher profits and prices are rising. They could increase their purchases of raw materials and labour. No changes in prices and wages are to be expected if the supply of these inputs is high and demand is not yet too strong. If, however, an expected scarcity of these inputs is a problem, this can lead to higher prices. In that case, firms would try to roll over higher costs onto consumers by increasing their prices.

Since consumers are funded by family members who are recipients of wages, this might work. Under pressure of rising prices, workers will probably have tried to enforce a rise in wages. This would increase their purchasing power in the short run, but in the medium term further price rises of consumption goods might destroy this advantage. The worst-case scenario is a wage–price spiral.

Banks, for their part, have lower profits than before the rise of the price level, if one considers the purchasing power of their net profits. They too could raise their prices, i.e. the interest rate they charge borrowers (the price of credit is the going interest rate). A rise in the interest rate would increase profits, at least as long as the base rate of the central bank is not moved. Obviously, the central bank could increase the base rate, which would certainly lead to banks increasing the interest rates on loans. This would increase costs for firms that have to finance operations on credit, and might lead to a fall in production. Due to weaker demand on the goods and labour markets, prices would stop rising as quickly, or even start falling.

Apart from the consequences for production, a change in the rate of inflation also has consequences for the distribution of wealth and debt in an economy. Let's consider a household and a bank that has extended a mortgage to that household. The mortgage is worth €100, and so is the house whose purchase the household financed by taking on the mortgage.

bank			household		
mortgage	100	deposits 100	income	20	expenditures 10
reserves	20	loan (IB) 20	savings	10	
			house	100	mortgage 100
			deposits	20	net wealth 20
				(+10)	(+10)

If the household's breadwinners were to put all of their savings into debt repayment, it would take them ten years to repay the mortgage (which we assume is interest-free to avoid cluttering the balance sheet). We assume a one-time rise in the inflation rate by 10 per cent. The balance sheet of the bank is not affected, since the household still owes the bank the nominal mortgage debt of €100. However, the household experiences some changes. The value of its house has increased to €110, the yearly wage to €22 and expenditures to €11. This causes a rise in nominal savings (+€1), deposits (+€1) and net wealth (+€1).

bank			household		
mortgage	100	deposits 100	income	22	expenditures 11
reserves	20	loan (IB) 20	savings	11	
			house	110	mortgage 100
			deposits	21	net wealth 31
				(+11)	(+11)

Repayment of the mortgage would now take nine years instead of ten, since the household has higher savings. This increase is only nominal, as it has been caused by higher wages. The savings rate – savings divided by income – is still at 50 per cent, as the household did not reduce its consumption. The household is wealthier now, after the house price increased. If the household would like to use this increase in wealth to increase consumption, it would have to sell the house or take out another mortgage that is secured by the higher value of the house.

While this household would be representative for the middle class, other households would have other experiences. A relatively poor household that rents a flat would be neither better nor worse off. The wage has increased, but prices have been rising as well. If a household does not own any assets and does not owe any debts, the rise in the rate of inflation will not affect it. Recipients of rents and transfers, however, suffer from the increase in the price level if their nominal monetary income does not rise.

The situation is different if the household is relatively wealthy, like the following household, which owns a variety of assets:

household			
income	50	expenditures	11
		savings	39
house	110	net wealth	349
t-bonds	100		
stocks	100		
deposits	39		

Income paid as interest on savings will not change. The rise in consumer prices leads to a rise in expenditures, and hence to a reduction of savings by €1 to €39. The household has no debts, hence it will not benefit from more inflation. Perhaps its net wealth increases due to the rise in house prices, but price changes of sovereign securities or shares could neutralise this effect. Deposits held at the bank lose a part of their purchasing power.

Box 8.1 Expropriation of savers by falling interest rates?

Lower interest rates cannot be expropriation, many comments to the contrary notwithstanding. There is no right to a (positive) rate of interest, and a negative interest rate can be dodged by holding cash. Nobody is forced to hold wealth in the form of deposits at the bank. However, the nominal value of €100 cannot be reduced as long as there is a deposit insurance scheme. €100 invested in shares, bonds or real estate, in contrast, might very well incur a loss in the investor's nominal wealth, if the nominal price of these financial assets, as measured in euro, declines.

In certain circumstances, higher rates of inflation can lead to a rise in speculation. If households expect increases in prices of assets like real estate, they might be willing to borrow even if interest rates are high. Firms might come up with the idea of buying more raw materials than before. Since their price is on the rise, it would be profitable to build up loan-financed inventories. In principle, both cases of speculation are identical. The speculator borrows and hopes that the incremental rise in the price of the asset that he purchased is, over a given time-frame, higher than the rate of interest he pays on the loan he has taken out.

bank				speculator		
loan	100	deposits	0 asset	100	loan	100
reserves	0	loan (IB) 100				

The speculator transfers his deposits to the seller of the speculative asset. If the seller has his account with another bank, the bank will need to borrow reserves. The deposits are reduced to zero, since the speculator has no more deposits and the seller of the asset keeps his deposits at another bank. The bank pays an interest rate on the interbank market and gets an interest rate from the speculator. As long as the latter is higher than the former, the bank makes a profit. The speculator turns a profit if the asset value increases more than the interest rate. Let's assume that the asset increases in value by 10 per cent and the loan's interest rate is 5 per cent. The loan matures, but the speculator borrows again in order to repay the old loan. The following balance sheets display this development.

bank				speculator		
loan	105	deposits	0 asset	110	loan	105
reserves	0	loan (IB) 100			net wealth	5
		equity	5			

On paper, the bank has made a profit. It is based on a loan of €105, which depends on the market value of the speculator's asset. If that market value falls below €105, then the speculator will not be able to repay the loan without recourse to other wealth. Net wealth is solely based on the evaluation of this asset's value. Note that the only thing that is happening here is a change in the monetary valuation of the asset, without any equivalent changes in reality. An asset's value always depends on subjective assessments on which market participants act. There is no such thing as a fundamental or intrinsic value.

The distributionary consequences of a change in the rate of inflation can be significant. For one thing, high inflation has a rather expansionary effect on the economy. If the inflation rate rises to more than 50 per cent per month, we speak of hyperinflation. Capital markets mostly come to a standstill. Uncertainty with respect to the future inflation rate will cause banks to lend only at significantly more than 50 per cent per month, and only for short maturities, to reduce the risk of a complete loss in the case of higher inflation.

Historical cases of hyperinflation were not set off by an increase in the quantity of money, as popular opinion has it, but by a strong reduction of production capacities. This was the cause of the hyperinflation in the Weimar

Republic. In the aftermath of the First World War and the unfortunate Versailles Treaty, French troops occupied the Rhineland from 1919 onwards, and from January 1923 also the Ruhr area – the industrial heartland of Germany. Workers there opposed France's attempt to annex the region, and called a general strike. The German government decided to grant workers in that area continued payment of wages, even though most of them were on strike, and production had therefore plummeted. This is what led to a rise in the inflation rate. In September 1923, the government stopped its support for the workers. One year later, in January 1924, hyperinflation ended with the introduction of a new currency (Rentenmark), and in 1925 the last foreign troops left the Ruhr area.

Another circumstance that can lead to hyperinflation is government debt in foreign currency. If a government has debts of this kind, and can neither create the foreign currency itself nor gain sufficient access to credit, it could try to exchange large amounts of domestic for foreign currency in order to repay its debts. This exchange of currencies will lead to first subtle, then serious changes in the exchange rate of the currencies used. The domestic currency will fall in value, which leads to imports becoming more expensive. This causes the price level to shift upward; this phenomenon is called 'imported inflation'. Conversely, the fall in the value of the domestic currency will make it cheaper to buy goods produced in the country by workers paid in domestic currency, leading to a rise in competitiveness on global markets; this will cause an outflow of goods and services.

Government access to central bank reserves is crucial for these kinds of operations. In most countries, the government is not allowed to go into debt in foreign currency. The countries of the Eurozone are an exception. Germany issues almost all bonds in euro, and the same goes for public organisations like the German Bank for Reconstruction (*Kreditanstalt für Wiederaufbau*). Developing and emerging economies sometimes need US dollars to buy oil or weapons. Since these governments see their political power threatened, they accept the long-run problems of foreign currency denominated debt in order to arm themselves. The crucial issue is that the debt is denominated in foreign and not domestic currency. In times of need, the central bank can provide unlimited quantities of domestic currency, but not foreign currency.

The problem with deflation

The opposite of inflation is deflation. Deflation is just as problematic as hyperinflation, since it destroys the foundations of the monetary circuit. Let's return to the example above. We assume that a firm takes out a loan from its bank and procures factors of production. However, the value of production now sinks, because of a drop in the level of prices. If we assume that prices dropped by 10 per cent on average, the price the firm can obtain for its output once it's done producing it is not €110 but only €99.

The firm will not be able to repay the loan it took up to finance production. It has to transfer €105 in deposits, but possesses only €99. The fall in the price level has led to a reduction of revenue, and this now exacerbates the repayment of the loan. Apart from this, the firm is insolvent, because its liabilities exceed its assets.

The bank that financed the firm's production by extending a loan to it has incurred a loss, since it issued €100 in deposits but only €99 were returned. It probably borrowed some reserves during settlement with other banks. The €100 in reserves were drained when the firm spent the deposits. The bank was forced to borrow €100 on the interbank market.

bank				firm		
loan	105	deposits	99	deposits	99	loan	105
reserves	0	loan (IB)	6			equity	−6
		equity	0				

The €99 in revenues of the firm mean that reserves of the same quantity flow back to the bank. While the firm cannot repay the loan and is insolvent, the situation of the bank depends on accounting. The bank can almost repay the interbank market loan (interest rate: 3 per cent), but not quite. The question is whether the loan has to be written down. The deposits transferred by the firm have reduced the outstanding loan from €105 to €6. As it stands, the bank has no negative equity, since the loan was not written down. If it does get written down, equity would be negative (€0−€6=−€6). The bank would be insolvent as well.

Deflation often develops in an environment of declining wages and revenues, and hence falling profits. Deflation makes debt repayment more difficult. Creditors can gain, since the purchasing power of one unit of currency rises. After all, €1 buys more if the price level has been falling. On the other hand, if wages are declining, this means workers have to work longer to pay off a fixed amount of debt. The higher the level of debt, the more relevant is this issue for an economy.

Macroeconomics and business cycles

The monetary circuit of a monetary economy depicted in Figure 3.1 is somewhat oversimplified, but nevertheless can be used to explain some essential functions. Firms borrow from banks, which extend loans, which they use to purchase the input factors. This creates incomes at households that these then use to buy the output. If households withdraw some deposits from circulation by building up savings, then the circuit might falter. Deposits at banks that are not spent reduce the potential income of other market participants.

Rising incomes, however, are a precondition for economic growth. Growth is reduced because the saving of the private sector reduces demand – since money not spent is essentially hoarded in economically inactive pools. This effect is more likely when income and wealth inequality are high: the fact that relatively wealthy persons save relatively more of their income than the rest of us means they use proportionately less of their income for purchasing goods and services. Instead, as people get wealthier, their savings calculated as a proportion of their income tends to increase. This occurs without any effect on loan-financed investments, because as we've seen, banks do not on-lend money from savers to borrowers: in balance sheet terms, bank lending has nothing to do with savers' saving.

Additional saving thus leads to a fall in production via the resultant decrease in consumer demand. In times of strong demand and inflation, this can be advantageous; in times of weak demand, this weakens the economy further. A fall in production can lead to a vicious cycle: firms are not able to sell their production, and hence they shed workers, which consequently see their collective income fall as unemployment rises. This leads to further downward adjustment of prices, as sellers slash prices to try to attract buyers in the face of weak demand.

The increase in uncertainty leads to increased hoarding and debt repayment in the private sector – especially by firms – and that leads to the next step in the downward spiral. After all, there's no incentive to invest in expanding production capacity or hiring more workers if your factory is already half-idle and everyone knows consumer demand is weak.

Another difficulty arises from stagnation or fall in the amount of credit owed by the private sector. The latter happens when borrowers use more deposits to repay loans than they add by taking out new loans. Too few deposits circulate and production cannot be sold at established prices. Prices will have to come down, or some of the goods produced will not be sold. In the medium term this leads to a fall in production, to allow firms to sell-off accumulated inventories. This leads to more unemployment and lower incomes, while the price adjustment could also lead to lower wages. A lower price is something that a firm can only afford if the prices of inputs have fallen or productivity has increased.

The foregoing makes it clear why deflation should be avoided at all costs – and why ECB chief Mario Draghi has, at time of writing, been taking steps that seem almost desperate to prevent deflation in the Eurozone.

Hoarding of money can also happen at firms that build up a precautionary fund or repay debts. It could be real economy firms (non-financial companies) that do this to reduce their risk of insolvency in turbulent times.

Banks can also cause a decline in net outstanding loans, at times when fundamental macroeconomic uncertainty makes them unwilling to expand their loan portfolios. Sometimes banks themselves have to repay loans soon, or sometimes they're unable to assess the risk of investment projects.

Today, Figure 3.1 would be more realistic if the model balance sheet were adjusted to show that households can also borrow from banks and firms are also able to save. The key issue, however, is that as long as more loans are taken out than repaid, additional deposits enter the monetary circuit. If investment falls or saving rises, the amount of circulating deposits that contribute to effective aggregate demand will be lower.

Some economists claim that saving would be good for the economy. While this might be so in times of strong demand, it is not the case when the economy suffers from a lack of demand. If I decide to save more of my income, I accordingly need

---

Box 8.2 The Japanese sickness

The economist Richard Koo coined the term 'Japanese sickness', which he associates with stagnating loan demand in Japan and resulting weak economic growth. After a stock and real estate bubble burst in the early 1990s, aggregate private sector demand in Japan was weak. However, government spending stabilised the economy. While Japan is often described as the 'sick man of Asia', its economic growth rate has been low but positive over the years. Compared with Greece, Ireland or Spain, the country has done well.

---

to spend less. Saving is income not spent. Since my spending is somebody else's income, the reduced demand will induce a fall in economic activity.

A look at our model balance sheets does not reveal anything positive to be gained for the economy as a whole from increased savings, either. If I use my €5 to increase my deposits at the bank instead of spending them on a restaurant visit, the bank has more disposable cash. However, the bank had not been faced with any lack of cash on hand, and therefore the bank will bring the cash to the nearest branch of the central bank. It does so because the bank can exchange the cash for reserves, which it can lend out on the interbank market.

This will push down the short-term interest rate on the interbank market, which triggers automatic intervention by the central bank. The latter engages in open market operations by selling bonds to the bank in return for 'my' reserves. Alternatively, the bank uses 'my' reserves to pay down debt vis-à-vis the central bank. It thus reduces interest rate costs. This result shows that a rise in savings is not generally beneficial to the economy. It is not true that more loans are made, since banks do not need reserves to create loans and deposits.

A more precise view of credit and debt mediated macroeconomic relationships is necessary to understand the dynamics of an economy. The relation between debt and demand, which is created by debt-financed expenditures, is essential. Since today the external sector (trade with foreign countries) plays a large macroeconomic role, we will move from our balance sheet models of a closed economy to balance sheet models of an open economy in the next chapter.

Part III

Analysis

The GFC of 2007–8 started with the US sub-prime crisis of 2007, but over time it seized the whole world. The insight that global financial contract interconnections resulting from modern portfolio management can result in a situation in which speculative bubbles in the US real estate market lead to bank failures in Germany has come at a steep price. With hindsight, it became clear that hundreds of billions of euro in foreign assets had been grossly (and fraudulently) overvalued. Apart from US financial assets connected to real estate, Spanish and Irish assets were affected in a similar way.

A crucial issue here is foreign debt. As we have seen, it increased in countries that had imported more than they exported. Conversely, total foreign debts were reduced or foreign assets were built up in countries where exports exceeded imports. Hence, high foreign debts in some European countries went hand in hand with German export surpluses. Why have these surpluses and deficits been so high?

The next two sections shed some light on these questions of international trade. We'll look at adjustment processes in the European Union in the lead-up to the introduction of the euro, first by examining a system of fixed exchange rates (the Bretton Woods system), and then a system of flexible exchange rates. These will serve as benchmark scenarios to understand adjustment processes in the Eurozone.

It will become clear that the euro suffers from a faulty design. The underlying problem seems to be a poor understanding of monetary theory. While Eurozone regulations to limit increases in government debt were quite strict, there were no limits at all on how much credit commercial banks could extend to borrowers, or for what purposes. Moreover, current account imbalances were ignored. These issues will be explored in the next two chapters.

9 A macroeconomic model

In an open economy, we complement the demand equation – production equals the sum of consumption, investment and government spending – by an additional term that adds the external demand components: exports and imports. This is especially relevant for countries that engage in active trading and build up or run down assets and liabilities vis-à-vis foreign countries.

In an open economy, domestic demand is supplemented by exports (EX) and diminished by imports (IM).

$$Y = C + I + G + EX - IM$$

An increase in demand for imports does not increase domestic income, since a larger share of consumption, investment, government spending and even some of the inputs to goods produced for export is now covered by imports. On the other side of the deal, exports are added to demand, which do increase national income.

Given the above equation, it becomes clear that an economy does not have to absorb its entire production. The difference between production (Y) and domestic demand ($C + I + G$) matches the current account surplus or deficit ($EX - IM$).

The savings of an economy are defined as the part of income which has not been spent on goods and services. The following formula expresses this relation for an open economy:

$$S = I + EX - IM$$

Savings are equal to investment plus exports minus imports. This is a result of the possibility for a country's savers to run up savings in the form of foreign assets. If an economy has a current account surplus (exports exceed imports), then the private sector will build up a stock of foreign assets, or will reduce the stock of liabilities its economic actors owe to foreign countries. An example will shed light on this situation.

Assume that country D with the dollar as its currency dollar trades with country P that uses pound sterling as its currency. To keep things simple, we'll set the exchange rate at parity (one dollar equals one pound). Both countries use their own currencies to purchase imports. Assume the exports of D to P exceed those of P to D. At the end of a given time period, people in D hold more pounds than people in P hold dollars. After exchanging currencies so that people hold domestic currency and not foreign currency, the people of D are still holding some pounds. They have earned more pounds than people of P earned dollars, so when P has swapped all dollars for pounds some pounds are left in the hands of the people of D. These holdings correspond to net savings arising from international trade.

The foreign money held by successful exporters from country D can be used in different ways: pay workers or suppliers, or reduce foreign debts denominated in foreign currency. Alternatively, interest-bearing (domestic or foreign) securities could be purchased. Or some land, firms, corporate shares or other assets in the foreign country in which one holds some foreign currency could be purchased. Last but not least, foreign currency can be exchanged into other currencies.

In any case, country D's positive current account means that net savings will rise by the difference between exports and imports, because somebody holds more assets than before. These assets might be used to pay down (foreign) debt, which does not change the fact that it is income not spent – savings – that has been used to achieve that. Whether the assets that have appeared because of the net exports are foreign or domestic depends on the portfolio preferences of international investors. Vice versa, P, the foreign country with the negative current account, sees its foreign debt increase or its foreign assets fall or a combination of both.

Since exports of one country are the imports of another, not all countries can have a current account surplus. Who or what determines this question of surplus or deficit?

As we've seen, domestic production is partially used up domestically. Government spending that falls on domestic production as well as consumption and investment; as long as these are not based on imported products, government spending will increase demand for domestic purposes.

If, for instance, given some fixed level of incomes, there is an increase of consumption of domestically produced goods and services and a decrease in exports, then savings will adjust as well. The fall in exports will translate into a fall in savings, since the private sector will have consumed goods that otherwise would have led to the accumulation of claims vis-à-vis foreigners. Selling to a domestic resident does not increase private sector savings because one party has a higher income, but the other has higher expenses. If one household saves more and another saves less, then private sector savings are unchanged.

The opposite happens when consumption is diminished. This is why consumption plays a major role in the economy. Consumption depends on income; and this means that political reforms can have some leverage. Increasing VAT while lowering taxes for the affluent probably has the effect of diminishing domestic demand, because workers will have to pay higher prices and the affluent will probably not increase their spending to overcompensate this fall in demand. Also, weakening unions will change their power in wage negotiations and lead to relatively less wage growth. This can lead to a loss of purchasing power and hence force companies to export their surplus production if productivity grows faster than nominal wages.

Falling real wages will probably lead to lower consumption. The same goes for a fall in the exchange rate. In the short term, the adverse movement in the exchange rate will increase the price of imports, whereas domestic goods prices (unless they are produced using a large amount of imported inputs) will hold relatively steady. So, consumption will shift towards domestically produced goods and services and away from imports. The result is a positive current account as exports rise above imports. The rest of the world is now in a debtor position vis-à-vis the country we are looking at.

On the other hand, a strong increase of investment can lead to higher consumption. As we've seen, a rise in investment leads to a rise in national income. The workers producing investment goods will save some proportion of their increased income, and will spend some larger fraction of their increased income. This will lead to a current account deficit as imports rise above exports. Our country becomes a net debtor to the rest of the world. Its foreign debts are increasing, or its foreign assets decreasing, or both. This usually cannot go on forever and hence will at some point stop.

As we saw in the last chapter, when net private debt starts to grow more slowly or even falls, imports collapse, and the private sector struggles to increase savings. These negative effects on demand, as we've seen in Spain among other countries, can lead to economic trouble. Countries using their own sovereign currency will likely see their exchange rate fall, which leads to instant changes in relative prices – including dearer oil and foreign machines as well as cheaper domestic labour – with negative consequences for production in the short run. As people spend more money on imports they have less money to spend on domestic goods, given that international goods like oil are preferred to domestic goods.

Also, a fall in the exchange rate will lead international investors to sell domestic assets, which will further depress the exchange rate. This might result in imported inflation as everything produced in the rest of the world is more expensive. Since prices of domestic assets, like real estate, are depressed, it is very probable that investment slows down. This seems to be happening in Brazil now, where real estate prices grow slower than consumer goods prices. It makes sense to investment money in some financial asset that pays an interest rate higher than the inflation rate and wait with the purchase or construction of real estate. This depresses demand and hence the economy will grow more slowly.

Sectoral balances

So far we've looked at national savings, but it might be useful to look a bit closer. Rearranging the balance of payments identity, we get:

$$(S_P - I) + (T - G) + (IM - EX) = 0$$

This sectoral identity says that the change in net financial debt of the private sector (households and firms) plus that of the public sector (government and central bank) and that of the external sector (rest of the world) add up to zero. The private sector net-saves when its savings – income minus consumption minus taxes – are higher than its investment. The public sector net-saves when taxes are higher than government spending. The rest of the world net-saves when our country's imports are higher than its exports.

What for our country is a rising debt caused by a negative current account must be a rise in foreign wealth for the rest of the world. The flow of net savings over one year is added to the financial wealth of the nation or subtracted from its debts or a combination of both. This is how flows of net savings connect with stocks of wealth and debt. In order to build up wealth or repay debt, an economy needs positive net savings. If they are negative, the economy is building up foreign debt or reducing its foreign assets or a combination of both.

An increase in net savings of one sector always goes hand in hand with a rise in the net debts of another. This is a fundamental insight derived from double-entry bookkeeping. It's necessarily so, since savings are composed of claims on another (natural or legal) person residing domestically or in a foreign country.

Households and firms can save by accumulating claims against the state (domestic sovereign securities), or against the rest of the world (foreign assets), or by paying down claims made on them by the government (outstanding taxes, loans) or by the rest of the world (loans from foreign banks, shares held by foreigners). They cannot increase their aggregate savings by building up claims among themselves; within the private sector, it's a zero-sum game, since the savings of one player are the debts of another.

This becomes a question of distribution. Inevitably, for every asset we have a liability, because an asset is a claim to a (potential) monetary stream, which must come from somewhere. This is often forgotten in debates over whether the government is too deeply in debt. In debt to whom? The government's debt is someone's asset.

Understanding the sectoral balances allows us to better assess policy proposals. For instance, in recent years there was a proposal for Eurozone countries to 'tighten their belts', i.e. to reduce private household debt while simultaneously running a government budget surplus and a current account surplus. That is unrealistic, since not all countries can have a current account surplus vis-à-vis the rest of the world at the same time. Within the Eurozone – just as for the world as a whole – the exports of one country are another's imports.

In terms of internal trade within the Eurozone, long-term export surpluses would have to be achieved by individual Eurozone member countries without any exchange rate movement being available to neutralise the increase in 'competitiveness' achieved by wage suppression. This is unlikely to happen. Therefore, the belt-tightening proposal seems misguided, because the only way for it to be consistent with economic growth is for countries outside of the Eurozone to tolerate a sustained increase in their debt (piled up through many years of trade deficits vis-à-vis Eurozone countries). Nevertheless this is the political rhetoric that we have in the Eurozone.

An increase in debt in any one sector could in some cases be traced back to a rise in spending. Higher investment increases private sector debt, higher government spending increases public sector debt, and more exports means one's trading partners in the external sector must increase their debt.

However, a rise in indebtedness of any one sector might also be due to a fall in spending. The private sector may have tried to increase its savings by spending less at a given level of aggregate income. The resulting fall in production will lead to lower incomes for workers, which means less taxes for government and more expenses when unemployment insurance and other social payments kick in to compensate, thus leaving the state with more debts. A fall of imports caused by lower incomes might affect the rest of the world, and changes the balance-of-trade figures. Government might reduce demand further by increasing taxes, or the external sector might do so through a reduction of its imports, which are the exports of the counterparty economy. All of this would lead to a fall in income, but not a fall in debt of the three sectors.

An important insight is that the reduction of spending of one sector will not automatically lead to an increase in spending of another. In neoclassical economics, which is still dominant at universities, it is assumed that a rise in savings will lead to a rise in investment. If we look at this more closely, we will discover an adjustment process triggered by less consumption that leaves the public and external sector as the counterparties, with falling taxes and falling imports causing rises in net debt of these sectors. The rise of net savings of the private sector certainly does not increase expenditures of other sectors. There is no mechanism on the demand side that leads to any kind of equilibrium.

When a person buys an existing asset, like a house or some shares or bonds, bank deposits are usually transferred. The seller is likely to spend the deposits thus acquired, so that a whole chain of purchases and according sales of assets will follow. This portfolio adjustment will go on until the deposits are either destroyed or rest idle in some bank account. Deposits might be destroyed because of taxes that are paid when assets are bought, or the deposits end up in the hands of an indebted party that uses them to reduce its debts. Repayment of a bank loan thus causes deposits to vanish from circulation.

The same logic also applies to increases in expenditures. Neoclassical economics postulates a displacement of private demand (investment and consumption) in case of a rise in government expenditure. The assumption of a so-called *crowding out effect* is based on a misguided understanding of money (called *loanable funds theory*), which assumes that the amount of money is fixed and that market participants compete for it. In consequence, a rise of government spending would not lead to an increase in demand or national income, because it would be compensated by an equally sized fall in private sector demand.

In light of the sectoral identity above, we arrive at a different result. An increase in government spending creates additional income for the private sector. As we have seen, this additional income exists in the form of additional bank deposits owned by the private sector, which was paid to it for delivery of goods, services or labour services. These deposits will be spent onward until such time as someone decides to 'save' the money (hoard it, take it out of active circulation), whether in the form of domestic or foreign savings, or it gets used up in debt settlement (repayment of bank loans or payment of taxes). An increase in public debt hence leads to an increase in private sector and external sector wealth. These sectors do not necessarily reduce their expenditures as a consequence.

Price signals are also not clear. If an increase in government spending were to increase the CPI rate, then private expenses might be reduced. In normal times, however, this is not to be expected. In some cases, additional government spending channelled into goods markets could translate into higher wages, which would pull workers towards the sectors concerned. This could reduce the supply of other goods and services if (and only if) it robs other sectors of workforce resources. The effect assumes a situation of or near full employment, with private firms substituting workers only by paying higher wages or not substituting them at all.

Another kind of price signal are the interest rates on money markets and capital markets. As we've seen, an increase in government spending leads to a fall in the short-term interbank market interest rate if the central bank does not engage in open market operations. No reduction of private investment is to be expected as a result of this.

In summary, it is only when the economy is at or near full employment that a rise in government spending can crowd out private demand. But the displacement of demand would be effected through claims on real resources, not by displacement of credit. Whether such a displacement is reasonable and worthwhile, in light of society's higher objectives, would have to be decided through the political process.

An increase in debt is obviously not the only way of increasing the different varieties of spending. An economy should be able to grow without an increase in sectoral debts. To achieve this, the velocity of money must increase – i.e. incomes must be spent rather than saved, and spent freely and quickly as they come in. A redistribution of society's flow of incomes from relatively poor people to relatively wealthy people tends to lead to less consumption and more savings, since wealthy people already have what they need and have a proportionately lower 'propensity to consume'. In other words, households with relatively low income tend to spend more of their incomes on consumption goods than households that are relatively wealthy. Let's return to the sectoral balances equation for a moment:

$$(S_P - I) + (T - G) + (IM - EX) = 0$$

Some additional logical conclusions can be derived from this equation. Caution is recommended, however – since this is an accounting identity, it does not say anything about causality. We only know what the position of the sectors look like with hindsight, and guessing what would happen to the sectoral balances if investment/government spending/taxes/exports were to rise (fall) would be very speculative. We also cannot assume that a change in one variable has no influence on income and hence economic growth. For instance, a rise in government spending will increase incomes, and this will have an effect on private savings, taxation and imports. A rise in private investment might also result, so that a rise in government spending does not automatically lead to a budget deficit of the public sector.

Let's assume the change in net debt of each sector is exactly zero. Consider a country with over-indebted households in the aftermath of a financial crisis. Households will be anxious to pay down some of their debt. In order to spend less and save more, they reduce investment, but that leads to a fall in national income. In addition, households could try to increase their private savings as a percentage of their income. If private debt is to fall, what must happen to the other variables?

Private sector deleveraging

If $(S_P - I)$ is positive then either $(T - G)$ or $(IM - EX)$ or both should be negative. In other words, high net savings of households are achieved by their possession of additional sovereign securities or additional foreign assets. Hence if the entire equation is to balance out to zero, the government must either lower the tax rates or increases its spending (or a combination of the two); or a fall in imports or rise of exports (or some combination of the two) enables households to buy more foreign assets, which might include sovereign securities. Alternatively, the foreign debts of households can be reduced.

But where do we end up when government does not increase its deficit and neither imports fall nor exports pick up?

Adjustment towards the private sector's target level of savings will happen in any event. Without any intervention of the government's economic policies, something like the following might take place:

The intent of households to save more leads to less consumption. This weakens demand, and hence weakens production and national income as well as imports. The lower income feeds back into consumption, which falls further because households whose income is declining generally spend less.

On the other hand, the declines in production and national income lead to increased government spending, since spending on the social system and unemployment benefits will increase. Tax revenues will fall as well, since a lower level of employment causes income taxes and value-added taxes to fall. This reaction of the public sector is called the *automatic stabiliser*.

Eventually, we have a paradox. The attempt of households to increase their savings has led to less consumption and less income. The fall in demand probably leads to less investment as well. In cases like these, the private sector's attempt to reduce its net debt $(S_P - I > 0)$ cannot succeed. The result is a fall in income and hence not an increase in saving, which depends on income. Inside the private sector, we might end up in a situation in which households save more, but firms are unable to sell as much of their production as previously.

Thus household debt is reduced at the firms' expense. The private sector taken as a whole would not improve its position. Indeed, the increase in debt carried by the firms might lead to an increase in bankruptcies. Firms cannot force households to spend, so given that they produced too much, a buyer's strike will lead to less revenues for firms. Given that many of them are indebted and have pre-financed their production, their debt at the end of the period will be higher than planned. Hence, the debt of the aggregate of all the firms increases.

Since the adjustment process includes a decline in production, it leads to an increase in government debt ($T-G<0$) through the automatic stabiliser, and a slight improvement in the current account ($IM-EX<0$) because of a drop in imports (assuming that both balances had been zero before). Two more adjustments would be possible, in which either the government deficit or current account surplus would bear the brunt while national income remains stable.

The government could facilitate private sector consolidation by increasing its spending. The increase in demand by government will compensate the decrease in demand from the private sector. This enables households to save more without causing national income and production to collapse. Unemployment need not rise. This policy is called 'expansionary fiscal policy'.

The question of which projects the government will spend the additional money on is political. In the short run, the main thing is to stabilise household income so that households can repay their debts. However, obviously the government should use its additional spending wisely to increase the long-run growth rate. Among other things, investments in infrastructure can be useful. Alternatively, the government could lower the tax bill it imposes on households and thus increase available household income directly. A combination of the two policies is also possible. That said, only increases in government spending are a sure way to increase the level of demand, since increased incomes through lower taxation might be used to build up savings or pay down previously accrued debt rather than for consumption spending. If the private sector uses the financial room made available by means of tax cuts to repay debt, then the amount of deposits will be the same as before the policy was enacted.

Another economic policy option is expansionary monetary policy. A decrease in the central bank's short-term interest rate might lead to an increase in private sector investment. Investments financed by loans pay off better when interest rates are low. Additionally, financial market investors might be willing to run higher risks if the interest rate of the risk-free asset falls, forcing them to cast about for other investment opportunities.

An increase in demand caused by higher investment motivated by lower interest rates could compensate for a trend towards household restraint in consumption. Households could increase their savings by investing in liabilities issued by firms, and so the economy could provide households with an opportunity to increase savings without necessarily engendering a fall in production.

However, monetary policy (attempts to stimulate investment by reducing interest rates in an environment of weak aggregate demand) does not seem to work when interest rates are already very low, since the weak level of demand cannot be compensated by further, rather minor and marginal, decreases in interest rates. Firms refrain from investing more, since even if interest rates approach the zero lower bound, they do not expect to profitably sell any increase in production with profit, given the prevailing weakness in aggregate purchasing power. Economists label this situation an *investment trap*.

If the price level falls (i.e. if deflation occurs), then the real interest rate would be positive even if the nominal interest rate is very low. The real interest rate is calculated *ex post facto* by subtracting inflation from the nominal interest rate. Subtracting a negative rate of inflation from a nominal interest rate that is close to zero must result in a positive number.

If we assume that the prices of financial assets grow at the same rate as those of consumer price goods, a negative real interest rates means that the inflation rate lies above the nominal interest rate. In other words, the price of financial assets rises at a percentage that is higher than interest paid on debt. Financing purchases of financial assets with debt would make sense in such a world.

This is why investment financed by loans is profitable. If the real interest rate is positive, then the nominal interest rate lies above the inflation rate – the investment does not pay off. Hence the expected rate of inflation is crucial for investment. If it lies above the expected rise in the value of assets, investment is postponed; if it lies below it, investment is forthcoming.

Another pathological condition that restricts the effectiveness of monetary policy is the so-called liquidity trap. In contrast to the investment trap, the focus here is on the behaviour of banks. Banks command liquid funds (reserves). Since these do not yield any returns, individual banks try to minimise their holdings of reserves by investing them in financial assets or lending them out. The latter takes place on the interbank market; the former includes parking the funds at the central bank, but also purchasing shares or other assets. Note that one bank or another will always be left holding the bag (i.e. sitting on excess reserves), once they're in the system. They can only be reduced in total circulating volume by using them to buy something from the central bank, like physical cash or bonds (or to repay reserve money owed to the central bank).

At very low interest rates, banks will be less and less inclined to invest their liquid funds in short-term interest-bearing securities. After all, the rate of return that can be achieved is low. At the same time, there is some non-negligible risk.

Market prices of sovereign securities in the market typically rise significantly after substantial reductions in the base rate. The crux of the matter is the relationship between bond price and yield. Let's explore a scenario: we'll assume that in early 2007, US investors expected a recession would arrive any time soon. They knew that in the case of recession, the central bank would decrease the base rate. This will cause nominal interest rates on government bonds newly issued during the recession to fall. Government bonds already on the market, by comparison, bear relatively high nominal interest rates. Two government bonds with a nominal value of $100 but differing in the nominal interest rate, which is hardwired into the bond, should be priced differently. Who would buy a government bond carrying a nominal interest rate of 2 per cent if there are older government bonds on the market, with an identical term to maturity, that carry a 5 per cent interest rate?

Hence US investors will invest their money in government bonds to capitalise on the relatively high yields. Higher demand for these bonds drives up their price, because a $100 bond being priced at $101 with a 5 per cent nominal interest rate still looks attractive if compared with a (hypothetical) bond with a 2 per cent interest rate. The increase in price leads to a fall in yield (which expresses the ratio of return to market price), assuming a maturity of one year, to about 4 per cent, since $101 invested leads to a payment of $105 at maturity. If a longer recession is expected, then investors will buy mostly long-term government bonds with maturities of several years.

As a result, medium- to long-term government bond prices will be relatively high, which means that their yields will be relatively low. When the economy comes out of recession, these government bonds with low yields would be relatively unattractive. A flourishing economy will cause interest rates to go up again, and new government bonds will be far more attractive than old ones. This does not mean that the owners of the old government bonds will make losses. The bonds are paid off at maturity and the investors have more money than they invested. However, the investors could have made more money by investing in new government bonds carrying higher nominal interest rates later on. The interim loss that results from the fall in the bond price only exists on the balance sheet – it need never be 'realised', never cashed out.

This is why banks will increase their holdings of liquid funds when interest rates are low instead of investing them in government bonds. The same goes for bonds from the private sector.

Given that we are in an investment trap, it is highly unlikely that further monetary policy in the form of reducing interest rates which are already at historic lows could achieve an expansionary effect in bank lending. The base rate of the ECB in June 2016 stands at 0.00 per cent. It is not to be expected that households and firms will react to any further falls in the base rate by expanding their demand for loans.

In Spain, for instance, the real estate market has collapsed; housing and land prices in the whole country fell from 2007 until 2014. Investment in Spain is at a very low level, since a large part of investment consisted of real estate construction, both residential and commercial. If a Spaniard wanted to buy a house in 2012, she would look at the real estate market and conclude that average prices were still falling. Thus she would refrain from purchasing a house, and instead wait until prices have fallen further. The cheap loans currently available (at the time of writing in 2016) will not change this.

Given the negative dynamic in house prices, an increase in capital requirements must be reckoned with, because banks can expect to make further losses on their portfolios of mortgage loans. Spanish real estate buyers don't borrow directly from the central bank, but from a commercial bank, which charges some mark-up on the interest rate.

Likewise, entrepreneurs will not undertake any big investment projects given a prevailing environment of weak demand. The cost side isn't crucial. As long as Spanish households save a lot and consume sparsely, effective purchasing power in the economy will remain weak.

Firms could alternatively try to increase their export activities. This also could lead to some balance sheet consolidation in the private sector. If the private sector saves and the public sector does not change its net debt, then an increase in net exports could stabilise demand so that an increase in private sector net savings can be achieved without a fall in national income.

The post-financial-crisis adjustment process after a bubble bursts and domestic demand crashes depends on the exchange rate regime. The two most important categories are 'flexible' and 'fixed' exchange rate regimes. When the exchange rate is flexible, relative prices depend on the exchange rate. Foreign currencies are traded, with their prices determined by supply and demand on the market. The ECB intervenes in the market infrequently. Differences in the inflation rate – read: expected changes in wages – are compensated continuously through movements in the exchange rate, so that a rise in wages will not lead to a one-to-one loss of competitiveness for the net exporting country. Conversely, domestic wage suppression will not automatically lead to more exports, but will be partly compensated by a rise in the exchange rate. This is roughly the story of the Deutschmark. The Federal Republic of Germany had a low interest rate and the DM revalued against the US dollar over time.

With a fixed exchange rate system, macroeconomic adjustment works somewhat differently. The central bank announces an exchange rate at which it will exchange domestic into foreign currency, and vice versa. Maybe not everyone is allowed to hold or trade foreign currencies. Tight restrictions ('exchange controls' or 'capital controls') often cause the rise of a black market in currencies.

The Eurozone is a kind of currency system in which exchange rates of the participating currencies are fixed. This is hidden by the fact that all currencies in the Eurozone are named euro. A euro in a bank that holds a lot of German sovereign securities, however, is worth more than one in a bank that holds a lot of Cypriot sovereign securities, as investors in the latter learned to their dismay in 2013. Since deposit insurance and bank insolvency are regulated at a national level, some of the smaller countries in the Eurozone with dodgy banks and weak deposit insurance schemes cannot fully protect their depositors against losses.

Let's return to the private sector and its efforts to increase savings. If domestic demand is weak, an increase in external demand could compensate the gap and thus prevent a fall of aggregate production. Given a flexible exchange rate, the domestic currency usually drops in value when the central bank lowers the base rate to fight the recession. Investors react to lower interest rates by investing elsewhere, causing capital to flow out of the country and the exchange rate to depreciate. Foreign products increase in price. Since domestic prices and household income (as measured in domestic currency) did not change, purchasing power for imports is likely to fall.

As a consequence, households will reduce their consumption of imported goods. After imports have increased in price relative to domestic goods, a higher share of demand will fall on domestic production. This means that domestic production will probably sink more slowly than imports.

Exports are also affected. Given the drop in the exchange rate, domestic goods can now be sold at lower prices on global markets. If the price of exports falls, as denominated in foreign currency, then exports can rise. Whether this leads to higher total export earnings as measured in domestic currency depends on the net effect of changes in the exchange rate and export volumes.

Positive net exports can increase foreign assets or decrease foreign debt, since the rest of the world has demanded more domestic goods than vice versa, and resulting financial claims parallel this. The difference must be paid for by increases in debt, often in the form of foreign currency. If a German company exports to Sweden, the Swedish importer will pay for his imports with either Swedish crowns or euro. Hence, either foreign debts of the Eurozone are reduced (if euro held by Swedes flow back to Germany), or foreign assets have risen because the exporter now has some additional Swedish crowns with which he could go buy something in Sweden (Swedish goods, land or a factory, say). This mechanism is quite similar in a system of fixed exchange rates.

Exchange rates can be fixed by the central bank. The central bank can proclaim that it commits to exchanging domestic into foreign currency at the fixed rate (in both directions). In order to be able to sustain this commitment, it has to ensure that it doesn't run out of foreign currencies. It's no problem coming up with adequate amounts of domestic currency, which the central bank can produce in unlimited amounts. If, however, demand for foreign currency exceeds the foreign reserves held by the central bank, then the fixed exchange rate cannot be sustained. Central banks therefore build up foreign reserves in order to increase confidence in the stability of the fixed exchange rate.

The build up of foreign reserves is usually achieved through net exports. Since export earnings often take the form of foreign currency (like US dollars), but exporters pay their domestic costs in domestic currency, the central bank is asked to exchange the two currencies. This is how a stock of foreign currency is built up at the central bank.

In the context of an export surplus, the real exchange rate is very important. It describes the price of the same basket of goods purchased either in Spain or in Sweden (for example), expressed in one currency. Both nominal exchange rate, like €1 = $1, and nominal price level play a role in this. If, for instance, the domestic inflation rate is above that of a country's trade partner (e.g. higher in Sweden than in Germany), the real exchange rate will move up. The same effect is caused by a rise in the nominal exchange rate, which causes a change in the real exchange rate without any change in the price level.

Changes in exchange rates affect not only international trade, but also financial assets. The daily turnover on global financial markets has increased enormously in recent decades and is now a multiple of turnover of actual trade in goods and services. Portfolio adjustments are often the cause of exchange rate movements, rather than the effect.

A European investor in financial assets denominated in US dollars incurs a loss when the euro appreciates. The value of the asset will be lower, as denominated in euro, so a part of the investor's purchasing power has been lost. On the other side, liabilities are affected as well. Someone who owes debts denominated in US dollars now needs fewer euro to repay those debts. As long as the investor's income streams are paid in euro, the real burden of debt is reduced.

Exchange rate effects on a country's balance sheet

It is quite interesting what the effects of a change in the exchange rate are for the economy as a whole. To get some insight into this, it's useful to add up foreign financial assets and foreign financial liabilities of all domestic residents – individuals, firms and the state. On the left side of the balance sheet, we find the value of foreign assets in their respective currency; on the right side, the foreign liabilities. The currency depends on the denomination of the asset or liability. Theoretically, a domestic household can move into debt vis-à-vis a foreign institution in both domestic and foreign currency.

In the following we look at a stylised balance sheet showing foreign assets and foreign liabilities for the US.

	total economy	
assets	€1,000	liabilities $1,000

We see that liabilities are denominated in US dollars, and assets in foreign currency. What would happen to this balance sheet if the US dollar were to fall vis-à-vis other currencies? Liabilities denominated in US dollars remain unchanged, but assets rise in value as measured in US dollars, since it's possible to buy more of them with the same €1,000 worth of non-US currency holdings one has. This is very convenient, as we will see soon.

In contrast, we look at the balance sheet of a developing country. This country cannot issue debt in international markets denominated in domestic currency – no one wants to buy such debt, the 'country risk' is too high. The reason might lay in strong devaluations or public debt defaults in the past. So it needs to hold assets in both euro and US dollars in order to be able to do business internationally.

	total economy	
assets	€500	liabilities $2,500
assets	$500	net wealth–$1,500

This economy will experience problems when the domestic currency drops in value. The depreciation has increased the value of liabilities, now that more domestic currency is needed to pay off each unit of foreign currency debt. On the other side, the value of assets only increases partially. Since the country has net foreign debts, some trouble might result. Debt service in US dollars becomes more burdensome, since incomes continue to be denominated in domestic currency. Only export incomes lead to foreign currency inflows of US dollars or other hard currencies.

Since liabilities lead to interest rate payments in the respective currency, the country has to export more now that the exchange rate has dropped, in order to service its foreign debts – assuming that prices do not change. This constitutes a real transfer of resources from this country to the rest of the world. Entering into foreign debts denominated in foreign currency is labelled *original sin* in the language of economists.

If a country is in arrears with interest payments on foreign debt denominated in foreign currency, extreme measures might be undertaken. The government might ask the central bank to create the necessary amount of money in domestic currency and exchange it into foreign currency so that the interest instalment can be paid. This type of policy would push down the exchange rate and cause imports to become more expensive. The increase in import prices can lead to a rise in domestic prices as well. After all, the purchasing power of domestic currency is diminished, and workers might be trying to compensate for this through higher nominal wages. Pressure to raise domestic prices would result, since firms will try to pass increases in costs on to consumers. In the extreme case, a spiral of doom can result that leads to hyperinflation. This adds high foreign currency denominated debt as an additional cause of hyperinflations, other reasons for which, as we've seen, can include large-scale reductions in a country's aggregate production as a result of civil war or international conflict, e.g. the occupation of the Rhineland by French troops in the last German hyperinflation in the early 1920s.

Alternative currencies

In times of hyperinflation, the nominal value of noble metals invariably increases because they're bought as a store of value. Investors speculate on the retention of purchasing power, hoping that as the inflation rate increases, so does the price of gold. This also works with other metals and raw materials. However, one should not consider gold a sensible choice as a store of value outside of a hyperinflationary context. Even though the US dollar was to some extent backed by gold up until the beginning of the 1970s, that's no longer the case, and a return to a metallic standard is very unlikely.

It's even more unlikely that virtual currencies like bitcoin, which are not issued by banks, can preserve their store-of-value function over time. Whereas normal currencies can be used to discharge tax liabilities with the government, virtual currencies like bitcoin are not guaranteed by any law to discharge any future liabilities at all. This, however, is an essential function of money. As long as there are no larger quantities of bitcoin-denominated debt whose value is backed up by legally enforceable contracts, one cannot speak of a sovereign currency.

The value of bitcoins arises from emotional bonds to the object, just like with trading cards. Another reason to buy bitcoins could lie with the illegal goods and services that can be purchased with it. Bitcoin is a currency, but it is built on very shaky foundations. Let's return now to the currency that many Europeans use today to pay their taxes and its current problems.

10   Europe before the euro

It always must be kept in mind that the euro crisis that first emerged in the wake of the GFC and re-ignited starting in 2010 was a result of unhealthy macroeconomic processes, a symptom of weaknesses that had accumulated over years, weaknesses with multiple causes rooted in complex, historically contingent sociopolitical processes. 'Saving the euro' is a misguided metaphor – the euro does not need to be saved. It is merely a tool, a currency shared by a group of countries. What needs to be saved is the capacity of this group of countries to produce goods and services that increase the welfare of their populations.

With mass unemployment of 21 per cent and 24 per cent in Spain and Greece at the time of writing, it should be clear that the issue is not saving the currency but saving the people. In Spain, about two million people in one million households have no income at all. At the same time, the suicide rate in the crisis countries has risen drastically. Cost-cutting 'reforms' in the healthcare system have led to an increase in the mortality rate. Unemployment in the Eurozone set records starting in 2011, and over the last three years has fallen very slowly from 12 per cent to just below 11 per cent. This sort of thing destroys people's confidence in society and in the political system, especially in a democracy.

Adam Smith, in his book *The Wealth of Nations* warned that 'Civil government, so far as it is instituted for the security of property, is in reality instituted for the defense of the rich against the poor, or of those who have some property against those who have none at all.'

In the Eurozone, in the wake of the GFC, only banks and investors were bailed out, while millions of citizens were thrown into unemployment through no fault of their own. Even those that bought houses and flats by borrowing a lot of money should be assigned only partial blame. It takes two to agree on a loan contract – a borrower and a lender – and a non-zero interest rate exists because there is a risk of default. It cannot be justified that only banks have been protected from the consequences of their mistakes while borrowers have been left high and dry. It seems unlikely that by acting in this way a government will increase the wealth and welfare of its citizens.

The Bretton Woods system

Even before the end of the Second World War, Allied leaders met at a hotel in Bretton Woods, New Hampshire in the US, to design a currency exchange regime intended to stabilise global trade and support peace and security in the world after the end of the war. Exchange rates of participating countries were pegged to the US dollar, which itself was pegged against gold. The exchange rate of the Deutschmark was fixed at a level that left German products competitive on the world market. As long as the inflation rate in West Germany did not surpass that of the US, Germany was able to achieve a current account surplus.

The inflation rate is mostly determined by changes in productivity (output per worker per year) and changes in wages. If in the US and elsewhere wages and productivity were to increase in lockstep, whereas in Germany wages grow a little more slowly than productivity, then the real exchange rate of the DM would fall. So, German products would get cheaper compared to foreign products. In a system of fixed exchange rates, changes in the price level do not lead to changes in the exchange rate, but rather to changes in the current account balance. Since prices of commodity inputs in global markets are the same for all importers, changes in relative prices of finished consumer products are mostly due to changes in unit labour costs.

Given that productivity increased strongly year after year in post-Second World War West Germany, it was not very difficult to keep wage increases a little bit lower. This wage policy stabilised the current account. The real exchange rate was favourable for exporters, while imports were relatively dear. The export sector created additional employment, and as reconstruction of the country's industrial capacities progressed, output grew and grew. A so-called *Wirtschaftswunder* (economic miracle) was achieved.

The 1953 London agreement on German legacy debts, which wrote down a considerable portion of debts that were incurred during the war, also helped the young *Bundesrepublik* get back on its feet in the 1950s and 1960s. Millions of Germans had good incomes and moved up the socioeconomic ladder into the middle class. Distribution of incomes and wealth became more egalitarian and tax revenues rose. Domestic demand supported economic growth, which led to full employment.

European nations, to a greater or lesser extent, undertook national industrial policies in the postwar era. Firms were set up systematically, infrastructure was constructed and workers were educated. When a leading industry such as car manufacturing experienced trouble, companies were sometimes nationalised and restructured. While this failed in the UK in the 1970s, it was successful in France in the 1980s. Also during that time, Japanese car manufacturers bowed to pressure from Brussels and limited their sales in Europe.

In the background of this industrial policy lay the insight that with rising output, average unit production costs fall. If output falls, unit costs will rise. Under-utilisation of production capacities thus leads to higher prices, falling sales and thus a further increase in under-utilisation. This is why it can make economic sense to come to the aid of an industry in times of economic drought. Once output is reduced, production might cease completely and devalue both physical and human capital. In good times workers can find employment elsewhere, but in bad times it can be a sensible policy to support an industry in financial trouble. After all, the production of industrial goods was and still is a key for good jobs and prosperity.

Current account surpluses racked up year after year meant that Germany built up foreign reserves in the post-Second World War era. But these were unwarranted under the Bretton Woods system, since it wasn't really necessary to defend the value of the currency as it can be with free-floating exchange rates. Nevertheless, the German central bank held copious amounts of US dollars on its balance sheet, since exporters exchanged their US dollars into DM in order to pay their domestic bills.

Rising exports created additional jobs in Germany, whereas the US lost some as a result of imports. The DM was revalued upwards a few times over the years to ensure the current account surplus would not grow too large. Holiday trips to the rest of the world were reduced in price, and export goods sold a bit dearer on the global market.

Nevertheless, Germany was a country with an export surplus, and the losses incurred on the central bank's excess holdings of US dollars were deemed the price of a slightly undervalued currency.

Europe after Bretton Woods

After the end of the Bretton Woods system in 1973, exchange rates between European currencies were administered by the continent's several central banks. Initially, so-called corridors were established inside which exchange rates could move up or down slightly relative to the other currencies. This was developed further into a European exchange rate mechanism. This system was plagued by problems of adjustment as well.

For instance, economic growth rates of the Italian economy were below those of Germany, because the annual rate of Italian wage increases tended to surpass the country's rate of productivity increases. The resulting inflation in unit prices reduced competitiveness of the Italian exporters. Policy-makers urged devaluation of the Italian lira in order to improve the current account. Such devaluations were able to restore the international price competitiveness of Italian firms, particularly those of the north, quite quickly and easily. Competing firms, in Germany and elsewhere, saw their price advantage dwindle.

The affected industry perceived this process of adjustment to be unfair, since a constant threat of devaluation led to fundamental uncertainty. It complicated long-term investments because it was very difficult to estimate future revenues. Another effect of the process was that the constant danger of devaluation meant that German banks did not add a lot of foreign assets to their portfolio.

This was why the very old idea of establishing European currency was taken up some years before the rather unexpected reunification of Germany. In 1992, immediately after reunification, the detailed plan for a European currency union was agreed in the Maastricht Treaty, and a little later the name 'euro' was chosen. Exchange rates were fixed in 1999, and three years later euro coins and notes were introduced. The members of the Eurozone were united in a currency union. Based on the theoretical foundations from the first part of this book, we will now examine and assess the economic development of the Eurozone from 1999 to 2014.

11 The situation with the euro

With the introduction of the euro, the nominal exchange rates of the countries had been fixed, interest rates harmonised, and the scope for increases in government indebtedness limited. These were the three main technical features of the introduction of the euro. All three play a major role in the economic analysis of the Eurozone from 1999 to 2014. In the following, a panorama is developed using data from Germany, Greece, Ireland and Spain.

We'll start with the standardisation of interest rates. Figure 11.1 shows the interest rates (in per cent) of three ECB facilities: marginal lending, main refinancing and deposits. Banks operating in the Eurozone can borrow reserves against collateral from the first two of these facilities. They can also borrow in the interbank market. In order to do so, they must offer an interest rate that lies above the deposit rate.

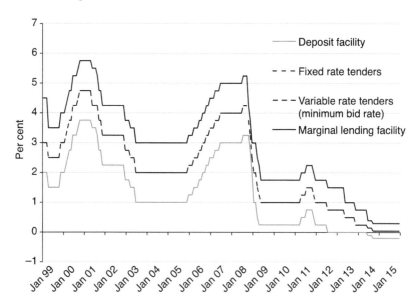

Figure 11.1 Marginal lending, main refinancing and deposit rates, in per cent (source: Eurostat (irt_cb_m)).

The base (main refinancing) rate of the Eurozone stood at about 3 per cent in the first few years of the common currency. For countries like Spain and Ireland this was a significantly lower rate than those that had applied when they had their own currencies. In both countries, people were generally optimistic. Unemployment fell during the 1990s, rates of GDP growth picked up, and people looked ahead with great expectations.

Construction and purchases of real estate, financed by mortgages, were particularly popular. Real estate statistics in Spain, it was said, never recorded a year of falling real estate prices since the start of their collection. In the wake of the bursting of the dot-com bubble in 2001/2, the US Federal Reserve Bank adopted a policy of low interest rates (the *Greenspan put*), which put downward pressure on interest rates in Europe too. The net effect of these several factors was a constantly rising demand for mortgages. The resulting increase in debt is shown in Figure 11.2.

While the private sector – firms and especially households – increased their debt in Spain, Ireland and Greece, for a number of reasons that didn't happen in Germany. On the one hand, real wages were flat or on the decline, with purchasing power of households falling. In such an environment, households did not want to increase their indebtedness. On the other hand, the unemployment rate was in the double digits, notwithstanding or perhaps because of the short-run labour market adjustments caused by the introduction of Hartz IV reforms in the early 2000s, which reduced job security.

Loan demand from German firms was weak as well. Reasons included the high interest rate policy of the German central bank in the middle of the 1990s; restrictive fiscal policy – two-thirds of the years between 1982 and 2002 show a

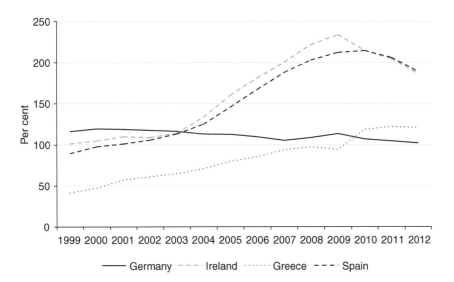

Figure 11.2 Domestic credit to the private sector, in percentage of GDP (source: European Central Bank, Statistical Data Warehouse).

primary surplus; considerable negative balances for the private sector between 1994 and 2002, especially after Hans Eichel took office; and a constant appreciation of the Deutschmark after the crisis of the European monetary system in 1992. Then in 2002, the *Neuer Markt* crashed; launched in 1997, it was Germany's equivalent of the NASDAQ, a segment of the stock market which listed emerging new technology.

The Nemax-50 index reached an all-time high in 2000 with more than 9,500 points, but plummeted when the dot-com boom came to an end, and in September 2002 stood at only 1,000 points. Investors who got in at the peak had lost about 90 per cent of their portfolio. This caused some big gaps in balance sheets of the German corporate sector, part of which had participated in the speculation by financing some purchases with debt. Some firms therefore used their cash flows to reduce their level of debt. Given the low level of domestic consumer demand and the combination of these several other factors, business investment fell.

In Spain and Ireland, rising real estate prices led to the insight that a lot of money can be made with speculation. Apart from demand from people who wanted to live in the houses, there was additional demand from speculators that hoped to make some money 'flipping houses'. Figure 11.3 shows the development of house prices in the four countries from 2005 until 2013. There are no older data available, which is why it cannot be seen that, especially in the case of Spain, house prices had been rising for quite some time.

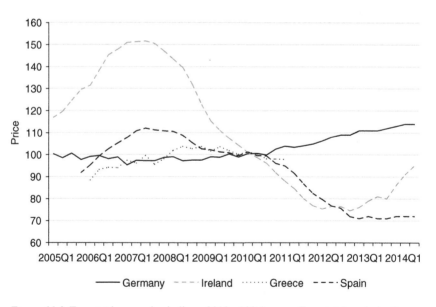

Figure 11.3 Eurostat house price indices, 2010 = 100 (source: Eurostat (prc_hpi_q)).

Macroeconomic consequences

What are the macroeconomic consequences of real estate bubbles? The fundamental macroeconomic identity is:

$$Y = C + I + G + EX - IM$$

GDP is calculated as the sum (over a given time-frame, usually one calendar year) of consumption, investment, government spending and current account balance (exports minus imports). Construction of both residential and commercial real estate falls under investment. Investment can be financed by personal savings or retained earnings, but also directly by credit. As we saw in Figure 11.2, credit expansion in Spain, Greece and Ireland was relatively high, whereas it was stable in Germany. This is reflected in the statistics on gross fixed capital formation, a technical term for investment in capital goods, per inhabitant. Figure 11.4 shows that these had risen in countries with a pronounced real estate boom.

The rise of investment was financed by loans. Spanish, Irish and Greek banks expanded their loan portfolio, since they thought themselves to be on the safe side. The respective economies showed relatively high and stable growth, real estate prices were rising, and in cases of mortgage loan default the banks would be able to appropriate the house or flat and sell it on. The perceived risk was low.

The granting of loans, as we have seen in the theoretical part of this text, does not require savings. Banks extend credit, and thereby create deposits in equal

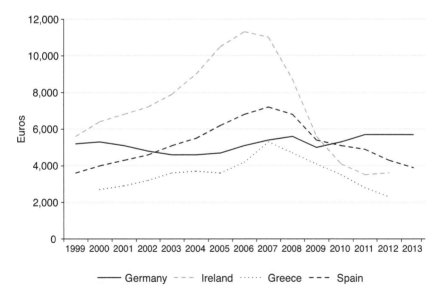

Figure 11.4 Gross fixed capital formation, € per inhabitant (source: Eurostat (nama_gdp_c)).

measure with debt owed to banks by borrowers. If they need reserves or cash, they can borrow them at the central bank.

As long as the newly added deposits created were spent in Spain only, they were transferred from one Spanish bank to another. Banks with temporary excess reserves could lend them out to those with a temporary deficit. Since the real estate boom affected regions quite differently, it is quite likely that some regional banks held more than enough liquid funds, while others held not enough.

In consequence of the real estate boom, the construction sector's share of the economy's 'total value added' increased. This effect can be seen in Figure 11.5. The construction sector's share reached as high as 14 per cent in Spain, while in Germany it fell from just under 6 per cent to a little above 4 per cent.

The construction sector built public real estate projects as well as commercial and residential buildings. In Spain, public real estate increased the value of adjacent residential real estate in a systematic way (new public infrastructure often creates 'positive externalities' for adjacent private real estate owners). Spanish newspapers report on new details of multiple corruption scandals on a daily basis, often linking building tycoons to local and national politicians. Local tax income depends heavily on the quantity of new real estate projects, since new constructions are taxed. In boom times, these taxes became a growing share of municipalities' total tax income.

As long as a lot of credit-financed investment is undertaken, the GDP of the concerned countries will rise more strongly than elsewhere. Figure 11.6 shows

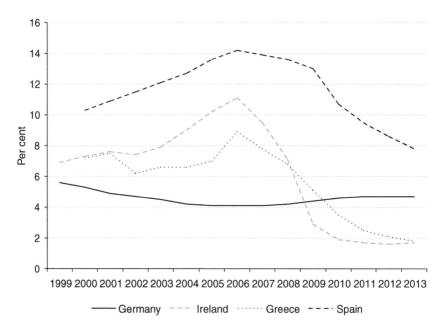

Figure 11.5 Share of construction in total value added, in per cent (source: Eurostat (nama_nace10_c)).

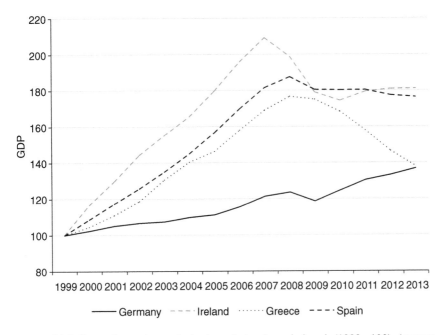

Figure 11.6 Gross domestic product at market prices, indexed (1999 = 100) (source: Eurostat (nama_gdp_c)).

GDP (at market prices), with GDP in 1999 indexed at 100. Spain and Ireland experienced phases of strong and sustained economic growth before the crisis; Greece's GDP trajectory looks quite similar. Germany's development of GDP was rather weak in comparison, showing no evidence of a boom, but it was nevertheless positive.

The elevated growth rates in Ireland, Greece and Spain led to a fall in unemployment rates. Figure 11.7 shows that unemployment rates in these countries were reduced to below 10 per cent. This was due to the construction sector, among other things, which employed workers who had previously been difficult to integrate into the labour market. The decrease in unemployment led to a scarcity of labour; this led to a rise in wages. Employers noticed that workers had different employment opportunities and offered higher wages to bind their own workers.

Firms inside industries competed for labour, and also industries competed for labour. In Spain, starting salaries in the construction sector were above those of academics. Workers were more and more optimistic. There were an increasing number of well-paid jobs. Spain and Ireland became the target of net immigration, and immigrants found jobs as well. This led to a further increase in consumer demand. Both consumption and investment increased further, since people had good incomes and money to spend, as well as improving creditworthiness on that basis.

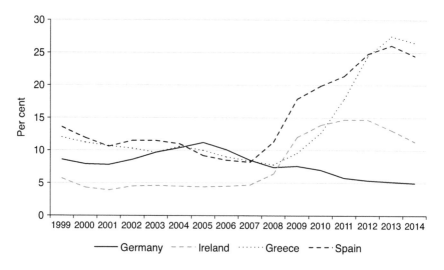

Figure 11.7 Unemployment, in per cent (source: Eurostat (un_rt_a)).

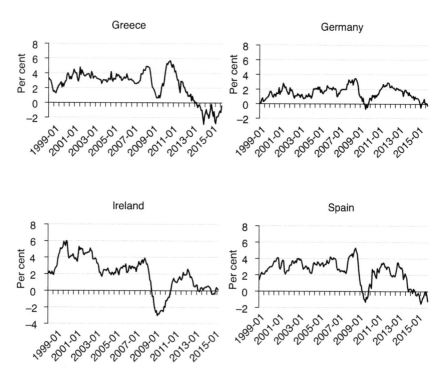

Figure 11.8 Change in consumer price indices, in per cent (source: European Central Bank (ICP.M.DE.N.000000.4.ANR)).

In consequence, the inflation rate in these countries rose higher than in the rest of the Eurozone. The ECB's 2 per cent inflation target was surpassed year after year. Inflation rates in Ireland and Spain were between 3 per cent and 4 per cent, while they were between 1 per cent and 2 per cent in Germany (Figure 11.8). The cause was differing growth rates in those countries. While in Spain, Ireland and Greece, credit-financed investment was relatively large, in Germany the quantity of lending was flat. Germany was hit by economic stagnation from 2001 until 2006. The level of investment was low, and firms were managing the debt overhang that had resulted from the dot-com bust instead of investing in growth of production capacity.

The inflation rate calculated for the whole Eurozone concealed significant internal divergences between inflation rates in Eurozone member states. From 1999 until 2012, the Eurozone's overall inflation rate fluctuated around 2 per cent, causing the ECB to declare that it was doing its job well. In the background, however, diverging rates of economic growth led to growing imbalances in the current accounts of member countries – imbalances that were destined eventually to cause problems.

Figure 11.9 shows developments in the external balance of traded goods and services. Irish, Greek and Spanish GDP grew relatively more strongly than Germany's between 1999 and 2007. The rise in the relative share of incomes in these countries is a consequence of this trend. Consumption and investment also rose relatively more strongly, which led to a rise in imports. This doesn't necessarily mean that imports from Germany into those countries rose, since

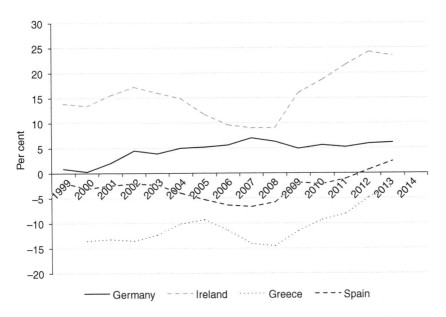

Figure 11.9 External balance of goods and services, as a percentage of GDP (source: Eurostat (nama_exi_c)).

their external trade relationships were diverse. But higher incomes led to more consumption, which partly falls on higher consumption of imports.

The weakness of economic growth in Germany led to a current account surplus, since domestic demand was not sufficient to absorb domestic production. This was due to the restrictive wage policies. Political reforms – key words: non-labour wage costs and taxation – shifted costs from firms to workers. In contrast, the situation in Greece and Spain was shaped by strong domestic demand.

Spain especially saw its current account move into negative territory. The largest share in imports was energy. Ireland is a special case, since it is the home of many multinationals, particularly from the US, which have offshored their European headquarters and revenue streams into Ireland simply to minimise their tax bill – even as they maintain actual production elsewhere. Ireland offers corporations extremely low tax rates specifically in order to lure multinationals to do this.

A key factor in country X's export performance is the income of its trading partners. If the latter's economies grow stronger than X's own, then X's current account is likely to improve, as exports grow faster than imports. Since there is no role for exchange rates within the Eurozone and commodity prices on global markets are the same for every country, it is wage policy that determines countries' respective rates of inflation and hence the effective exchange rates (which are relevant for external trade) of Eurozone member states (think back to our explanation of 'real exchange rates' defined in terms of the differing prices of a basket full of identical goods and services in country A vs. country B).

Wage policies depend on what stage of the business cycle a country is in: in a boom there are scarcities in the labour market, leading to increases in wages. While real wages in Ireland, Spain and Greece grew relatively more strongly than in Germany, Germany's exports to those countries tended to increase.

This explanation should be separated from the narrative of unit labour costs. As can be seen in Figure 11.10, the latter focuses on competitiveness of countries. Countries with rising unit labour costs export less; countries with falling or stagnating labour costs export more. The problem with this narrative is causality. Unit labour costs are, as we have seen above, not independent of the stage of the business cycle. The real estate boom in Ireland and Spain explained these countries' rising unit labour costs. These, then, are a symptom of credit expansion, and not an isolated cause for trends in the development of the current account. Moreover, a rise of wages in times of falling unemployment increases households' aggregate income. Higher incomes usually lead to more consumption, of which a part consists of imported goods.

Summing up, unit labour costs were not the single cause of current account deficits of Greece and Spain and were not the single cause of the German current account surplus. They were a symptom of differences in aggregate demand in the Eurozone member countries, which led to stronger bargaining positions for workers in countries like Spain and Ireland and a relatively weaker one in Germany. Where wages expanded more rapidly, consumption was increasing

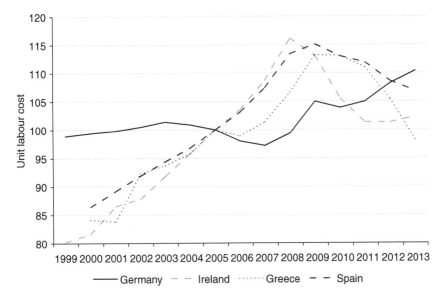

Figure 11.10 Nominal unit labour cost, 2005 = 100 (source: Eurostat (nama_aux_ulc)).

faster, thus leading to higher imports and a deteriorating current account. Germany's export miracle was not based on competitiveness, but on the increase in private debt elsewhere.

Another myth about the alleged causation of the Eurozone crisis is a story about government overspending. It has been claimed that governments overspent and should now tighten their belts. Figure 11.11 shows government surplus/ deficit trends of the four countries we've been comparing. Greece is the obvious outlier. It is the only country that had a deficit over the whole period. Ireland and Spain, on the other hand, had reached budget surpluses almost every year between 1999 and 2007. The idea that government deficits had something to do with the crisis has to be rejected for Ireland and Spain. Meanwhile, Germany experienced budget deficits over these years, often above the 3 per cent of GDP officially allowed under EU Treaty rules. We've already seen in the theoretical part of this text why government deficits are generally necessary in order to provide room for private savings. Now we see that neither Latin government budget profligacy nor German government budget restraint actually took place in the lead-up to the GFC.

It was only after the outbreak of the global financial crisis in 2007 that government budget surpluses turned into deficits in Spain and Ireland. This was due to automatic macroeconomic stabilisers kicking in. The social security system had to spend more on benefits as a consequence of higher unemployment, even as tax income decreased, which led automatically to government budget deficits. Moreover, Ireland nationalised its banks and reached a deficit of more than 30

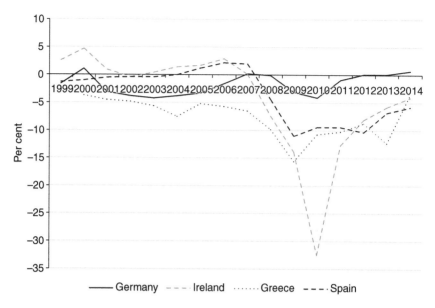

Figure 11.11 Government surplus/deficit as a percentage of GDP (source: Eurostat (gov_dd_edpt1)).

per cent in 2010 by taking the banks' debts onto the public balance sheet. There was never any excess in government spending on public goods and services.

The first reaction of markets after the *sub-prime crisis* started was an appreciation of the euro (see Figure 11.12). The US dollar weakened, the euro became more expensive and not a few commentators expected the crisis to be limited to the US. This perception was wrong. Financial assets in the whole world had been dispersed via globalised financial markets. In 2008–9 it became clear that several important German banks held a substantial amount of the sub-prime US financial assets concerned, which had been fraudulently labelled AAA by US ratings agencies and marketed by Wall Street banks to suckers worldwide. WestLB stocked up with doubtful paper from the US; Hypo Real Estate did the same in Ireland with Irish paper. IKB and Nord LB too had US financial assets in their respective balance sheets that had to be radically marked down in their market values.

The mood in the foreign exchange market swung back, and the US dollar regained its value. This development had some benefit, at least for European exporters, since they could offer lower prices on global markets. It is important to note at this point that exchange rates have little to do with the real economy, or more precisely, the state of the current account is not the primary driver of swings in exchange rates – rather, the reverse is often the case. It could be hypothesised that imports and exports trigger flows of foreign exchange that subsequently determine exchange rates. This is not the case. The daily turnover on

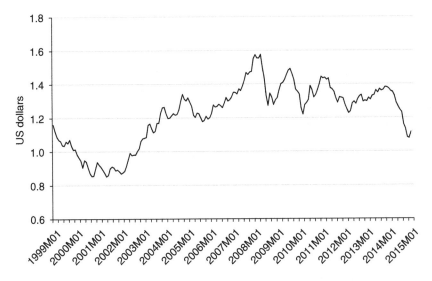

Figure 11.12 Euro exchange rate to the US dollar, in US dollars (source: Eurostat (ert_bil_eur_m)).

global foreign exchange markets is bigger than annual turnover on the global goods and services markets. Exchange rate swings are driven mostly by the activities of forex speculators.

The financial crisis started in the US in 2007 when it became widely known that huge amounts of sub-prime loans were fraudulent, and that derivatives (collateralised bonds) built out of bundles of mortgage loans were vastly overvalued as a result. The crisis exploded with full force when Lehman Brothers, one of the world's biggest investment banks, collapsed in September 2008. This bankruptcy made investors realise that there were loads of non-performing loans on banks' balance sheets, and that no one knew how much or how many banks were really insolvent.

The traditional answer to a financial crisis is to nationalise affected banks. The banks' shareholders are wiped out, its creditors take partial write-downs ('haircuts'), and government takes over all remaining liabilities and thus increases its own debts. After ridding banks of so-called toxic assets – with the taxpayer footing the bill – the banks are eventually sold back to the private sector. But with huge, globally active financial entities like Lehman Brothers, the list of counterparties is so enormous and the deals so complex that it's extremely difficult to untangle the balance sheets and apportion losses. That's why the failure of such banks can lead to systemic crisis, and why they're generally treated as 'too big to fail' and propped up, no matter how much financial crime they've been involved in, charged with or convicted of.

Credit bubble, not sovereign debt crisis

Expectations in the Eurozone were that countries with credit-financed real estate bubbles would face huge costs after the bubbles burst, and that these costs would be put on the public budget. This would lead to a rise in government debt. Since in the Eurosystem the central bank is prohibited from financing public spending (by the Lisbon Treaty on European Union, Article 123), Eurozone member countries must finance themselves by borrowing from commercial banks in the European financial market. This causes the possibility of public default to arise – and it also links the solvency of governments and commercial banks.

As Figure 11.13 shows, the secondary market yields of government bonds with maturities close to ten years increased for Greek, Irish and Spanish bonds in the wake of the GFC. The yield moves inversely to the price. If market participants expect that Greece cannot repay its government debt, the prices of Greek bonds fall, which increases their effective yield. If the secondary market price of government bonds sinks from €100 to €80 with an expected nominal repayment of €100 plus interest (which is fixed), then yield will rise, from the point of view of the secondary market buyer of such a bond at its new price. After all, only €80 are now required to collect the repayment at maturity.

The reason for the rise of yield in Greek, Spanish and Irish bond yields (among others) was the change in the perceived risk of the underlying sovereign security. Investors were nervous about the possibility that some European governments might declare insolvency at some point in the future, as Argentina did

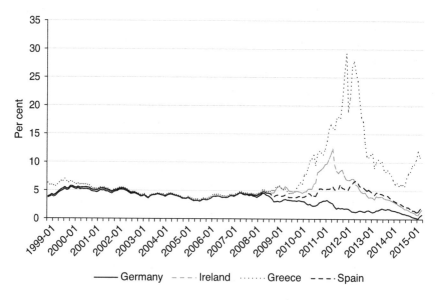

Figure 11.13 Secondary market yields of government bonds with maturities of close to ten years, period averages in percentage per year (source: European Central Bank (11.15 Harmonised long-term interest rates for convergence assessment purposes)).

in 2002. Ironically, this nervousness had a self-reinforcing effect: the more expensive it got for struggling Eurozone member governments to raise fresh money from investors by issuing fresh bonds in order to roll over old debt, the closer to insolvency those governments actually got, since rising interest rates meant governments had to pay out a larger share of their tax revenues for interest payments, leaving less available to invest in stimulating their domestic real economies, leading to a further weakening of their economies, and so on in a vicious circle.

As we can see in Figure 11.13, yields of the different bonds had almost been identical since the introduction of the euro. A Greek government bond was not ranked as more risky than a German one. This shows distinctly that market participants had been wrong. Investors had been ignoring the so-called *no bail-out clause*, which forbids the ECB from directly financing any Eurozone member state government or fiscal agency. The possibility of a sovereign bankruptcy was not taken into account. This shows that investors had not understood a major element of the Eurosystem's design correctly. As a consequence of the ECB not being allowed to directly finance Eurozone member governments, these governments are forced to incur debts in what amounts to a quasi-foreign currency, i.e. a currency they have no control over, no ability to create in whatever quantities needed at will. They are players in someone else's casino, not the owners of their own; they are no longer in control of their financial fate. They run the risk of becoming illiquid if (expected) tax income is not sufficient to repay the debt.

The dwindling confidence in some governments' capacity to repay public debts was mirrored in the private financial sector by a breakdown of the interbank market in the Eurozone. Figure 11.14 shows the so-called TARGET2 balances in the Eurozone. The balances show the debt situation of NCBs. They are purely passive accounting entries tracking specific capital flows in the Eurozone. If, for instance, a Spaniard distrusts the solvency of domestic banks and moves his money from a bank in Spain to a bank in Germany, a deposit is created in favour of *Bundesbank* that matches a liability of *Banco de España*. The black line shows that since mid-2007, a capital flight has taken place from the European South towards Germany.

German banks inadvertently played a significant role in causing this capital flight. Over several years, they had been actively net lending to Spanish banks, to the cumulative tune of €600–800 billion. This was a consequence of Spain's long-standing current account deficit, which as we've seen was caused by Spain's relatively strong economic growth. Spanish banks issued more and more mortgages. As long as the resulting deposits circulated in Spain, banks could borrow reserves needed for settlement among them. However, Spain's negative current account balance meant that more reserves were draining out of the country as a consequence of payments for imports into Spain than were coming back in through foreigners' payments for Spanish exports. As a result, reserves in the Spanish banking system were scarce. However, Spanish banks were able to borrow reserves through the European interbank market, and this is exactly what happened.

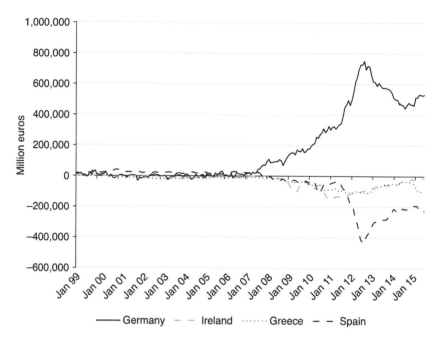

Figure 11.14 TARGET2 balances, in millions of euro (source: ECB: http://sdw.ecb. europa.eu/browse.do?node=9689638).

When the huge risks in balance sheets of Spanish banks generated by massive mortgage over-lending on overpriced real estate became clearly visible after the country's real estate bubble burst, loans on the interbank market stopped being rolled over and no new loans were made available. Spanish banks could access liquidity only through the Spanish central bank, acting for the ECB, by borrowing against collateral. This is what prevented a bankruptcy of Spanish banks. Since such a bankruptcy would have led to a default on a large share of the payments due to German banks, German banks would probably have faced insolvency as well.

The example of Cyprus shows some other possible consequences of banking crises. Rating agencies had progressively marked down Greek and Cypriot government securities until the ECB decided their quality was so low that they could no longer accept them as collateral. In summer 2012 it was already clearly recognisable that Cypriot banks would not receive additional reserves from the ECB using Greek and Cypriot bonds as collateral. The quantity of liquid funds shrunk steadily, since the country had a current account deficit and some investors pulled their money out. Eventually, the quantity of reserves at Cypriot banks was so low that they could not go into clearing anymore. Consequently, the Cypriot banking system crashed in spring 2013.

Banks were not bailed out by public funds in Cyprus, but instead banks were shrunk through a 'bail-in' of depositors and other debt holders – which is to say, their claims on Cypriot banks were partially cancelled, or written down. A Cypriot bank's balance sheet might have looked somewhat like this:

_____Cypriot bank Z_____			
assets	€900	liabilities	€1,000
		equity	–€100

To shrink the bank down to solvency, two possibilities exist. The government could bail-out the bank and transfer €100. This would buy it a 10 per cent share in the bank. Liabilities stay at €1,000, but assets are increased by €100 in liquid funds, to reach €1,000. The bank is returned to solvency. This is what the Irish did when their government took over bank liabilities. While the money of investors is secured, taxpayers foot the bill.

A non-negligible part of the reserves in Irish banks originated from German banks that had made interbank loans to Irish banks. So the Irish taxpayer ended up paying for the results of speculation done by its own banks using German money. Spain faced the choice of either nationalising banks and hence socialising private losses, or using European institutions like the EFSF and now the ESM to solve the problem.

The second possibility is a *bail-in* of private creditors of the insolvent bank. This is what happened in Cyprus. All persons that have a stake in the bank will be made worse off by partial write-downs. The Cypriot bank's balance sheet after the bail-in now looks like this:

_____Cypriot bank Z_____		
assets	€900	liabilities	€900

The bank is solvent, but counterparties to its liabilities have had to stomach losses. In this case, 10 per cent of the balance sheet was erased. Liabilities of the bank are, among other things, loans from other banks, but also deposits from legal and real persons.

While this procedure might seem fair enough at first sight, it is problematic in terms of its macroeconomic impacts. First of all, an incentive is created that makes depositors pull out their money when a bank is suspected of hovering on the edge of insolvency. Especially given that interest rates are near zero, this provides little incentive to keep savings in the form of deposits at a bank.

The second reason is the bank's reaction to this policy. Since it is in constant fear of a large-scale withdrawal of deposits, it increases its holdings of liquid funds. That's necessary to ensure the bank can supply an amount of cash and reserves sufficient to counter any bank run by depositors. The bank can increase cash holdings by selling illiquid assets like shares, bonds and real estate. If many of a country's banks act like this, however, prices of financial assets will plummet. The banking system will be bankrupt if the financial assets of the economy fall in price while liabilities are stable. There will be enough liquid funds to make payments, but the balance sheet will show that the value of assets has fallen below that of liabilities.

Measured against the possibilities of a sovereign modern monetary system that's controlled by a sovereign government, as described in the theoretical part of this text, the euro crisis has demonstrated that the current design of the Eurozone suffers from a number of important shortcomings:

1 If a government has debts in a foreign currency, it has a problem, since it cannot determine the interest rate on that debt, nor can it ensure an appropriate supply of money from the central bank. Most modern monetary systems, like the US or Canadian dollar, the British pound sterling, the Swiss franc or the Swedish crown, do not have these problems. The euro is in essence a foreign currency even for members of the Eurozone, since they do not have a national central bank that can supply money as needed at all times, but instead have to compete with private borrowers to borrow euro on financial markets.

2 Differences in credit growth over several years in various parts of the Eurozone led to widely divergent levels of demand. This led to macroeconomic imbalances: some countries exported more than they imported, and conversely, others exported less than they imported. German firms didn't increase their pace of investments after the year 2000 even though interest rates were low. German households didn't see any room to increase their debt (and therefore spending), given that real wages were falling and unemployment relatively high. At the same time, low interest rates facilitated a real estate boom in several countries, especially in Spain and Ireland.

3 The disadvantage of a common currency is national governments' sacrifice of independent monetary and fiscal policy, as well as the loss of the nominal exchange rate as an instrument for steering demand. If some countries are in crisis and others in a boom, the central bank is faced with an irresolvable conundrum: crisis countries need low interest rates, booming countries need high interest rates. Additionally, crisis countries need active fiscal policy to increase aggregate demand. The use of the nominal exchange rate to change purchasing power and counter trade imbalances is a powerful and important tool for most countries, but it's no longer available within the Eurozone.

4 Banks have in recent decades taken to speculating with huge sums, making loans not just to mortgage borrowers or non-financial firms, but also to financial firms (including 'off-balance sheet vehicles', letterbox firms set up by banks themselves) who use borrowed credit (i.e. newly created money and debt) to speculate on various financial assets, not to invest in the real economy. This presents enormous risks to the stability of the financial system. In many countries, the summed balance sheets of a country's banks far surpass the country's GDP in scale. Although this phenomenon is not limited to the Eurozone, we've seen how misallocation of financial capital can lead to financial crises that spread globally. Furthermore, banks seem to have used their powerful influence to make dubious arrangements to their

sectoral benefit on many regulatory issues, and command an oligopoly in some cases. Profits are distributed privately and losses are borne by the public. Banks have few incentives to pay attention to the quality of their borrowers if they later 'securitize' and sell on their loan portfolios to third parties, thus removing loans (and the consequences of defaults on those loans) from their own balance sheets. This use of securitisation does not lead to a better distribution of risks, but instead disguises and disperses them, laying the basis for systemic crises through financial contagion when large quantities of loans prove to have been bad. The losses and problems show up in the next crisis where third-party investors had scant knowledge, or where investors have been misled outright. The hopes of former Federal Reserve chairman Alan Greenspan that companies would regulate themselves have been replaced by the certainty that bankers engage in highly risky and therefore short-term-profitable transactions with the knowledge that the public bail-out fund will save financial institutions that are too big to fail because they would cause a contagious systemic collapse if allowed to do so.

5   The idea of an inflation target as the single and only legitimate goal of an independent central bank has served its time. The inflation rate in the Eurozone in the period of 1999–2012 never veered far from the target rate of close to but below 2 per cent. Nevertheless, Europe experienced its biggest financial crisis since the end of the Second World War. Central banks clearly need to adopt several core goals and learn to integrate them into successful monetary and macroprudential policies.

Financial crises and business cycles have been around for centuries. They are part and parcel of a modern monetary system. Ever since the Great Depression, it has been understood how the business cycle can be tamed. In the following chapters, solutions are offered for how to solve the problem of mass unemployment – or at least lessen it – and how to prevent a rerun of the Depression. Whether a redesign of our existing modern monetary system could or should be undertaken will not be discussed.

Part IV

Reform

The euro was a political project that was supposed to bring Europe together. It was expected that countries would converge towards the wealthiest countries of the currency area. A political union was what was thought to follow. This did not happen. The euro is just a currency, so it is not the singular cause of all the economic bads of our times. However, it is a fixed exchange rate regime that does not allow countries to devalue their currency.

Many economists warned Europe against going ahead with the euro since they thought it would not work. Some European countries preferred to watch from the sidelines, like the UK and Sweden. Both have very old central banks and profound economic knowledge about how the monetary system works.

The Eurozone countries should now rethink the institutions of the Eurozone 1.1 – some reforms did happen since the start of the crisis – and move towards a new direction. The Eurozone institutions have a deflationary bias, and this must be cured. In the next chapters, I revisit the lessons of the crisis and describe possible solutions. One strategy would be to reform the euro, another to dissolve it. Discussion on both is needed, and the following chapters should be understood as a starting point, not as the final word.

12   How do we restore demand?

When the real estate boom in the US turned to a bust, the investment bank Lehman Brothers went under. Lehman had a vast portfolio of complex contracts and derivatives deals with counterparties around the world, so financiers and bankers didn't know which other banks might be rendered insolvent by Lehman's failure to repay its creditors and settle its debts. Unable to assess which banks were solvent and which were not, banks stopped lending to each other – especially banks in the US and Europe whose portfolios were closely interconnected by myriad deals.

A liquidity crisis resulted as banks tried to call in loans while hitting the brakes on making new loans. Acting on the resulting expectation of a weakening global economy, policy-makers first reacted with caution, then with public spending programmes, extensive liquidity facilities (like TARP) and a comprehensive national deposit guarantee scheme. Germany's 'cash for clunkers' programme, which offered people a subsidy if they traded in old cars and bought new ones instead, was set up to increase consumption spending. The measure was part of a package of successful measures, which also included government subsidies to firms to encourage them to retain workers on shorter hours rather than laying them off altogether. After the crisis year 2009, Germany's rate of economic growth turned positive in 2010. However, elsewhere the situation deteriorated more and more quickly.

After Europe's political elite agreed – wrongly – on government debt as the cause of the crisis, Greece, Ireland and Portugal were punished with austerity policies. Governments of these countries were cut-off from financial markets, and had to rely on help from public sector international financial institutions. A 'troika' of institutions consisting of the EC, ECB and IMF forced the respective governments to enact drastic measures, which supposedly were needed to bring these economies back on track. The new loans granted to the countries in trouble were largely used to pay off older loans. Therefore, these loans had the character of a bail-out. Had they not accepted the loans, the countries at risk would have had to declare at least a partial default on their debt.

This policy was not successful. The economic growth rate collapsed in the bailed-out countries, and government debt increased further. Greece has by now written off half of the debt it had owed private investors when the crisis broke out.

Historically, this is not an isolated incident. Whoever lends money or extends credit to an institution that might declare bankruptcy should be aware that there is a risk of default. After all, the interest rate is supposed to compensate creditors for this risk.

The European problem is not excessive public debt, but rather excessive private debt. Today, resulting weakness of demand, which also has some structural causes, has led to stagnation replacing economic growth supported by heavy mortgage lending that inflated real estate bubbles just a few years earlier. A glimpse at the balance sheet of a Spanish household reveals the problem:

	Spanish household		
real estate	€200,000	mortgage	€300,000
(value in 2007:	*€500,000)*	net wealth	−€100,000

The household was wealthy before the crisis. The mortgage of €300,000 had its counterweight in €500,000 worth of real estate. Net wealth of the Spanish household was €200,000. Since the Spanish welfare system is not very extensively developed, the typical household needs to have at least €100,000 in savings when its members reach retirement age in order to keep up their lifestyle.

The balance sheet as of today looks rather grim. The value of the real estate has sunk below that of the mortgage. The household's net wealth is a negative €100,000, but the target remains accumulating a positive €100,000 before reaching retirement age. To reach this goal, the household will reduce consumption so that more can be saved. If all households do this, consumer demand will take a hit. The consumption spending of one household is the income of another. If Spanish households economise on restaurant visits, then owners of restaurants and their employees will have to forgo some income.

This is exactly what happened in countries like Spain and Ireland. Firms laid off employees; the laid-off ex-workers were forced to reduce their consumption; and this triggered the vicious circle described above. As we have seen, a macroeconomic accounting identity says that income is made up of consumption, investment, government spending and the trade account (exports minus imports):

$$Y = C + I + G + EX - IM$$

As we saw earlier in this text, issuance of government bonds finances public expenditures. If the state has control of its own sovereign currency there is no inherent limit to its spending powers.

Investment expenditures of the private sector are mostly credit-financed. Since banks can create unlimited amounts of loans in their books, this is also theoretically without limit. However, rising private debt was the problem in the ongoing financial crisis in which banks and households loaded up with too much debt.

Three possibilities remain available to increase demand. Increasing exports or lowering imports, or both, could improve the external balance. This only works in a system of fixed exchange rates, since otherwise the foreign exchange market will set some rather random exchange rate. An export surplus is nothing but a share of aggregate consumer demand grabbed away from the importing country's own domestic producers. The importing country's net trade deficit means it has not sent an equivalent value of goods in the other direction – it has instead provided an IOU to the exporting country – which means the surplus enjoyed by net exporting countries is also based on credit.

Export surpluses can only arise between individual trade partners. The world as a whole cannot run a surplus, since all surpluses and deficits have to sum up to zero.

Consumption depends mostly on disposable income. The latter consists of wage income and capital income minus taxes. Given that interest rates are very close to zero at the time of writing, capital income from interest is relatively low, whereas capital gains are a relatively large share of capital income as a result of high stock prices caused by the flood of investment money looking for investible assets that has resulted from central banks' 'quantitative easing' policies.

To increase capital income accruing to savers, the central bank could increase interest rates. This, however, would have a negative effect on the economy and create additional unemployment, because investment will react negatively. The additional capital income would be neutralised by lower wage income.

The problem associated with an enduring lack of credit-financed investment is the consequent demand gap. If investment falls and other variables do not change, then income falls as well. The economy shrinks, unemployment rises. This is not socially sustainable.

Two options for restoring demand remain. First, a wage increase would lead to higher wage income and hence increased consumption. Second, an increase in government spending would increase demand directly. The advantage of increased government spending is that it increases incomes and profits and encourages further investment. It also creates more saving for the private sector, which means that it has fewer problems with any existing debts.

Since money does not vanish from circulation when it has been spent – but rather stays in circulation – increases in government spending create more purchasing power and are not just a flash in the pan. But it's worth considering a change in how government finances its deficit spending. There's a good argument to be made that government should borrow from itself (i.e. the Treasury should borrow from the central bank) instead of from the private sector, since interest rates for public borrowing are lower than those offered by the private sector in a modern monetary system. Moreover, interest accrues for the holders of sovereign securities, among them the central bank if it has them on its balance sheet. If a larger share of sovereign securities is held by the central bank, interest payments are neutralised. The Treasury pays interest to the central bank, which leads to central bank profits. These are disbursed to the Treasury.

Such a system would, however, deprive institutional investors like pension funds of safe sovereign bonds where they could park their money. This is not necessarily a bad thing, since it will force private investment funds to find other investment opportunities. However, it could increase the level of risk associated with private savings pools, and there is also a risk that large pools of savings chasing a diminished pool of investment opportunities (if sovereign bonds are no longer available for purchase) could lead to asset bubbles in other categories of financial asset, e.g. real estate.

13 The future
With or without the euro?

Before the euro was introduced, each European country had its own currency. These currencies were integrated into fixed exchange rate regimes after the end of the Bretton Woods system. European currencies floated freely against the US dollar and the Japanese yen, but moved only inside pre-determined bands against each other.

Central banks guaranteed solvency of national governments by financing the budget, either directly or indirectly. This meant that even relatively high levels of public debt could be financed without difficulty. This is not to say there were no problems – of course there were, for example in regards to interest rates and the current account.

Countries with relatively weak annual rates of increase in per capita productivity experienced a relative increase of the price of their products over time, compared to similar products produced more efficiently elsewhere. Foreign competition gained a price advantage over domestic producers, and this shifted production and jobs abroad.

Rising unemployment led to political pressure to adjust. This often entailed devaluation of the currency. A cheaper currency meant that foreign products would increase in price, while domestic products would become relatively cheaper. Employment started to rise again as domestic production substituted for imports, and production returned.

However, the owners of financial assets denominated in the devaluating country's domestic currency lost out in these devaluations. This is why a country with relatively weak productivity growth had to offer an additional incentive to international investors to hold their assets (corporate shares, government bonds, etc.), given that the danger of another devaluation always lurked: an attractive interest rate, higher than what could be found in jurisdictions with more stable currencies. This higher interest rate, however, had the downside that it also kept domestic investment subdued.

A return to sovereign national currencies

Two exit scenarios exist regarding the euro. In the first scenario, countries with serious economic problems (Spain, Portugal, Ireland, Greece, etc.) would exit the euro in order to regain currency sovereignty and once again become able to use currency devaluation as a policy tool.

In the second scenario, it would be Germany that leaves the euro.

It's not easy to estimate the economic consequences of an exit from the euro under either scenario. The uncertainty is exacerbated by the fact that, as it stands, a country can only leave the European Monetary Union by leaving the European Union.

Good crisis management is based on bending or ignoring rules that, given the circumstances, don't work well, so the latter constraint shouldn't be overestimated. If the political will exists, a country could be quickly invited to re-join the European Union, even if it has unilaterally exited in order to leave the common currency area.

A crisis country exits the Eurozone

What would the economic costs of a euro exit be for a crisis country? All euro-denominated debts contracted under domestic law would be redenominated to the new currency. That's the easy bit.

Debt instruments contracted under foreign law, however, might not be easily redenominated. If this affects sovereign securities, the government could negotiate a swap. A default on part of the government's debt would also be possible. Since the country will already have annoyed international investors, the additional inconveniences should be manageable. In contrast, private debts of households and firms denominated in euro under foreign law could not be redenominated. This would impose a significant burden on private debtors, if – as is expected – the new domestic currency undergoes a devaluation.

On the sunny side, the national central bank would regain the full powers and privileges it had before the euro was introduced. This would erase any default risk in the context of sovereign securities issued in domestic currency under domestic law. The government's requirement that taxes be paid in its new currency would create demand for the new currency and ensure its general acceptance as the primary means of payment domestically.

The central bank would be responsible for setting interest rates, which given that government issues its own money, can lead to lower interest rate payments even in the case of increased government spending. The government would regain its access to liquidity. Interest rate payments would be lower – or nonexistent with an interest rate at zero – and the government's policy option of financing its spending via the central bank means that spending could be increased. As long as mass unemployment exists, the government could hire workers at the going wage rate, or place orders with private sector firms that would hire workers.

This would lead to increased production of goods and services, higher total income for the population as a whole (thanks to banishment of involuntary unemployment), and hence a boost in aggregate demand. Higher inflation rates should not result, since supply would increase in tandem with demand.

The exchange rate of the new currency against the euro would depreciate. This would lead to fewer imports and more exports in the medium term. In the short term, imports of desperately needed primary goods that could not be obtained domestically would increase in price, but this cost must be weighed against the fall in the quantity of imports if the country were to stay in the Eurozone. As it stands, economic adjustment in the Eurozone works via deliberate decreases in workers' incomes in order to try to regain unit-cost competitiveness. This suppresses domestic demand, which leads to a decrease in imports.

The current account would turn positive over the medium term, since imports would become dearer and exports cheaper. This would eventually create an annual surplus of foreign currency that could be used to repay debts denominated in foreign currency.

If required, the central bank could fix the exchange rate against the euro at an artificially low rate, so that a persistent current account surplus results. Perhaps a system of fixed exchange rates would be a good way to allow indebted countries to reduce their foreign debts, by having them keep their currencies undervalued for many years. In this way, debt repayments in foreign currency could be sustained.

Some historical cases suggest that a country's exit from the European Monetary Union would likely lead to relatively high rates of economic growth in that country, since the resulting increase in employment would go hand in hand with higher income and production. Between 1991 and 2002, Argentina maintained a currency peg (fixed exchange rate) between the Argentine peso and the US dollar. After the country ran into economic trouble due to mismanagement, it abandoned the peg, and it was quickly rewarded with economic growth rates of 8 per cent. Countries that went 'off gold' in the Great Depression also experienced higher rates of growth. The effect of lower interest rates on economic growth is, in general, also positive.

Impacts on the remaining Eurozone

What would the exit of country A from the Eurozone mean for the remaining members – let's call them country B – of the monetary union? In the medium term, the reversal of B's current account – it moves from surplus into deficit – with A would increase the part of B's purchasing power that falls on imports from A. In other words, everything bought from the country that has left the euro is now cheaper because of the new exchange rate. B's demand for imported products from economies other than A might hence rise somewhat.

In principle, this could be compensated through economic policies, if the fall in aggregate demand is too steep. Interest rates could be decreased to stimulate investment; or government spending could be increased directly, which would probably trigger more private investment as well.

However, the Eurozone's core interest rate, the rate the central bank charges commercial banks for loans, is already at zero, yet no investment boom has resulted. Moreover, Maastricht rules include ceilings on new government debt –

3 per cent of GDP per annum, at most. That constraint would still be at work. Their having passed national laws, in some cases even constitutional amendments, imposing 'debt brakes' on themselves, has further reduced the fiscal flexibility of several Eurozone member governments.

For these several reasons, because of the Eurozone's design flaws, under current institutional arrangements the exit of a relatively large country from the European Monetary Union might lead to an aggregate demand gap in the Eurozone as a whole that could not be readily compensated.

Multiple exits from the Eurozone

Another problem might be a succession of exits from the common currency area. If the first country to leave ends up experiencing high rates of economic growth, other countries would likely follow suit. This would cause a sudden change in relative incomes and prices. The net effect would be to increase the probability of internal demand weakness for the remaining Eurozone countries – because consumers in the remaining Eurozone countries would suddenly be faced with supply offers from several European countries with newly devalued currencies, while consumers in those ex-Eurozone countries would be faced with increases in the price of euro-denominated products, as measured in their new domestic currencies.

Could exports to countries outside the Eurozone compensate for the reduced demand, from the point of view of remaining Eurozone countries? It seems unlikely. If a succession of countries with relatively weak economies were to leave the Eurozone, that means the remaining countries will be the stronger, more creditworthy countries. That would tend to cause the value of the euro to increase on global currency markets, which would dampen global exports from the Eurozone.

A German exit from the Eurozone

Instead of an exit of crisis countries, Germany's exit from the Eurozone is a second possibility. In this scenario, all domestic debt contracts would be redenominated in the domestic currency, the renascent Deutschmark. The new DM would appreciate in value against the euro, since Germany exports much more than she imports, which would add to the demand for her domestic currency. The appreciation would increase the relative income of Germans as measured in other currencies, which would lead, among many other things, to cheaper holidays in other European countries.

However, the purchasing power of foreign countries as measured in DM would sink, so production would shift towards the newly cheaper Eurozone countries. Consequent reductions in demand for German products and services would again have to be compensated with expansionary domestic fiscal and monetary policy. Since Germany would not be bound by Maastricht rules, there would be space for such economic policies – but it's an open question whether German policy-makers would have the sense to make use of them.

German financial assets would be very attractive to global investors. Her currency would be relatively dear, and as long as Germany sustains her current account surplus, the DM would probably continue to appreciate. This would mean that the currency would be very attractive as a store of value. Germany could hence offer relatively low interest rates, and still many investors would buy her financial assets and thereby drive their prices up. This would lead to owners of these financial assets feeling richer, and maybe they would be more willing to increase their own private debt levels in order to borrow money to invest in machines or real estate.

Designing the new post-euro monetary system

An important issue in Eurozone exit scenarios is the design of the monetary system. The highest goals of an economy should be high levels of employment and income with as high a standard of living as possible. A low rate of inflation would be helpful too.

However, the new monetary system should not follow the design of the Eurozone. Otherwise, the government and people of Germany will be forced to watch the country's economy go under. In the new system, government must be able to borrow without limit from the central bank, at least theoretically, both to eliminate any threat of default on sovereign debts and so remove the ability of bond markets to attack the currency, and also to equip the government with the ability to spend enough money to restore full employment whenever necessary. It's very unlikely, particularly in a German context, that this monetary power will be overused – voters will punish governments that create unwanted levels of inflation through excessive government spending. The country's legion of assiduous savers has a lot of political clout, and that will remain the case in a country once again blessed by a sovereign currency.

A reform of the Eurozone

The macroeconomic problems of the Eurozone today are inadequate aggregate demand and, as a consequence, an excessively low rate of inflation and excessively high rates of unemployment. While the ECB could fight elevated rates of inflation at any time by increasing interest rates, it cannot easily fight too-low rates of inflation.

Given the ECB's zero core interest rate policy – the base rate stands at 0.00 per cent as of March 2016 – commercial loan rates are already very low, even if commercial lending rates relevant for private sector investment remain higher in the periphery (Spain, Portugal, Greece, etc.) than in the core (Germany).

Since the credit supply side is now pretty much as flexible as it can realistically ever be, the problem of credit stagnation in the Eurozone must be with the credit demand side. Firms and households still aren't borrowing as much as they used to – because they don't want to.

The causes of weak demand can be found among both firms and households. In Germany, real wages had been stagnating or falling for many years – and the purchasing power of wages, in terms of the proportion of the national economy's total production of goods and services a worker's annual wage packet can buy, had thus been falling, since wages had increased less than productivity. Only recently did German real wages start to increase as a result of very low inflation rates.

In the Eurozone's southern countries, high unemployment in conjunction with a low willingness to invest have led to falling demand. As we have seen in the theoretical part of this book, the monetary circuit is based on the deposits the private sector holds in the banking system. These deposits can be increased, in aggregate, only by a net increase in private sector borrowing, or by increased government spending in conjunction with budget deficits.

As was previously explained, government deficits are necessary to compensate for demand gaps in times of weak private sector demand, and to allow the private sector to accumulate wealth if it so wishes (that is, if it wants to save a bit of money rather than spending all its income on consumption).

The austerity policies enacted in the Eurozone forced government spending to decrease below the level that would have been necessary to compensate for a period of weak private sector demand. Austerity did not lead to an improvement in the real economy, nor did it mitigate problems in financial markets. The recovery of the economy promised by the then ECB president, Jean Trichet, a stern advocate for austerity, has not materialised even six years after the Greek sovereign debt crisis broke out.

It was only Mario Draghi's July 2012 announcement that he would do 'whatever it takes' to protect the euro that helped stabilise the Eurozone, at least in regards to ending the financial turbulence caused by speculation against some Eurozone member governments. Without this step, austerity policies would surely have led to a number of sovereign defaults in addition to that of Greece.

The question the Eurozone needs to tackle is how to restart the monetary circuit in times of economic weakness. As we've seen, simply on the basis of balance sheet arithmetic, one of the three sectors (Eurozone households, Eurozone governments or trading partners in the rest of the world) has to go into debt in order to increase aggregate demand.

The private sector shows little desire to increase its net indebtedness at the moment. Many households are already burdened with more debt than they're comfortable with, and private companies have little incentive to load up on debt for purposes of investing in increased production, given stagnant consumer demand.

The external sector could increase its demand for European products, but this would lead to an appreciation of the value of the euro. If the ECB intervenes to push the exchange rate of the euro down, other regions will fight back sooner or later by initiating interventions of their own. It is hence unlikely that the Eurozone can turn into a huge (net) exporter in today's world economy, much of which is plagued by weakening demand.

Even if an export-focused strategy were to work for a while, it would eventually run into the same sort of problems we've seen inside the Eurozone. Countries with current account deficits that are stuck in fixed exchange-rate regimes will be driven into debt, and eventually encounter problems of debt repayment. Alternatively, countries with flexible exchange rates will see their currencies depreciate over time, which will move their current account towards balance. Since the exchange rate of the euro against the rest of the world is not stable, these depreciations will cause the financial value of assets accumulated as a result of current account surpluses, where those assets are denominated in foreign currencies, to fall.

The only remaining potential sources of increased demand are governments. This could mean the national governments of Eurozone member states – or perhaps the European Union as a whole, if it could bring itself to issue Eurobonds and raise money to spend money on infrastructure.

As was shown in this book's theoretical sections, a government can increase the amount of the private sector's deposits in the banking system by increasing government spending. This adds purchasing power for households and thus should increase demand. Obviously households could alternatively use the additional income to repay debts, so the demand effect will not be identical everywhere.

As it stands, government spending in the Eurozone is regulated by restrictive laws at European and national levels. Among these are the Maastricht rules regarding government deficits and national 'debt brakes'. Enabling a proper stimulus policy may require rule changes.

If additional demand created by higher private and external sector indebtedness does not suffice to fully mobilise the economy's production capacity – or enough of it, at least, to ensure everyone who wants a job can get one – then government spending remains a last resort.

As we have seen above, Eurozone countries can default on their sovereign debts *de jure*, but de facto it will not be allowed to occur. Mario Draghi's decision of July 2012, creating a programme named *outright monetary transactions* enabling the ECB to buy sovereign bonds of crisis countries on secondary bond markets, led to a fall in risk mark-ups and hence yields.

Access to OMT is only granted when a government makes use of the ESM. The ECB has also set up a *Securities Market Programme* enabling it to buy sovereign securities on the secondary market. What is needed today is an institutional arrangement that allows the Eurozone to increase demand through higher government spending. This must be financed through an institution that cannot go bankrupt.

Technically, as we have seen above, there are two alternatives. The ECB could set up such a programme either directly or indirectly. However, this would be a one-off in historical terms, since under normal circumstances democratically elected government is responsible for fiscal policy (spending on goods and services and collecting income through taxes and duties), whereas the central bank deals with monetary policy exclusively. It 'merely' buys and sells financial assets with a view towards public goals and not profit.

In the context of QE, the ECB can try to create additional deposits for the private sector. However, the results of this instrument have proven rather disappointing. First, the receivers of these deposits are usually not willing to spend them on consumption goods. Often the receivers are relatively wealthy and will use the deposits coming into their bank accounts from the sale of an existing asset sale to buy another one. The effect is a rise in asset prices, and thus a strong redistribution of wealth in favour of banks and owners of financial assets.

In addition, the private sector will have lower interest income when interest rates are lower, and that might result in lower consumption and possibly increased efforts to save more. The driving force behind this is the interest paid on government bonds. If government prefers to spend less on interest and not increase spending elsewhere in its budget, then it takes deposits out of circulation.

As a last resort, the government could stimulate the monetary circuit by creating additional deposits. This could be done through lower taxes, which would leave more deposits for the private sector. Although this would drive the government deeper into debt, it should improve the economic situation.

Alternatively, the government can spend more. Since government spending corresponds to the wishes of the parliament, it's democratically legitimated. However, some national governments have run into barriers because they're already heavily indebted, and they aren't monetarily sovereign – they don't control a currency of their own – so in principle, they could become insolvent if they issued large amounts of fresh debt for sale to private institutional investors (if those investors start charging excessively high interest rates). The implication is that if the Eurozone is to be preserved, Eurozone fiscal institutions are needed that can increase spending without burdening themselves with the risk of insolvency, bankruptcy or default.

Generally there are two ways this could be achieved. First, national parliaments could pass laws redesigning Eurozone institutions such that Eurozone member government sovereign default risks are all zero. This could be achieved by allowing the OMT programme that was discussed above. Any default risk of sovereign securities would be a thing of the past.

The question of how much each government is allowed to spend remains open. It's an important question that requires a political answer. Some proposals are already on the table; eventual compromises and agreements are likely. All parties concerned should understand that further postponement of the decision about additional government spending in the Eurozone will lengthen the ongoing period of weakness. It's high time to raise and spend a great deal of money to get the monetary circuit moving vigorously again.

Eurobonds are a solution that does not necessarily entail removing the risk of default from national governments. Eurobonds are sovereign securities that all Eurozone governments would be jointly liable for. This would put European nation-states on an equal footing with US states, which also have to balance their budget, but have a federal government able to run large deficits.

Eurobonds would not solve the problems connected to the possible default of member states governments. However, a European institution could take care to ensure a level and regional distribution of spending and aggregate demand consistent with balanced budgets at the national level.

Alternatively, the EC could be expanded to become a true European federal-level government, with a European Parliament worthy of its name. As it stands, these institutions exhibit serious democratic deficits. The parliament cannot depose the president of the Commission from office, Commission members are nominated by national governments and the idea of 'one citizen, one vote' is not in operation either. Today Germany has 96 seats in the European Parliament and Luxembourg has 6. Given that Luxembourg has a little less than 550,000 inhabitants, one Luxembourg seat represents somewhat less than 100,000 people. Given the same ratio of seats to voters, Germany would have 800 seats, given that her population stands at more than 80 million.

A reform of the Eurozone and, if necessary, the European Union towards establishing a strong European government requires the trust of its citizens. One should think about a new institutional framework in which Brussels – representing the EU as a whole, or just the Eurozone – would finance some level of expenditure in the member states, financed by European taxes. This would relieve nation-states and guarantee the provision of certain public goods like education, health or infrastructure. National governments forced to cut spending would not be forced into a downward spiral of spending cuts that lead to lower tax income and hence a new round of spending cuts.

At the end of such a development, we would have a Europe that institutionally resembles other federal systems, like Canada, Australia or the US. A European government would stand above its member nation-states, which would remain very powerful, with many areas of exclusive jurisdiction (similarly to Canadian provinces), but nevertheless would be united in a confederation.

Whereas the member nation-states would have to balance their national budgets, the former would be able to increase spending when needed in order to stabilise the economy. Note that the question of the relative size of public and private sectors does not hinge on the absolute size of government spending. After all, any government can choose to organise production through public companies or by buying from private sector suppliers, or any mix of these two options. So, this is not about the size of government, but about the question of whether the state, through the government that represents it, should be held responsible for economic growth and employment. I think the answer is definitely in the affirmative.

Conclusion

I hope that with this book I've been able to increase the reader's knowledge about the role of credit and money in a modern economy. This knowledge surely is not original, but much of it has been forgotten. The goal of this book was to empower the reader by explaining some of the basic rules of a modern financial system.

As I pointed out at the beginning, institutions of money and credit creation didn't emerge from nothing. The existing institutional arrangement in the Eurozone is flawed, and badly in need of reform or redesign, but it isn't the only cause of recent European financial and economic crises. The structural weakness of demand has been caused in part by restrictive monetary and fiscal policy, but also by policies that have led to a gradual proportional redistribution of income and wealth from middle and working classes to wealthy elites, which reduced the disposable incomes of most Europeans.

Since a variety of factors play a role in determining aggregate demand (for instance, government spending, wage and pension policies), the central bank is not powerful enough to improve the economic situation with purely monetary policies. Periods of weak demand can be papered over by credit bubbles as in Ireland or Spain, but in the long run domestic demand needs to be sufficient to absorb domestic production. Everything else is beggar-thy-neighbour economic policy made at the expense of one's trade partners.

A variety of different reforms are possible that would increase European domestic demand. Higher wages can increase demand by increasing the purchasing power of the bulk of the population, since wage earners normally spend the largest part of their income. Alternatively, working hours could be reduced further, without reducing monthly wage packets. Germany would consequently import more and see its current account surplus decrease. There's an additional motivation for decreasing weekly work-hours: in many European countries we see annual total of hours worked by employed people rising at the same time that unemployment rates have risen. Obviously, work is not distributed well.

Another issue we need to solve is climate destabilisation. This will cost a lot of money – but spending money is a good thing, not a bad thing, particularly when there's a huge reservoir of unemployed and underemployed workers sitting idle. In the monetary circuit, all spending is also income.

Neither a scarcity of monetary means nor any pernicious burden of aggregate debt on future generations can be substantiated in monetary theory, since money can always be created (or destroyed) and intragenerational redistribution through taxation is always possible. The same goes for the fairy tale that demographic problems could render the repayment of the national debt impossible. No it couldn't! If society wants to do more in terms of protecting the environment or stabilising the income of pensioners, then this can and should be decided upon via democratic political processes.

This does not necessarily mean that an increase in government spending is always the solution to every problem. As has been shown, an increase in government spending can under some circumstances (i.e. when full employment has already been attained) lead to inefficiencies, crowding out useful private production, causing undesirably high rates of inflation or long-term problems of a negative current account.

Right now, though, we're nowhere near full employment. Moreover, every situation is different. An increase in government spending can lead to more efficiency, by crowding out harmful private production, restoring desired (higher) rates of inflation or generating medium-term current account surpluses or even deficits, depending on economic conditions and goals.

From a balance sheet perspective, an increase in demand can only arise when at least one sector (private, government or external) accepts additional net debt. The question is not *if* we want debt, but rather *who* is to be moved further into debt. Not all debts are bad; most of them are actually very useful for society (extremes of mortgage debt, however, are pernicious, as are debts incurred for asset speculation or for most leveraged buyouts).

Government, households and firms move into debt by choice, and as long as the income of the private sector is sufficient to service its debts it is not a bad system. If, however, debt repayment is unexpectedly or extremely difficult or even impossible, then debt becomes a major problem.

The GDP as an economic measuring tool was not originally designed with an intention to measure the wealth of a nation. However, there's a connection between GDP growth and the rate of unemployment, as well as of disposable household income that enables us to use GDP as a mirror of the strength of an economy. Falling GDP goes hand in hand with rising unemployment.

This is a social problem, since work is still a very important point of reference for most people. Studies on happiness have shown that there is a certain level of income at which happiness does not increase any more with income. However, unemployment almost always leads to less happiness.

A clear basic understanding of the empirical reality of how money, credit and debt are created and circulated is important for citizens to be able to recognise the potential of our society. The future is open. It can be shaped and moulded. The oft-claimed scarcity of money and credit is a chimera, a mirage; it doesn't need to exist at all. We must not let a false comprehension of the nature of money, credit and debt continue to be an obstacle to full employment and widespread prosperity.

Further reading

I am indebted to many authors, among them Carl Föhl, John Kenneth Galbraith, Wynne Godley, Mitchell Innes, Michal Kalecki, John Maynard Keynes, Charles Kindleberger, Georg Friedrich Knapp, Marc Lavoie, Axel Leijonhufvud, Abba Lerner, Perry Mehrling, Hyman Minsky, Knut Wicksell and Randall Wray (in alphabetical order).

Remarks in Part 1 are based on, among others, Tony Lawson, George Soros and some older philosophers. Part 2 is based on monetary theory developed by Knut Wicksell, Joseph Schumpeter, British economists William Stanley Jevons and Walter Bagehot, as well as ideas of Wynne Godley and Hyman Minsky, which I partially acquired via Marc Lavoie and Randall Wray.

Some of the authors named above were representatives of the so-called banking school or Chartalists, including Georg Friedrich Knapp or David Graeber. Modern representatives are, among others, post-Keynesians, to which I would also count economists who work on modern monetary theory. The latter are also called neo-Chartalists. There are many researchers who do not belong to any of these schools, yet still write excellent papers and books.

Part 3 is based on macroeconomic ideas of Wynne Godley, Richard Koo, John Maynard Keynes, Abba Lerner and others. The fundamental problem of an economy is usually demand, which does not automatically correspond to supply. Economic policy intervention is necessary to keep the level of employment high. One can argue about what the best instruments of economic policy might be, but it's clear that mass unemployment is a disease that governments with sovereign money systems can cure if they want to (unless they just don't understand how the monetary system really works). The last part is based on the first three parts, with the insights applied to the Eurozone.

Bagehot, Walter (1873), *Lombard Street: A Description of the Money Market*. London: Henry S. King and Co.

Föhl, Carl (1937), *Geldschöpfung und Wirtschaftskreislauf.* München und Leipzig: von Duncker & Humblot.

Galbraith, John Kenneth (1954), *The Great Crash, 1929*. Boston: Houghton Mifflin.

Godley, Wynne (1992), Maastricht and All That. *London Review of Books*, 14(19), pp. 3–4.

Godley, Wynne (1999), *Seven Unsustainable Processes: Medium-term Prospects and Policies for the United States and the World*, Levy Economics Institute Special Report.

Graeber, David (2012), *Debt: The First 5000 Years.* New York: Melville House Publishing.

Jevons, William Stanley (1876), *Money and the Mechanism of Exchange.* New York: D. Appleton and Co.

Kalecki, Michal (1943), Political Aspects of Full Employment. *The Political Quarterly*, 14(4), pp. 322–330.

Kelton, Stephanie and Edward Nell (2003), *The State, the Market, and the Euro: Chartalism Versus Metallism in the Theory of Money.* Cheltenham: Edward Elgar.

Keynes, John Maynard (1936), *The General Theory of Employment, Interest and Money*, London: Palgrave Macmillan.

Kindleberger, Charles (1978), *Manias, Panics, and Crashes: A History of Financial Crises*, London: Macmillan.

Knapp, Georg Friedrich (1905), *Staatliche Theorie des Geldes.* München und Leipzig: von Duncker & Humblot.

Koo, Richard (2008), *The Holy Grail of Macroeconomics: Lessons from Japan's Great Recession.* Singapore: Wiley.

Lawson, Tony (1997), *Economics and Reality.* London: Routledge.

Leijonhufvud, Axel (1981), *Information and Coordination: Essays in Macroeconomic Theory.* Oxford: Oxford University Press.

Lerner, Abba (1943), Functional Finance and the Federal Debt. *Social Research*, 10(1), pp. 38–51.

Mackay, Charles (1841), *Extraordinary Popular Delusions and the Madness of Crowds.* London: Richard Bentley.

Mehrling, Perry (2011), *The New Lombard Street: How the Fed Became the Dealer of Last Resort.* Princeton: Princeton University Press.

Minsky, Hyman (1975), *John Maynard Keynes.* New York: McGraw Hill.

Minsky, Hyman (1982), *Can 'It' Happen Again? Essays on Instability and Finance.* Armonk: M.E. Sharpe.

Minsky, Hyman (1986), *Stabilizing an Unstable Economy.* New Haven: Yale University Press.

Minsky, Hyman (1992), *The Financial Instability Hypothesis*, Levy Economics Institute Working Paper No. 74.

Mitchell-Innes, Alfred (1913), What is Money. *The Banking Law Journal*, May, pp. 377–408.

Mosler, Warren (2010), *The 7 Deadly Innocent Frauds of Economic Policy.* St. Croix: Valance Co., Inc.

Newman, Frank (2013), *Freedom from National Debt.* Minneapolis: Two Harbors Press.

Schumpeter, Josef (2006) [1912], *Theorie der wirtschaftlichen Entwicklung.* Berlin: Duncker and Humblot.

Soros, George (1987), *The Alchemy of Finance: Reading the Mind of the Market.* New York: Simon and Schuster.

Wicksell, Knut (2006) [1898], *Geldzins und Güterpreise.* München: Finanz-Buch Verlag.

Wray, Randall (2012), *Modern Money Theory: A Primer on Macroeconomics for Sovereign Monetary Systems.* New York: Palgrave Macmillan.

Index

Page numbers in *italics* denote tables, those in **bold** denote figures.

For Product Safety Concerns and Information please contact our
EU representative GPSR@taylorandfrancis.com Taylor & Francis
Verlag GmbH, Kaufingerstraße 24, 80331 München, Germany